Discovering Galloway

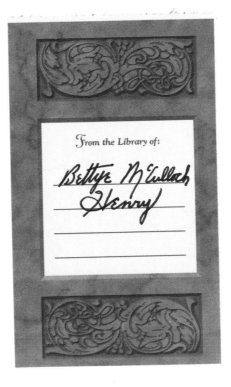

For Sally

Discovering
Galloway

INNES MACLEOD

JOHN DONALD PUBLISHERS LTD
EDINBURGH

ISBN 0 85976 114 2

Exclusive distribution in the United States of America and Canada by Humanities Press Inc., Atlantic Highlands, NJ 07716, USA.

Reprinted 1988

Phototypeset by Key Phototypes, Edinburgh and Printed in Great Britain by Bell & Bain Ltd., Glasgow.

Acknowledgements

We are very grateful for the helpful co-operation received and permission to reproduce photographs from:

The Stewartry Museum, Kirkcudbright (photographs on pages) 7, 10, 11, 27, 51 and 108

Dr. W. Kissling, Dumfries 8 and 156

Newton Stewart and District Museum 25 (front cover) and 200

Mr. J. McDavid, Creetown 33 and 110

The Committee for Aerial Photography, University of Cambridge 80

Mr. D. Nelson, *Wigtown Free Press* 255, 266 and 269

The Biggar Museum Trust (G. Allan Collection) 102, 123 and 138

Miss Purdie, Newton Stewart 198

The University Library, University of Glasgow 212.

Other photographs and plates are by the author or from his collection.

Contents

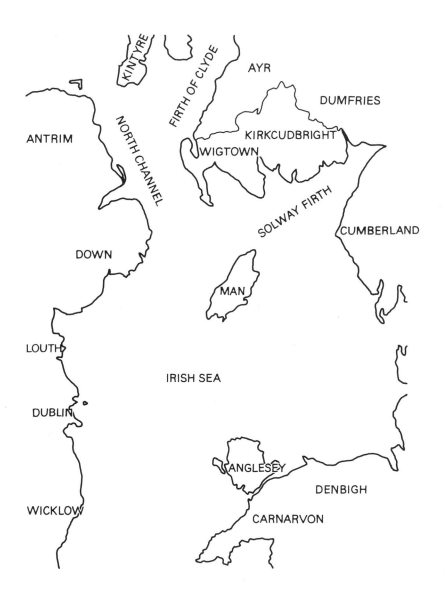

Old Galloway

Introduction

This is a vast subject, for to truly discover Galloway is the 'velvet study and recreation work' of many years. Hopefully this book will offer something new on occasion to Gallovidians born and bred and to those with the sense and sensibility to live there, and will also be an entertainment and a practical useful tool for visitors 'doing' Galloway, whether in a weekend, a week, or at intervals over a lifetime.

Galloway is admirable. It is not, however, Arcadia, and it is surely better to describe it without engaging in too many gushing superlatives. A certain austerity and calm may be preferable. My own tendency is to admire rather the honest and classical turn of phrase demonstrated in an advertisement in a prestigious journal in which a local caravan site was described as 'within spitting distance of the Solway'. That seemed to me to be as neat and precise and graphic a description as could possibly be achieved.

Galloway means geographically the area from the Mull of Galloway and Loch Ryan in the west to the Solway and the Nith at Dumfries in the east. Although for centuries this meant Wigtownshire and the Stewartry of Kirkcudbright, in the era dating from regionalisation in 1975 this has meant a larger Wigtown District, a truncated Stewartry District, and part of Nithsdale District. These constitutional niceties need not concern us here. Perhaps the really important point anyway is that they are definitely not part of Strathclyde. In spite of that, Ayrshire as far north as Ballantrae, Loch Doon and Dalmellington, and the area east of Dumfries along the northern shore of the Solway have been included in the topographical section in this book.

Galloway is compact. Distances are not enormous—Stranraer to Drummore 18 miles; Stranraer to Newton Stewart 26 miles; Newton Stewart to Girvan 30 miles; Newton Stewart to Whithorn 18 miles; Newton Stewart to Kirkcudbright 27 miles; Kirkcudbright to Dumfries 28 miles; Castle-Douglas to Carsphairn 25 miles; and New Galloway to Thornhill 24 miles. But this small area embraces a diversity of scenery and interest which makes the term 'Scotland in miniature' a good and fair description.

A rather endearing debate has been pursued over the years about the best way to promote Galloway as a holiday area and a leisure-orientated society. Should it be 'Grey Galloway', the older phrase and still romantically evocative of the land and its history, but no doubt seen now as being too

1

'elitist'? or 'Bonnie Gallowa', direct and more in line with the populist approach perhaps more relevant in the 1980s? or 'The Quiet Country', sweet, but too reminiscent of John Wayne in John Ford's *The Quiet Man?* The mildly amusing 'Costa Geriatrica', although it does reflect an important and valuable trend in many villages and towns which have been revived as havens for retired gentlefolk, is hardly acceptable! The 'Scotch Riviera' of the Glasgow Boys is rather fun though.

The more overwhelming memories of this little Galloway world are of orderly landscapes, green fat farming land and wooded hills softly and gently rippling along the sky, and grey and white painted houses and cottages. Here 'peace *is* the tranquillity of order'. This is held between on the south the mud flats and salt marshes and liquid blue-grey of the Solway and the Irish Sea, and to the north the vaster wastes of brown-grey moor and hill land, this invaded by drystane dykes and settled with blue-black lochs and scythed now with platoons and brigades of forests. And we remember the favourite lanes and roads, the Old Military Road from Castle-Douglas to Lochfoot, Mochrum Loch to Kirkcowan, Gatehouse-of-Fleet to Creetown by Rusko and the Moneypool Burn, and Beeswing to New Abbey. And the gorgeous place-names, New Luce, Elrig, Whauphill, Curleywee, Balmaclellan, Kirkpatrick Durham, Kells, Ferrytown of Cree, Palnackie, Kirkbean, and Carsethorn. And the rich archaeology and history behind it all, the old stone circles and early crosses, the castles and towers and abbeys, and the witches and warriors, the miners and smugglers and tinkler gypsies. And the great appeal of being the John Buchan country of *The Thirty-Nine Steps*—do you remember the literary innkeeper, the spectacled roadman, and the radical candidate whom I'm *quite* sure was not sent to the House of Commons? and the splendid Donat, Carroll, Laurie, Tearle film?

In Galloway terms only an incomer, having been brought up in Sutherlandshire, Deeside and Aberdeen, it was my very good fortune to work from August 1962 to March 1975 as Resident Tutor in the counties of Wigtownshire and Kirkcudbrightshire for the Department of Extra-Mural Studies of the University of Glasgow. This time was passed living variously in Creebridge (the perfect address to satisfy the preferences of both Education Committees as although actually in the Stewartry the postal address was Wigtownshire), Newton Stewart, Cardoness (as 'Cardoness Stables, Gatehouse-of-Fleet, Stewartry of Kirkcudbright' perhaps the longest address in the University Diary), and in Kirkcudbright. A unique posting to which distance lends enchantment, in reality the job was a sort of cross between being a rather superior kind of commercial traveller, with a quality product from a good firm established in 1451, and a district commissioner for

Culture and Good Works. It was a long way from Glasgow, and the highlights of the week were not the *Times Literary or Educational Supplements* of polite academic circles, but the *Free Press* on Thursdays and the *Gazette* and *News* on Fridays. Now, of course, Galloway is full of the ghosts of those years, for in this rural context students were generally two or three times older than tutors. But life goes on, and that in many ways is a more profound lesson from history than most of the pseudo-scientific Marxist class-conflict terminology-jargon inflicted all too often on readers these days.

This may seem unduly like a soliloquy, but this book has to be to some extent a matter of personal choices and preferences. It is not possible or really desirable to try to cover everything there is to see or do in Galloway. Now Galloway, like the Borders, has more than its ample share of local rivalries and jealousies. The two counties, now districts, are very distinct entities with their own character, and few visitors can fail to notice the marked differences in style and appearance encountered in the various towns and villages; or how dialect and pronunciation change from west to east; and how the climate alters from the soft and gentle in the Rhins of Wigtownshire to the brisk and invigorating in New Luce and Carsphairn. Although you have, after all, to actually experience the somewhat limited attraction of — on a wet evening in February to see Galloway at its worst, I have tried to steer a course which makes it difficult to detect my own dislikes and prejudices against localities or topics. May I add, at the danger of appearing patronising, that most Gallovidians, if not all incomers, have a good deal of brisk common sense, a wholly admirable reticence, and can deliver a jolly good put-down. As 'the man with the kilt and the white labrador' (this was Sally 1963-1976), the most brilliant cat-call received was from a street urchin in Kirkcudbright who hailed the approaching apparition with 'here comes the pipe band'! Either a very clever or a very silly little boy!

This is intended to be a practical guide for visitors. This does not imply, nevertheless, an even marginal enthusiasm for any great expansion or proliferation of tourist facilities. Much that is rare and precious in Galloway is also very vulnerable to damage and destruction from over-exploitation. The yaboos who want haggis hunts and welly boot throwing competitions should go elsewhere.

There is still room, however, for more good hotel accommodation and for attracting people of the right sort in Spring and Autumn, and for the development of more outdoor activities involving pony trekking and walking. The opening of the 212-mile Southern Upland Way from Cockburnspath in Berwickshire to Portpatrick will be an interesting test case. Will it prove to be an over-publicised circuit for those who need to be told where to walk, possibly even with eventually 'branch lines' to link up with the Pennine Way and the West Highland Way? Will it produce serious congestion and erosion problems, for example at the Portpatrick end or at the section joined from the A74? Or will the Galloway route, just because it is far enough from urban areas, escape these problems? More positively it does 'open up' (in the sense of making more people aware of their existence) very important sites, for example the Wells of the Rees and the Laggangairn complex.

Chapters 1 to 7 provide an introduction to environment and history. Chapters 8 to 21 are essentially topographical, but also include extended discussion of some subjects as they appear, for example early castles with the Motte of Urr. Routes are suggested for exploration of each area either by car or on foot.

Ordnance Survey Maps Sheets 76, 77, 82, 83 and 84 on the 1:50,000 scale provide a comprehensive coverage of the places mentioned in the text. Many map references have been given, using the simple-to-follow National Grid Reference System. All references are to be read as NX with the very few and specified exceptions in the far west of Wigtownshire. The first three numbers represent the distance from the left edge of the map and the second three represent the distance from the bottom edge.

Many of the sites and structures listed are visible from the roadside; some are officially Ancient Monuments open to the public; others are on land developed by the Forestry Commission; many are on private property, and permission for access should usually in these cases be obtained from the appropriate farm or estate. This is a matter of politeness and common sense, unless you want to be run down by a Galloway cow. 'Belties' look sweet, but are not always sweet-tempered. Animals are curious and often just playful — horses may well want to look inside a handbag or shopping bag, and goats may just eat your clothes! Obviously campers are usually only welcome at camping sites, dogs should always be kept on leads when there are or may be livestock in the vicinity, and visitors in general are not really wanted during the lambing season.

No suggestions have been made for the best touring centres, or for hotels and inns. Any hotel worth considering seriously, however, should be happy to serve, quickly and efficiently, coffee and biscuits in the morning— probably the best easy guide to comfort, quality and kitchen. Tastes do vary enormously: as a very sensible and well travelled lady observed on being offered the room where Burns had slept, she didn't really mind as long as she was not expected to sleep in the same bed!

CHAPTER 1

The Sea, the Shore and the Islands

To look at a map of Scotland on its own is a sure and certain way of starting with a false picture of the geography and history of this south-west corner. Seen from Glasgow or Edinburgh, Galloway looks remote and isolated. It still *is* unknown country to many Scots, and Scottish visitors usually make up about one-fifth of the total each year. So it does seem to be tucked away on its own, rather a long way from 'important' Scottish towns and cities, and involving a long journey through the moors and hills of Ayrshire and Dumfriesshire to get there.

Merely to glance, however, at a map of the Irish Sea area puts Galloway in a very different perspective. Until the coming of the railways what really mattered was the sea, and in these terms Galloway was readily accessible from the Clyde coast and Kintyre, and as easily from Lancashire, Cheshire and Cumberland, from Dublin, Down, Antrim, Derry and Donegal, from Denbigh, Caernarvon and Anglesey, and from the Isle of Man. If you doubt this, climb up into the hills behind Gatehouse and Creetown and look south to Cumberland and Man.

Historically, then, Galloway was part of this Irish Sea province with close economic, political and demographic links with its various countries and peoples. In the eighteenth century and for much of the nineteenth century men from Kirkcudbright and Wigtown looked for partners in trade and commerce and insurance to Whitehaven and Liverpool; even while at the same time church and university links and ties were with Edinburgh and Glasgow. Of course before the railways there were land routes, the mediaeval ways, the drove roads, the Old Military Road from Dumfries to Portpatrick, and some of these can still be followed in places, but it was still easier one hundred and fifty years ago to send heavy goods from Dumfries to Stranraer along the Solway and necessary to take the long sea route from Edinburgh round the coast of England to Gatehouse or Kirkcudbright. The development of the railways from the 1850s and the improvement of road links in the last sixty years have changed this balance almost completely so that to get now from Stranraer or Kirkcudbright to Bangor or Whitehaven or Barrow-in-Furness or Peel is an awkward journey seldom attempted. This is a great pity.

Galloway benefited fully from the Victorian enthusiasm for railways, and is perhaps fortunate in that it is still possible to go from Glasgow to Stranraer and from Glasgow and Carlisle to Dumfries by train. The run out of Girvan and over the moors from Barrhill and on to Stranraer makes an excellent leisurely excursion either from Newton Stewart or Stranraer, with possible variations on a triangle using the Western SMT bus services from Newton Stewart to Stranraer, Stranraer to Ballantrae and Girvan, and Newton Stewart to Barrhill and Girvan. On the old lines the section from Big Fleet Viaduct to Loch Skerrow is especially good walking.

Railway buffs will know all about the Galloway lines—Dumfries to Castle-Douglas opened in 1859, Castle-Douglas to Stranraer in 1861 and the section to Portpatrick for the Insh steamer in 1862, Castle-Douglas to Kirkcudbright in 1864, Newton Stewart to Whithorn in 1877, and Girvan to Portpatrick in 1877. There were also in Dumfriesshire the light railways from Elvanfoot to Leadhills and Wanlockhead opened in 1901 and the Cairn Valley line from Dumfries to Moniaive in 1905. Other projects and schemes which reached various stages of planning and surveying, but were never implemented, were for lines from Dalmellington to Castle-Douglas to Orchardton Tower to Balcary Point near Auchencairn (with branch lines to Gibbshole and Porterbelly!) in 1846, Stranraer/Dunragit to Drummore in 1878, Parton to Dalry, New Galloway to Dalry, Stranraer to New England Bay between Ardwell and Drummore, and in Ayrshire from Pinwherry to Ballantrae.

A common feature of most of these lines was the drive to the sea, to reach and serve ports and harbours and even creeks. There was also a pre-railway age plan for a Glenkens Canal on a route running west of New Galloway to Mossdale to the River Dee and hence to the harbour at Kirkcudbright. Every few miles along the Galloway coastline there seem to be creeks and inlets and natural harbours, as well as the Nith, Urr, Dee and Cree river estuaries. In the eighteenth century and for much of the nineteenth century sloops and schooners and brigs and snows and ships sailed from ports from Glencaple and Carsethorn to Creetown and Wigtown and Stranraer and Portpatrick on British coastal shipping routes and even for the Baltic, the Mediterranean, the Caribbean, and for North America. This has all gone, as has even the era of coasters coming in to Port William and Monrieth with coal to be collected by farmers with carts or (by the 1930s) lorries. Although these days are past, there is a current late twentieth-century revival of interest in the potential of the ports for commercial and leisure use.

Stranraer and Cairnryan, especially the former, surprise most visitors with the scale of the modern port facilities for traffic across the North Channel to Ireland. Annan, Kirkcudbright, Garlieston and Stranraer West Pier are

Little Ross Lighthouse, Kirkcudbright Bay, c.1900. Photograph by McConchie of Kirkcudbright.

likely to continue to have commercial cargo developments and possibly improvements; Glencaple, Kippford, Palnackie, Wigtown, Isle of Whithorn, Port William and Portpatrick seem likely to see some growth, mainly for leisure usage; the future of Port McAdam (Gatehouse-of-Fleet), Kirkmabreck (Creetown), Drummore, and The Wig (Kirkcolm) is more problematical. In the summer anyhow there is a great deal to see in the creeks and harbours. The lighthouses at Southerness, Corsewall, Killantringan (near Portpatrick) and the Mull of Galloway and on Hestan Island and Little Ross Island are sited at some of the most scenically dramatic and spectacular areas.

The breakers' yard at Cairnryan may have any size of warship up to an aircraft carrier being dismantled. The deep water facilities at Cairnryan were of major strategic importance from 1939 to 1945 (and you will see the remains of many wartime airfields and camps in Galloway). Cairnryan may become an important supply base for oil exploration and drilling areas in the Firth of Clyde (the BP Arran-Ailsa Craig block) and the Irish Sea. Other useful employment is provided by the Ministry of Defence, which has extensive bases at the Freugh on Luce Bay (RAF) and the Range east of Kirkcudbright

The tidal bore on the Nith at Glencaple.

(Army). Both are clearly indicated on O.S. maps with 'Danger Area' lettering.

The Galloway ports have not traditionally been great fishing centres, although Luce Bay was once famous for its oyster grounds, and Loch Ryan still has some of the last major oyster beds in the United Kingdom. However, commercial fishing has survived, and there have been some interesting recent developments. The most controversial is the decision announced by the Scottish Office in July 1985 to open Luce Bay with its important breeding and fishing grounds to commercial trawling. The consequences for local fishing and the tourist industry could be devastating. Loch Ryan is exempt.

A real change has taken place in Kirkcudbright where the harbour is now very much at saturation level and where upwards of 230 people are employed in fishing (some 70 at sea and 160 in a fish-processing factory). In 1983 there were nine 60 to 80 feet boats catching 'queenies' in the queen scallop grounds in the Solway and Irish Sea (four boats having their haul processed in Kirkcudbright and the other five sending their catch to Hull or Fleetwood); four 30 to 40 feet trawlers taking white fish; and one lobster boat working the local coastal area. The cash figures for landings at the harbour show an increase from £7,628 in 1969 to £219,035 in 1972 and to £1,232,990 in 1981.

Visitors perhaps will be more interested in the tidal stake-nets and traps in the Nith and Cree estuary mud-flats. Each fortnight some twenty-seven tides sweep over the mud and sand banks leaving channels and pools in which all kinds of fish, but especially salmon and flounders, can be taken. A number of stratagems and techniques are used. The *haaf nets* are a type of 'poke' net held and worked by fishermen standing in a slanting row and up to their chests in the river channel. The 'haafers', up to eight or nine men in a line standing in the running tide of the Nith, make a truly remarkable sight. The *stake nets* to take salmon on the ebbing or the flowing tide are striking features of the Galloway landscape. The net walls up to 100 yards in length and 8 feet to 12 feet high are stretched on stakes positioned close to the natural run of the sea or the river. They have enclosed chambers into which salmon or sea trout are guided from different directions by ebb, flood and cross-arms. The *paidle net* about 5 feet high is a smaller version of the stake-net with a barrel-shaped trap or 'paidle' for taking white fish. Another traditional way of getting salmon was the *yair* on the Dee, and also at one time at Spittal on the Cree. The 'yair' was the scaffold with a projecting platform sitting on stakes from which the fishermen worked the net, and this was set above the V-shaped enclosure into which salmon entered with the tidal flow.

You may also see shrimpers with nets and flounder-trampers with the multi-pronged 'leister'. The now annual flounder tramping competition at Palnackie is a rather jolly occasion.

The 210 miles of shoreline from Loch Ryan to Gretna have just about every possible variety of coastal scenery from cliffs and headlands, islands and caves, sand banks and mudflats, sand and shingle beaches, to sand dunes and saltmarshes. It can be a very dangerous coast, as the graveyards of old wooden ships remind us. Barnhourie off Southerness is almost certainly one of these. The powerful tidal runs can be vicious round the Mull of Galloway in the North Channel, but even in the Upper Solway when the tide races in over the flat-scape it has a frightening element of speed made more appalling by the shifting pattern of tidal channels and pools and the thought of welcoming quicksands. Detailed local knowledge is essential for yachtsmen, canoeists and wildfowlers. It is easy to be deceived in the land easing into water and sea into marsh. Unfortunately it also has more than its fair share of plastic waste and assorted debris. In addition nine bodies were washed ashore between Larbrax Bay and Southerness between 1972 and 1984.

The Upper Solway estuary from Carsethorn to Powfoot is a phenomenal place, perhaps especially when experienced in the full blast of a winter wind storm. It is literally a constantly moving landscape of mudflats and salt marshes. Over the centuries and decades the boundaries of land and sea change variously as in one place at one time the force of waves and tides and winds causes erosion, and at another place at the same time or the same place

Yair on the Dee at Castle Sod near Kirkcudbright, c.1900. Black water and silver-lavender-pink-yellow mud. The fish were caught in these enclosures by the tidal flow. The fisherman worked the net from above. See also page 11.

at another time silt deposits build up and accumulate on a sand bank, a shingle spit or a tidal merseland. The Caerlaverock and Bowhouse area is a classic example of this movement over the last seven hundred years, but there are many others along the coast. The Cree from Bladnoch to Machermore is another, although here land reclamation is rather the result of human endeavour.

Even on a British scale the Nith estuary and the Solway from Carsethorn to Kirkconnel and Glencaple and Ruthwell and Powfoot is a major area for ornithologists and wildfowlers and botanists and a rewarding area for photographers. The saltmarsh or merse land varies from dry and sometimes almost lawn tennis-like fresh water grass land where cattle graze and which is only covered by the sea for a few hours by the spring and autumn tides; to salt marsh with hummocks and tidal channels which has half its life under sea water, but is still home for marsh plants with deep and strong root formations, the common saltmarsh grass and thrift or sea pink and red fescue grass; and the straightforward mud flats and sandy banks full of a vast swarming invertebrate life—a feeding ground for birds which can probe

10

through the mud into the food banks of snails and ligworms and ragworms, which in turn feed on beds of algae and organic detritus. Great stuff!

The best sea cliff scenery is from Sandyhills with the Needles Eye and Lot's Wife to Port O'Warren, especially at Gillis Craig (875532), and to Rockcliffe and Kippford; at Balcary to Rascarrel (805482) near Auchencairn; Burrowhead near Whithorn; and at the Mull of Galloway, and with almost all of the west coast of the Rhins of interest. Nothing to rival Mingulay or Hoy or Foula of course, but the everchanging patterns of sky and sea and land looking over to Cumberland and Man and Ireland and Kintyre are always fascinating and will provoke plenty of arguments about which particular point of land you are seeing and describing.

There are some good sea-caves and caverns—but always check access and safety locally first—at Barlocco near Auchencairn, at Torrs and Borness east and west respectively of Kirkcudbright, St. Ninian's Cave at Physgill near Isle of Whithorn, Monrieth, St. Medan's Cave near the Mull of Galloway, and above the present shoreline on the old raised beach levels at various places including Loch Ryan.

For sea beaches, with variable qualities of sand, choose from Southerness, Sandyhills, Rockcliffe and Rough Firth, Auchencairn Bay, Doon Bay and Brighouse Bay in Borgue, Carrick and Sandgreen, Mossyard and Garvellan, Monrieth Bay, Maryport Bay, New England Bay, Ardwell, Sandhead, Port Logan, Portpatrick, and Loch Ryan. Always look for the smaller and less accessible beaches for the peace and privacy which is still often possible. Many of these are ideal for escapist beachcombing for stones and pebbles, which may include waste from old mines and debris washed up from wrecks, such as the green pebbles on the shore from Abbey Burnfoot and Barlocco to Auchencairn from the *Clynder* which had a cargo of Chilean phosphates. Those with an eye for these matters may spot coral and shell fossils on the Carsethorn to Arbigland shore and other fossil fragments at Balmae Ha'en on Kirkcudbright Bay. General collectors can assemble limpets and barnacles, cockle and mussel and whelk shells, scallop and tellin and long razor shells, all sorts of periwinkles, the auger or tower shell, and best of all the splendid pelican's foot shells and a few Hungarian cap or bonnet limpet shells (they look just like Disneyland dwarf hats), and perhaps oyster shells from Loch Ryan round to Corsewall. All sorts of flotsam and jetsam items might include mermaid's purses, i.e. egg capsules usually attached to seaweed by twisted tendrils. There is a neat reply here to the hotel bore— 'And what have you been doing today?' 'Oh—mm—collecting Hungarian caps and mermaid's purses—jolly good actually!'

For those who enjoy collecting islands and would like to puzzle a few native Gallovidians, try out the following list, which does not include sand bars or tidal offshore banks. 1. Rough Island (843532) near Rockcliffe. 2. Hestan Island (839502) near Auchencairn. 3. Inch (671483), a tidal island at the south end of 4. St. Mary's Isle (673492), which is not an island. 5. Little Ross (660432). 6. Barlocco Isle (578482), west of Borgue. 7. Ardwall (572493). 8. Murray's Isles (561502). 9. Isle of Whithorn (479362), but not an island except on rare occasions when a storm from the south-west can sweep a high tide through the houses. 10. St. Helena Island (192558), near Glenluce, only cut off at high spring tides. 11. The Little Scares (263345) and Big Scare (259333), or the Scar Rocks, in Luce Bay. 12. Emer's Isle (NW 973718) and Well Isle (NW 983728), north-west of Kirkcolm, to demonstrate quirky know-how!

Time and Tide Tables are published in the weekly *Dumfries and Galloway Standard* (for Hestan Island with adjustments for Drummore to Southerness), the *Galloway News* (Solway Tides), the *Galloway Gazette* (the Port William to Garlieston coastline), and the *Wigtown Free Press* (Stranraer Tides). These are essential for island goers, swimmers, and any of the sailing enthusiasts who are coming in ever-increasing numbers to Galloway centres. As the harbours dry out at low tide and there are almost no deepwater moorings, yachts should preferably be able to take the ground. For yachtsmen, getting to Galloway can be a tricky exercise, with the races off the Mull of Kintyre and the Mull of Galloway and Burrowhead, the Scares in Luce Bay, the RAF and Army Danger Areas, and the Craig Roan rocks off Rough Firth all to be avoided. Kippford and Isle of Whithorn with Loch Ryan (especially for dinghy sailing) are probably the most popular, with other stopping-off points and centres at Drummore, Port William, Garlieston, Creetown and Kirkcudbright. Owners of sailing dinghies operating out of the Wigtownshire centres in particular should check locally about weather and tide before venturing into more open water.

Perhaps the most exciting outdoor activity in the area is the inshore and deep sea angling, for which the Galloway waters, going out from Kippford, Kirkcudbright, Garlieston, Isle of Whithorn, Port William, Auchenmalg, Stranraer, Portpatrick and Drummore, are truly splendid. Over the years the seasons from May or June to September have produced many British or Scottish records for weight, and an extraordinary range and variety of species in both colder deeper and warmer inshore waters, with no doubt a number of varieties from the south coming up through the shallow Irish Sea to Luce Bay, Wigtown Bay and the Solway. More exotic occasional visitors include the leatherback turtle, octopus (recorded off Hestan Island), porpoises, Grey Atlantic seals, schools of squid, swordfish and tunny, sea lamprey (on the Cree), seahorses, and probably the highest proportion recorded of sharks caught off the Scottish coast.

The colder deeper water in the Outer Solway and off the Mull of Galloway and the west coast of the Rhins is the place for weight and size and the best sport. You may find excellent skate (120 lb. off Knockinan), ling, plaice, flounders, some of the finest tope in Britain (to 50 lb. and 6 feet), coalfish and pollack (to 15 lb.), conger eels off Burrowhead and the Mull (to 80 lb.), cod (to 22 and 36 and 40 lb.), turbot (to 21 lb.), dogfish or 'Blin Bitches' (to 2 feet 10 inches) off Portpatrick and Port Logan and, in Luce Bay, painted ray and sting ray and shagreen ray and thornback, and thresher shark, porbeagle shark, blue shark and basking shark. Four basking sharks taken in one day in

June 1984 between the Isle of Man and the Mull of Galloway were between 22 and 29 feet long and had a total weight of 13 tonnes.

The warmer inshore water in Luce Bay, Loch Ryan, Wigtown Bay and the Solway yields an immense variety of fish, including those moving back and forth between deeper and shallower water for food or in migration patterns. These may include shoals of cod, bass and mackerel and tope, smelt, ling, pollack or lythe, whiting, mullet, plaice, flounders, turbot, halibut, herring (formerly in large shoals in Loch Ryan), skate, sea trout, dab, gurnard, solenette, sturgeon (in Loch Ryan and Wigtown Bay), pipe fish, thornback rays, sand eels and sting rays in Wigtown Bay and Luce Bay and Loch Ryan, conger eels in Wigtown Bay, dogfish and blue sharks at Burnfoot and Innerwell, and huge numbers of spurling in the Cree estuary which is their most important breeding ground in British waters.

Perhaps this sounds too good to be true. And, yes, there is one problem that should not be ignored, summarised by the title of the 1983 Yorkshire TV programme on 'Windscale—the Nuclear Laundry', which included 'sampling' data from Kippford, Auchencairn, and Palnackie. This featured in local and national headlines in Winter 1983 and Spring 1984 under titles such as 'Tourist warning on nuclear scare stories', 'Call to Save Our Solway', 'Plutonium dust found in Kippford', 'Radiation report closes Solway beaches', 'Council to buy a Geiger counter', and 'Airborne radioactivity to be monitored'. This refers, of course, to the nuclear waste reprocessing and storage plant at Windscale or Sellafield in Cumbria, which has certainly been responsible for radioactive pollution of the Solway and the Irish Sea over the years, exacerbated by a major leak in 1983, although the most obviously damaging consequences seem to have been within a close radius of Sellafield itself. There is as yet no evidence of damage or danger to beaches or coastal areas in Galloway.

What is confusing is the amount of research conducted by a number of different agencies and organisations. Wigtown District Council Department of Environmental Health and the Department of Agriculture and Fisheries have been studying sprayborne radiation at sea and monitoring the North Channel, Larbrax Bay, Garlieston and Port William for many years in terms of the recommendations of the International Commission on Radiological Protection and the U.K. National Radiological Protection Board. This involves checking shoreline radiation levels and sampling sediments, seaweed, fish, shellfish and agricultural products. Shellfish in Loch Ryan, for example, showed a minimal level of radiation of about 0.1 per cent of the appropriate limit and most of this was natural radiation. The Stewartry District Council has also concluded that radiation in the area is not above natural background levels. Nithsdale District Council has been monitoring discharges from Chapelcross and has surveyed the Powfoot area. The H.M. Industrial Pollution Inspectorate of the Scottish Development Department in conjunction with the Ministry of Agriculture and Fisheries and Stewartry District Council conducted a post-1981 survey of Kippford, Palnackie and Auchencairn. The U.K. Atomic Energy Authority in conjunction with the Department of the Environment and the Scottish Office has been studying airborne contamination from seaspray. The Department of Agriculture and Fisheries has been sampling carcases of meat and offal from five sites in the Stewartry. And the National Radiological Protection Board began in 1984 a survey of houses in the Stewartry in areas where above-average levels of exposure to radon decay products might be expected, that is at Kirkmirren, Potterland, Sandyhills, Auchencairn, Palnackie, Screel, Dalbeattie, Kirkgunzeon, Lochend, Corsock, and Port O'Warren.

There seem to be two different issues here of sprayborne radiation at sea and of airborne pollution by dust blowing off silt. Evidently heavy concentrations can accumulate and remain concentrated in silt over considerable periods of time. There is, however, no evidence as yet that any section of the Galloway coastline has been affected by nuclear waste. There were suggestions in June 1984 that the publicity given to this issue might have reduced the number of visitors, and it does seem probable that some people have found statements by 'experts' alarming rather than reassuring. Nevertheless it is not an issue that can simply be swept like dust under a carpet and safely ignored. At the same time essentially pessimistic assessments by well-intentioned but largely self-appointed 'conservationist' and 'environmentalist' lobbies may attract too much attention. It is, of course, an immensely complex issue with all sorts of political and economic and scientific ramifications for the British state. In spite of the fact that discussion based on mutual ignorance of the subject is not necessarily particularly helpful, nevertheless it seems only right that individuals and families should reflect on the issue with whatever mixture of common sense and cautious optimism they can muster.

On a more positive note it is now possible to welcome the formal allocation by the Department of Energy in September 1984 of oil and gas exploration licences for the Solway area. Two blocks have been included, one a landward area to the east partly in Annandale and Eskdale, but mainly in Cumbria and including Silloth and Wigton and Maryport; the other a block in the middle of the Solway some three or four miles offshore between Kirkcudbright and Whitehaven and in a rectangle with parallel lines roughly running from Rascarrel Bay towards Workington and from Little

Ross to St. Bees Head. Seismic surveying began in 1985, with possible drilling in 1986 or, more probably, later.

In oil it is possible to be wildly over-optimistic, but the general assumption in this case is that the rock formations in the area are promising for hydrocarbon generation and entrapment. Since supply bases and terminals for bringing oil ashore are likely to be in Cumbria, the impact on Whitehaven, Workington and Wigton could be considerable. On the whole Dumfries and Galloway is less likely to benefit directly in initial stages of development. The 1990s, however, if exploration moves further west, could see a different pattern emerging. Regional and District councillors and landowners should take a tough line in negotiations with oil companies and their suppliers who will be in the area as welcome guests, but as ones whose presence is not essential to the economy of the area. On any sale or lease of land and property, think of a reasonable figure and multiply it by three or four. Offer no concessions or inducements to come to Dumfries and Galloway rather than Cumbria. Remember that compared with the North Sea Solway oil will have low exploration and development costs and possibly enormous profits, so insist on the companies paying for all harbour, port and road facilities required. After all, why should local ratepayers subsidise oil company profits and the U.K. economy? Don't worry too much about environmental disasters. Oil companies do not want expensive suits for damages or a bad public relations image and on the whole respond well to approaches from fishing and conservation pressure groups who have done their homework. 'Invite' companies to invest in a fund to cover long-term costs in the 2010s and 2020s to rehabilitate areas affected by oil development, to encourage the development of alternative employment resources, and to provide financial assistance for a wide range of ongoing local projects and concerns whether educational or leisure-orientated. Properly handled, as in Shetland and Orkney, the pluses will more than outweigh the minuses.

CHAPTER 2

The Rivers and the Lochs

There is another pollution headliner in Galloway. The phenomenon popularly referred to as 'acid rain' has been a matter of concern for some time and more particularly since 1983. People are worried about the impact on fish farming, loch and river fishing, and forestry, although it is now clear that this pollution is not by any means a new hazard. Galloway is vulnerable because of the granite geological base and the thin, rapidly draining soil in many hill areas: and perhaps because it is open to damage from industrial and urban areas in northern England, northern Ireland and central Scotland.

There are many difficulties. Acid pollution, for example, is not merely a matter of a wet fall as rainwater or snow, but is probably more significantly the *dry* deposition of material which is then washed into burns and lochs. As these are acidified, insect and plant life and fish stocks decline and disappear, leaving lochs looking strangely and idyllically clean and sparkling. Recently hatched larvae of trout and salmon are particularly vulnerable. It is at least conceivable that there might be secondary effects on the bird population.

Surprisingly, no damage has been recorded in the Galloway forests as yet, although soil acidification produces toxic metals such as aluminium which attack the roots of trees and reduce their ability to fend off diseases. It may be that this condition, widespread in southern Germany and other regions of central Europe, is due rather to ozone pollutants and oxides of nitrogen and to different atmospheric conditions.

There has been nothing remotely approaching the scale of the problem in Scandinavia, where evidently 2000 lakes in southern Norway now have no fish. But there have been incidents, in particular the acid surge (confirmed by the University of Stirling's aquaculture department) which destroyed 20,000 rainbow trout at Kenmure Fish Farm in November 1982. A Nature Conservancy Council report and a 1979 study of 72 lochs and 40 burns in Galloway and south Ayrshire by two Norwegian scientists, Wright and Henrikensen, have shown that a number of lochs and streams have high acidity levels with a fish population under stress or extinct. There is some evidence that the River Cree and Loch Ken are beginning to be affected, waters in the area west of Loch Dornal and in the Loch Doon area in general are approaching danger levels, Loch Neldricken and Clatteringshaws are poor, Loch Grannoch is badly affected, and Lochs Enoch and Fleet and Skerrow have been variously reported as barren. It might, on the other hand, be unwise to assume that all stress situations are due to the same causes. Loch Enoch is especially interesting, as a study of core samples has shown that acidification started about 1850, which coincides with the early stages of the 'Second Industrial Revolution', and accelerated from 1940. It is quite possible that Loch Enoch was an early casualty about 1900. Eglin Lane from Loch Enoch to Loch Doon, and which used to be a good spawning burn for salmon and also had a stock of brown trout, is now barren.

Clearly more research is needed, because it is by no means clear whether the causes are straightforward or complex and multiple. Is acid rain caused mainly by sulphur dioxide from power stations and heavy industrial plant burning fossil fuels even hundreds of miles away? Now these emissions have decreased by a third over the last decade, but then their distribution patterns skyways are different because chimneys and stacks are so much taller. There is also, however, a whole pot-pourri of pollutant gases, ozone, fluoride, and especially oxides of nitrogen from the petrol combustion engines of cars (a huge increase in the 1960s and 1970s), chemical works (as brown plumes), and from the oxidation at high temperatures of nitrogen in the atmosphere when fossil fuels are burnt.

Is the increasing use of nitrogen-based fertilisers another factor? Does the Forestry Commission policy of monoculture planting of huge numbers of conifers increase acidity? The answer to this last query is not clear, and the results may vary from one area to another and there might be different consequences at different times of the year, as research in the Loch Ard Forest and the Loch Grannoch area seems to have led to different conclusions. The use of sprays and gases to kill off life and growth before afforestation is another emotive and controversial issue.

Better management, including liming of water, can produce short-term and expensive improvements; but long-term feasible 'solutions', assuming, that is, that there is a 'problem', possibly mean hugely expensive operations to reduce pollution at its source at power stations and factories or instead more emphasis on nuclear power. Currently the Solway River Purification Board is continuing a ten-year study of the impact of acid rain on Loch Dee and the Black Water of Dee and examining sediments in a number of lochs. And the Scottish and English Electricity Boards and the National Coal Board are beginning a five-year programme of experiments to improve the water quality of Loch Fleet involving the construction of temporary lagoons.

Fish farming from tank and loch fishery systems is a fairly new industry in Galloway going back to the mid-1960s. The idea, of course, is an old one, and certainly the Cluniacs at Crossraguel Abbey near Maybole had fish ponds 500 or 600 years ago. The Kenmure Fisheries near New Galloway uses a system of earth ponds with water pumped from Loch Ken; another farm at Kendoon Loch near Carsphairn uses floating cages; and the farm at Kempleton Mill near Twynholm has tanks with water from the River Tarff. In spite of recent problems it seems an ideal growth industry with employment opportunities in the various processes in hatcheries and in production and packing operations.

Another successful and more obviously visible water-based enterprise is the Galloway Water Power Company hydro-electric scheme completed in 1936. There was already, surprisingly, a small private hydro scheme with water from Ornockenoch on Rusco estate near Gatehouse completed about 1930 and still in use. The Galloway Water Power Company was set up in 1929 specifically to build what was a major and quite revolutionary project at that time. Work began in 1931, and over the next five years five power stations were built at Kendoon, Carsfad, Earlstoun, Glenlee, and Tongland (another station has recently been completed at Drumjohn near Loch Doon). Major dams had to be built at Kendoon, Earlstoun, Carsfad, Tongland, and Clatteringshaws. The area and water level of Loch Doon were greatly increased, and the important castle on its now covered island site was reconstructed above the new shoreline on the west side of the loch. A new loch reservoir was completed on the wet marshland of Clatteringshaws for the Black Water of Dee and a $3\frac{1}{2}$ mile tunnel to Glenlee.

The main water route can be followed from the A713 and the B7000 from Loch Doon by Carsphairn Lane to Kendoon Loch, Carsfad Loch, Earlstoun Loch, the now much higher Loch Ken and the Loch Ken/River Dee to the eight-foot barrage at Glenlochar, and down to Tongland. Much of this work, especially Loch Ken, now looks so natural that it is easy to forget that so much of it is manmade reservoir rather than natural loch. The SSEB Power Station at Tongland is now a tourist attraction in the summer. The fish ladder and pass systems with sluices and pools at the power stations and dams are particularly interesting and rather beautiful new technology—quite important and pioneering work when first constructed. As well as Tongland there are also fish passes at Earlstoun and Carsfad Dams, a one-chamber fish pass at Glenlochar, and a unique fish ladder at the dam at Loch Doon, where the water level can go up and down by as much as forty feet and which is in the form of a spiral inside a circular tower.

The list of lochs might suggest an overabundance of water—and well, yes, it does usually rain a bit in August. Obviously there are within Galloway considerable variations in average annual rainfall figures, but these do not really matter all that much if you are on holiday. After all, if you wanted boring permanent sunshine you would not be coming to Galloway in the summer anyway. This is rather a place for an all-weather holiday and it is excellent in those terms, and not least of all for photographers who can do so much with the mixture of sun and shadow and cloud and mist and storm which can be expected and looked forward to.

Fishermen can usually be guaranteed some moist damp days. Details of the very moderately priced and even free loch and river fishing should be obtained locally as there are inevitably variations over the years in stocks of fish and water quality. Permits may be had from the Forestry Commission, angling associations in several towns, Galloway and Ayrshire estate offices, hotels, and also the South West Scotland Water Board for reservoirs. Many lochs have the local brown or Loch Leven trout, and for coarse fishing pike and perch are fairly plentiful in many lochs and slow-moving river stretches.

Loch Trool is probably the most visited and most generally admired of all the many lochs in Galloway. Perhaps its compact quality has something to do with this. It is indeed quite small, about a mile and a half in length from west to east, yet has the romantic characteristics of a Perthshire Highland loch; that is, there are some steep hill slopes running down to the loch, the surroundings are well wooded with a mixture of old 'natural' woodland and modern Commission plantations, and in autumn it is a blaze of golds, yellows, oranges, browns and reds. A good afternoon walk is to go along the north side of the loch, round the east end and back along the south side passing the traditional site of a battle in 1307 in the Wars of Independence.

Loch Trool at only 250 feet itself is an excellent starting point to explore some of the superb hill lochs. A long and very hard day's walk is to follow the hillside above the Gairland Burn up to the line of lochs set under the great granite hills of the Merrick on the west, Craiglee and Craignaw on the east, and Mullwharcher to the north. This takes you above Loch Valley which is at 1050 feet, Loch Neldricken at 1146 feet, and Loch Arron at 1450 feet. Neldricken and little Arron both have small pockets of granite silvery sand. Further on still and higher up again is the most remote and isolated of all, Loch Enoch at 1617 feet, also with silver sand which used to be collected for knife grinding or sharpening. Enoch also has its own Loch in Loch, that is a small island itself with a tiny lochan.

Another stiff trek is up past the Round and Long Lochs of the Dungeon, on past Loch Dee, and then south to Curleywee: then south to Auchenleck and the road in to Minnigaff, or back to Glen Trool by Lamachan and the Nick of the Lochans. This can be very hard and very wet indeed.

Loch Ken is very different, and some people may prefer the gentle wooded scenery, settled farmland and the charming villages of Parton and Crossmichael at the south end. An excellent viewing route is to circuit the loch by the A713 from Castle-Douglas, the A762 from New Galloway, and the side road of Willowbank north of Laurieston to the Mains of Duchrae junction and then along the waterside east of Livingstone Hill to Glenlochar. Perch, roach and pike are plentiful, and the loch is famous for the massive 70lb pike taken in 1880—the stuffed and mounted twelve inch long and nine inch wide head is at Airds House. This is defining Loch Ken as the present loch going past Parton and some ten miles long, as compared to the older loch of some five miles before hydro-electric developments. An unfortunate conflict of interests has developed recently between local people, ornithologists, fishermen, general holidaymakers, and power boat enthusiasts now banned from Windermere and controlled by speed limitations on Ullswater. Very different views are possible on how best to reconcile recreational and tourist activities with farming, forestry, and the preservation of wildlife habitats.

For a complete contrast may I suggest the Wigtownshire moorland lochs —rather more bare, bleak, black and yet still very beautiful under the sun or in rain-lashed and leaden skies? Lochs Ochiltree, Fyntalloch, Dornal and Maberry are reached by the B7027 from Newton Stewart to Barrhill, and there are some superb moorland landscapes with drystane dykes stretching miles into the distance. And the Fell, Black and Mochrum Lochs south-west of Kirkcowan take you into something like another world.

The many other lochs and lochans, mine and mill dams, water supply reservoirs and artificial lakes include some charming corners. For eighteenth-century formal landscaping for great houses, Cally Lake and the Black and White Lochs at Inch; for lochs with castle island sites, Loch Urr, Lochnaw Loch and Lochinvar Loch; for tiny delightful tucked away lochs, the Colvend lochs, Lilie's Loch and the Loch of the Lowes near the Old Edinburgh Road, and the lovely Bruntis Lochs which provided water power for the Blackcraig lead mines.

The map references for the lochs are given in terms of a roughly central location in each case: some names, such as Black Loch, appear several times. The artistic O.S. lettering in light blue is often difficult to read on the new 1:50,000 maps. A few important drained loch sites have been included.

Loch Kindar	969641	Lochaber Loch	920703
Loch Arthur	905689	Lochrutton Loch	898730
Milton Loch	840715	Auchenreoch Loch	820715
Glenkiln Reservoir	844780	Loch Fern	864624
White Loch, Colvend	863547	Barean Loch	861557

Clonyard Loch	857554	Auchensheen or Duff's Loch	851560
Dalbeattie Reservoir	806613	Dalbeattie (Plantation) Loch	841601
Edingham Loch	837633	Carlingwark Loch	763613
Loch Patrick	788708	Black Loch	782718
Lochenkit Loch	801757	Corsock Loch	752756
Arvie Loch	741758	Erncrogo Loch	745676
Loch Roan	742693	Loch Smaddy	734699
Loch Lurkie	730707	Falbae Loch	737718
Loch Urr	760845	Lowes Loch	705785
Loch Skae	710837	Loch Howie	696835
Loch Brack	683821	Barscobe Loch	668813
Moss Ruddock Loch	632815	Lochinvar Loch	658853
Knockman Loch	666836	Knocksting Loch	698882
Trostan Loch	701902	Kendoon Loch	607907
Carsfad Loch	606860	Earlstoun Loch	612831
Loch Ken	656732	Woodhall Loch	671674
Lochengower Loch	694659	Darnell Loch	703657
Blates Mill Dam	679671	Bargatton Loch	692618
Glentoo Loch	701625	Mossdale Loch	656710
Stroan Loch	644704	Loch Mannoch	663601
Culcaigrie Loch	663577	Tongland Loch	713568
Jordieland Loch	712537	Fellcroft Loch	758505
Bengairn Loch	788521	Loch Mackie	808489
Loch Fergus (drained)	698511	Cally Lake	600553
Orknockenoch	580591	Loch Whinyeon	624607
Lochenbreck Loch	642656	Loch Skerrow	604681
Loch Fleet	560697	Loch Grannoch	542700
Clatteringshaws Loch	542770	Loch Dungeon	525844
Loch Minnoch	530857	Loch Harrow	527866
Loch Doon	495988	Loch Muck	NS 512007
Loch Bradan	425970	Loch Riecawr	435935
Loch Macaterick	440914	Loch Enoch	446852
Dry Loch	467856	Round Loch of the Dungeon	465847
Long Loch of the Dungeon	466841	Loch Arron	443838
Loch Neldricken	446830	Loch Valley	443816
Loch Narroch	452815	Long Loch of Glenhead	446808
Round Loch of Glenhead	450803	Loch Dee	467789
White Lochan of Drigmorn	469758	Loch Trool	407798
Lilie's Loch	517747	Black Loch	496728
Loch of the Lowes	469704	Kirrieroch Loch	364866
Loch Moan	349858	Loch Middle	396741
Silver Rig Loch	379730	Loch Swad	351716
Dow Lochs	373717		

(The nearby 'Loch of Cree' is the slow-moving River Cree)

Loch of Glenmalloch	426691	Glenamour Loch	447673
Bruntis Loch	447652	Penninghame	374694
Loch Eldrig	352667	Garwachie Lochs	351688 and 343690
Barfad Loch	324662	Barnbarroch Loch	400514
Loch of Fyntalloch	312740	Loch Ochiltree	318745
Loch Dornal	292761	Loch Maberry	287750
Loch Derry	252736	Eldrig Loch	253693
Black Loch	280655	Loch Heron	272648
Loch Ronald	266642	Clugston Loch	345573
Barhapple Loch	260592	Dernaglar Loch	263582
Whitefield Loch	235550	Loch Robin	246558
Fell Loch	310551	Black Loch	302545
Castle Loch, Mochrum	286537	Mochrum Loch	301533
Loch Chesney	337541	Loch Gower	326546
Elrig Loch	324492	White Loch of Myrton	359436
Blairbuie Loch	363416	White Loch, Ravenstone	401440
Dowalton Loch (drained)	406468	Penwhirn Reservoir	123697
Loch Ree	103698	Lake Superior	086704
Black Loch (Loch Crindil)	113613	White Loch	106609
Cults Loch	121604	Soulseat Loch	102586
Loch Magillie	097595	Loch Connell	018682
Black Loch	001635	Lochnaw Loch	NW 992632
Dindinnie Reservoir	022605	Knockquhassen Reservoir	020594
Dunskey Loch	004565	Logan House	102431

Well! it is hardly now a surprise to discover that Galloway has a myriad number of water-courses, sometimes straightforwardly 'rivers', with others referred to as 'water of' (Luce, Fleet . . .), and 'lanes' which are burns or streams usually, but not exclusively, connecting lochs. The term 'lane' might seem to suggest a neat, placid ditch, but this is by no means usually so at all, as some have cascades and falls of fast-flowing water. Most rivers have salmon and seatrout, some with commercial fishing using stake-nets or by net and coble in the tidal estuaries. (The coble is taken out across the river in a semicircle, and the net on ropes to a fisherman on the shore is put out as the coble goes out and then comes back to its starting point.) The tidal limits are often surprisingly far up the rivers, certainly the case on the Cree and the Urr and the Nith up to the 'Cauld' at Dumfries.

Moving from west to east, note first the Piltanton Burn, starting on the hill slopes near Allandoo in Leswalt Parish, then moving east past Crailloch and Lochans just south of Stranraer, and then meandering on behind Droughdool motte south of Dunragit, and hence into Luce Bay north of the

Torrs Warren dunes. So insignificant on the map, it is perhaps a surprise to find that it has seatrout (to 12 lbs.).

The Water of Luce has salmon and seatrout, nearly all belonging to Stair Estates. The Main Water of Luce, starting up at Bennan Hill in Ayrshire and now collecting only a small flow from the Penwhirn Reservoir area, is perhaps not quite the water-course it used to be. At New Luce it is joined by the Cross Water of Luce and becomes the Water of Luce proper. The Cross Water comes from the north at Strawarren Fell and Kilmoray in Arecleoch Forest in Ayrshire and then follows the line of the railway south. It has some attractive sections near New Luce east past the Loups of Barnshangan waterfall. On the Water of Luce note the once famous pool under the old railway viaduct west of Glenluce village.

The main Wigtownshire river complex is that of the Bladnoch and its tributary, the Tarf Water, both with salmon and numerous pike and perch. The River Bladnoch runs south from Loch Maberry to Glassoch and Shennanton and over the Linn of Barhoise, and then south-east of the B733 round Wood Hill near Crows and Horse Hill to Torhouse, Bladnoch, Wigtown Sands and the Cree estuary, where there are stake nets at Innerwell. The Tarf Water runs from Bembrake Hill south to Laggangairn to join the Bladnoch east of Kirkcowan. The old mills on the Tarf below Kirkcowan enhance a very attractive and picturesque corner. Other tributaries with spawning waters are the Black Burn which comes into the Bladnoch north of Shennanton, and the longer Water of Malzie running from the Fell Loch and Muchrum Loch near Drumwalt and then east past Corsemalzie and into the Bladnoch at Horse Hill south-west of Torhouse.

The River Cree has some of the best salmon and seatrout, and pike of course. The Cree with its tributaries has a huge catchment area and tends now to rise very quickly indeed with the rapid drainage now general from forests and plantations. The Cree starts at Loch Moan and runs south to more or less follow the line of the A714 to Bargrennan and Newton Stewart. There are waterfalls at Birch Linn north-west of Bargrennan, and a complete contrast in the still, slow movement in the 'Loch of Cree'. The road north from Minnigaff along the eastern bank of the river through the Wood of Cree to Clachaneasy is a lovely and usually very peaceful walk. Note the various sets of stake nets in the estuary near Creetown, and the sites of mediaeval to nineteenth-century river ferries and crossing points between Creetown and Spittal. It was possible at one time to be guided across the sands at low tide to Wigtown, which is really quite a thought, and definitely not something that should be attempted as a solo effort.

The main tributaries running into the Cree have several attractive

The west bank of the Cree above Cree Bridge, Newton Stewart, c.1910. A lyrical waterfront composition, probably by Hunter of Newton Stewart.

stretches. The Water of Minnoch, which has salmon, starts further north than the Cree itself at Rowantree Hill south of the Nick of the Balloch, then south past Loch Roan to the west and Kirriereoch Loch to the east, picking up burns off the west side of the Merrick, to join the Cree south of Bargrennan. The short three-mile run of the Water of Trool from Loch Trool into the Water of Minnoch is a lovely water-burbling glen, but watch out for adders! The little Penkiln Burn starts off Curleywee and Lamachan and then runs south to Auchenleck and roughly parallel with the delightful road walk into Minnigaff. The Palnure Burn, which has salmon and seatrout, runs off the slopes of Round Fell and Brockloch Hill south-west of Clatteringshaws, then past Murray's Monument and south through Bargaly Glen collecting burns off Cairnsmore of Fleet, and into a long tidal stretch past Palnure and into the Cree. There are very nice walks on either road from Palnure and in Bargaly Glen itself. Lastly, there is the cheerful Moneypool Burn starting at Meikle Bennan and running beside the B796 and the old railway line, and with a very good road walk from Chain Wood into Creetown.

The Big Water of Fleet starts from the burns running off Benmeal, Craigwhinnie, Craiglowrie, and Cairnsmore of Fleet, coming together round about Maggie Ireland's Wa's north of Little Cullendoch Moss, and

Draught Net Salmon Fishers at Tongland on the Dee, c.1910. Four men working the net, two onlookers (one at each end of the group), three small boys, a man at the oars, and two wee dogs.

then it runs south under the magnificent Big Water of Fleet railway viaduct east of the Clints of Dromore until it becomes the Water of Fleet at Aikyhill Bridge. It is joined there by the Little Water of Fleet, which starts at Loch Fleet, and then runs round Benmeal and south over Craigie Linn. The Water of Fleet proper, which has salmon and seatrout, runs below the charming small reserve at Castramont Wood, and then winds on to Gatehouse-of-Fleet, becoming a canalised river from Port McAdam into Fleet Bay. There are very pleasant walks up to the Skyre Burn Valley, on either road up the Fleet valley towards Rusco Castle, and from Cardoness beyond Skyreburn Bay across Fleet Bay at low tide and back by Sandgreen.

The River Dee system with all its tributaries covers an immense area. Because of the hydro-electric works it is perhaps easier to follow it upwards on a map from Kirkcudbright. It is, of course, a very different river now from that of the 1920s and earlier when the gorge at Tongland, in particular, must have been a thrilling sight with fishermen working the doachs (salmon traps) and using ladle nets and draught nets and shoulder nets.

The River Dee proper now is the stretch from the estuary and Kirkcudbright and Tongland to Bridge of Dee and up to Glenlochar, where it really merges into Loch Ken. Especially in flood conditions it is a good experience to walk over the old bridge at Bridge of Dee and then go north on the side road at the crossroads on the A75 towards Glenlochar. It can be a real

Boat house or shelter ('heather hooses') at St. Mary's Isle on the Dee Estuary near Kirkcudbright, c.1900. Wooden frames were made by the estate workmen.

world of water vistas with Threave Castle looming out of the mist and rain from different points on the road.

The Tarff Water, which joins the Dee below Cumstoun, starts at Loch Mannoch—waterfalls at the loch and at Kirkconnel Linn—and then runs south towards Ringford and the saltings beyond the Low Bridge of Tarff. There are some very pleasing short walks between the Low Bridge of Tarff, Tongland Bridge, and the Old Bridge at Tongland just a short distance up the Dee.

The source of the Black Water of Dee is Loch Dee, and Cooran Lane also brings water tumbling in from the north. From Loch Dee the Black Water runs south-east and into Clatteringshaws Loch at the north-west corner, and then from the south end through King Edward Forest to Stroan Loch. It then collects the Crae Lane at Holland Isle from Woodhall Loch and joins Loch Ken/the River Dee below Loch Ken viaduct near Parton. The road walk from Little Duchrae to Holland Isle is rather splendid, as was the railway line east to Loch Ken.

North of Kenmure Castle the main water-course is called the Water of

East Cluden Mill on the Cluden Water near Dumfries. A late eighteenth/nineteenth-century grain mill with wooden breast-shot wheels. Photographed in 1972.

Ken. Notices warning about sudden rises in the river level should be taken seriously, as a nice shallow waterway can without any other warning become a five or six feet deep torrent, and you will feel distinctly foolish stranded having a picnic on a rock in mid-stream. It is a pleasant drive to follow the Water of Ken along the B7000 to the High Bridge of Ken, and then the B729 and the side road north to Craigengillan Bridge and Altry Hill. The B729 towards Stroanfreggan Bridge and the Image Pool is an excellent short walk.

The Water of Deugh comes into Kendoon Loch from the north-west. Drive along the B729 to Carsphairn, the A713 to the new bridge below the Green Well of Scotland, and hence up the A713 to the side road at 517997 opposite Loch Doon and into Carsphairn Forest. The Water of Deugh comes through the Forest by twists and turns from Jedburgh Knees and Wedder Hill.

Tributaries of the Water of Ken include the Trolane Burn, which takes you into a delightful valley east of St. John's Town of Dalry (normally just Dalry) off the A702 and the A769; the Polharrow Burn from Polharrow Bridge on the A713, offering excellent road walking to Burnhead Bridge below Forrest Lodge; the Polmaddy Burn off the A713 a few miles north of

Polharrow Bridge, coming down past the deserted settlement on the mediaeval pack road; and the Black Water, which comes down from Knocksting Loch and Greentop of Margree past Butterhole Bridge and into the Water of Ken above Carsfad Loch.

The Urr Water is a salmon and seatrout river, running some thirty-five miles from its source in Loch Urr south to Corsock, the Old Bridge of Urr, Haugh of Urr, Dalbeattie, Kippford, and Rough Firth. There are superb stretches from Palnackie to Kirkennan, at the Motte of Urr and nearby at the Haugh of Urr on the Old Military Road, and at the Old Bridge of Urr crossroads. Streams coming into the Urr include Kirkgunzeon Lane at Dalbeattie, and the Crogo Burn and the Craigenputtock Burn in the north.

Further east the Southwick Burn coming out from Caulkerbush onto the Mersehead Sands has seatrout. And the Cluden Water in the old Stewartry on the north of Terregles and Kirkpatrick Irongray Parishes joins the Nith at Lincluden College. The Nith itself, of course, is still a very good salmon and seatrout river.

CHAPTER 3

The Land, the Hills and the Forests

The next time a member of your party slips on a rocky beach or some hilly crag in Galloway you may well not be thanked for mentioning that he/she has tripped over and landed on a splendid example of Ordovician or Silurian greywacke. On the other hand it may be some consolation later over dinner to remind everyone that it was some 500 million years ago that the rock was deposited as layers and layers of mud. For indeed the basic bedrock in Galloway is the greywackes and shales laid down some 600 to 400 million years ago.

If you look at a geological map of southern Scotland you will see two main bands. One, running from the east coast near Dunbar and going all the way through the northern Stewartry and northern Wigtownshire, and including the Kirkcolm, Corsewall, Leswalt and Portpatrick area west and south-west of Stranraer, marks the Ordovician period. The other band runs from the east coast through most of the Stewartry and the Machars and southern Rhins of Wigtownshire and marks the Silurian period. Good examples of the latter can be seen at Portyerrock Bay to Port Allan east of Whithorn, at Burrow Head and at the Fell of Carleton, and at Meikle Ross and Balmae Ha'en (Silurian graptolites) on the Dee estuary.

The Old Red Sandstone period, some 400 million years ago, is probably more generally known because of the obviously recognisable evidence of igneous activity in the intrusions of the granite masses of Criffel, Cairnsmore of Fleet and Loch Doon. The Criffel mass, set in Silurian strata, covers a huge area from the Nith in the north-east to Dalbeattie and on to Bengairn north-west of Auchencairn. The Cairnsmore of Fleet mass, set mainly in Silurian, covers an oval area from Loch Ken in the north-east to Clatteringshaws in the north-west and to Cairnsmore itself on the south-west and to the hills beyond Loch Skerrow on the south-east. Outside this mass the Kells range to the east and the Merrick range to the west are made up of a mixture of greywackes and shales and gritty sediments. There are also two smaller granite masses at Cairnsmore of Carsphairn, and the area with cliffs up to 175 feet north-west of the Mull of Galloway between Laggantalluch Head and Portencorkrie Bay to Crummag Head.

The Lower Carboniferous period runs from 350 to 270 million years ago. In the south-west this is represented by millstone grits, coal measures, and limestone series, some with a positive abundance of marine fossils (coral, shells, fish, mosses, ferns) from the seas and swamps. Areas to note include a strip of basaltic lava—millstone grit—in Kirkcolm and Leswalt west of and parallel with Loch Ryan (fossils at Craigoch Burn); coal deposits in the Sanquhar area in Nithsdale and in the Canonbie area in Eskdale (with fossil plants and shells), and coal outcrops at Powillimont south of Kirkbean and (probably) at Rascarrel Bay; and, more important, the very extensive limestone series area along the northern Solway shoreline between Kirkcudbright and Dumfries (with some rich fossil beds including shingle beaches for easy collecting), and especially between Hogus Point and Borron Point near Carsethorn, Arbigland and Gilfoot and Southerness, Port O' Warren and Gutcher's Isle, and the Rascarrel to Barlocco to Orroland stretch.

Two areas of red sandstones and breccias from the New Red Sandstone period from 270 to 180 million years ago should be noted. In Wigtownshire there is the area from Stranraer to Luce Bay and also the western shore and cliffs along Loch Ryan, and in Dumfriesshire the large area in Nithsdale from the Solway to Sanquhar and Thornhill, including the Locharbriggs red sandstone quarries near Dumfries. There is another important strip between Bennane Head and Ballantrae in Ayrshire and the basin round Lochmaben in Dumfriesshire.

Recent geological features from the Pleistocene period two or three million years ago through various Ice Ages to the last ice sheet coverage about 30,000 years ago and the most recent glacial environment about 11,000 to 10,000 years ago and the early stages of the Post-Glacial period afterwards include the sands and gravels and boulder clays of (fluvioglacial) drift deposits, for example at Logan Bay, Clanyard Bay, and the peninsula joining the Rhins of Wigtownshire to the mainland; the drumlins or ridges up to 40 to 150 feet high shaped by the ice flowing southwards, very common in the Machars, for example between Newton Stewart and Kirkcowan and south to Burrow Head; and the various ice erosion patterns and effects, such as the corries on Benyellary and the Merrick, the hanging valleys at the Grey Mare's Tail between Moffat and St Mary's Loch and the Buchan Burn in Glentrool, and the deepened loch basins of which Loch Trool is a good example.

Over the last 10,000 years the natural environment in North Britain has been comparatively stable, with the exception of changes in sea level. The concept of 25 to 100 foot levels is a simplified version of a much more complex series of changes in the balance between land and sea. The raised beaches marking various sea levels from 6,000 to 12,000 years ago are another common feature, and examples include the line of the River Fleet with 25 to 100 foot levels up to Castramon, the terraces from Machermore to Creebridge or the River Cree near Newton Stewart, the levels from Auchenmalg to Chippermore to Port William on Luce Bay, and possibly, although difficult to distinguish from fluvioglacial features, the sand and gravel terraces from Loch Ryan south to Luce Bay.

Sand and gravel pits, then, are fairly common in Galloway, and especially in the Stranraer area. Peat deposits from 6000/7000 years ago, or earlier for upland areas, have been cut with flauchtering spades for hundreds of years. Some extensive mosses are now under forest, but there are still very considerable areas of peat, if not on a central Ireland or Caithness scale. Some are still worked, including sections of the probably six or seven square miles of twelve to fourteen-feet thick peat between Glenluce and Kirkcowan, at Barmeal east of Monrieth and the Whithorn Moss north-west of Whithorn, on the 25-feet raised beach at the Moss of Cree where it is eighteen to twenty feet deep, the area by Loch Lane and the Flesh Market south of Loch Skerrow, the Moss of Edingham near Dalbeattie, the Lochar Moss east of Dumfries, and the peat rigs above Dalry, Lochinvar and Glenshimmeroch. Recent developments in commercial cutting include a 70-acre site at Larbrax Moor, north of Portpatrick, and Glenshimmeroch Moss north-east of Dalry.

Brick clay, for making bricks and drain tiles, from deposits 11,000/12,000 years ago, has been worked throughout Galloway. These include the 10 to 15 feet deposits on the River Cree south of Newton Stewart at Carty Tile Works (431625); at Cairnbrock (NW 97 66) north-west of Leswalt and at Clashmahew (063593) south of Stranraer; and at the sites of nineteenth-century brick and tile works at Culmore (101515) near Stoneykirk, Black Parks (067603) near Stranraer's old Town Station, Terally (120407) north of Drummore, Monrieth (358413), Broughton Mains (454452), Kirkchrist (682518) near the River Dee at Kirkcudbright, Brickhouse (982603) near Carsethorn, Terregles (936767), Kirkbean (990589), and Rydedale (971750) in Maxweltown.

Granite has been extensively quarried for building and monumental stone and aggregate in the Craignair Quarries (821606) near Dalbeattie and the smaller granite mass near Creetown at the Kirkmabreck (481565) and Fell Quarries (488567). Roadstone has been widely obtained from quarrying greywackes over the area and from basalt lava porphyrite near Kirkcudbright. Roofing slate was quarried in the nineteenth century at Cairnryan Hill (067687) and Grennan (126394) north of Drummore.

Limestone, for fertiliser, was quarried at Torrorie (964570) near

Workmen at Kirkmabreck Granite Quarries near Creetown, c.1890? Carefully posed on an enormous single granite block.

Mainsriddle (kiln and shaft), and west of Southerness Point (970542) (kiln and quarry) in the nineteenth century.

In spite of many searches for coal, inspired no doubt by the proximity across the water at Whitehaven of the largest and most modern coalmine in Britain in the early nineteenth century, only one coalmine shaft seems to have been sunk. This was recorded on the 1849 O.S. Six Inch survey at Rascarrel Bay (809482). Lower Carboniferous in the same area near Auchencairn includes barytes (barium sulphide), which is used in making steel, and this was mined in the nineteenth century and at irregular intervals up to about 1960. There are old barytes mines at Airyhill (788474) near Barlocco Bay, and at Airds (817484) near Balcary Point. Spoil also includes malachite (copper carbonate).

It is surprising just how many, generally small-scale, lead and copper and iron mines there were in eighteenth and nineteenth-century Galloway, and just how many spoil heaps and remains of vertical and horizontal shafts, water power systems and structures can still be located. It is difficult to imagine what can have been the feelings of the Cornish and Welsh miners when they arrived at some of the more remote locations. It is even more strange to think of the men and boys, strangers and locals, in the shafts and tunnels under the ground. At Blackcraig in the 1870s they went down by a series of ladders, hand over hand, foot over foot, past the 30 and 60 and 80 fathom levels . . . until reaching the new cuttings at 132 fathoms, twenty minutes down, thirty minutes up. It is also extraordinary and amazing that some of the veins were ever found at all in the cliffs and rock faces and in the hill valleys.

The extensive lead-mining complexes at Leadhills and Wanlockhead with a history going back at least 700 years are on a different scale from most of the Galloway ventures. Here the most interesting are at Blackcraig (settlement sites, shafts, and water power systems), Pibble (spoil heaps, shafts and an engine house), and Woodhead (remains of rows of cottages and garden plots, a school, spoil heaps, shafts, a smelting house, and water power systems). Mines include, from west to east:

Knockibae (189665), north-east of New Luce;

Coldstream Burn (386697) at Cruive-End Bridge and Wood of Cree (386694) north of Newton Stewart;

The Craigton (433652) in Rough Park Wood and Path Hill and the Blackcraig mines (446646), south-east of Minnigaff;

Cairnsmore (464634), Bargaly (466682), and Wicklow Wood, Cuil (475635), near Palnure;

Balloch Burn (488588), Culchronchie (501608), and the Pibble mines (523608, 528604) near Creetown;

Meikle Bennan (551615), Lauchentyre (558572), Kirkbride (569567), and Bar Hill (603541), near Gatehouse-of-Fleet;

Woodhead mines (532936) on the Garryhorn Burn near Carsphairn, and in the far north the Clennochburn Head mine (NS 622006) north-east of Cairnsmore of Carsphairn.

Green Hill and Moorbrack Hill south of Clennochburn Head have recently (1982/83) been surveyed by BP Minerals International, who also planned to sink twenty bore holes in 1984/85 in the hunt for copper, lead, zinc, silver and gold. Were these to be successful, then this would count as one of the most intriguing and promising opportunities for economic development and employment in Galloway in the future.

The list of metals is interesting and serves as a reminder that although the old mines are labelled 'lead' or 'copper', in fact, as their spoil heaps show, they often yielded more than one useful metal. Silver, for example, was a byproduct from the processing of galena at Blackcraig, and Leadhills/Wanlockhead yielded silver, zinc and copper. The only 'silver' mine as such in Galloway was the Silver Rig mine (377728) near Cordorcan north of Newton Stewart. There was no gold mine, but gold panning was tried in streams near Woodhead, Carsphairn in the eighteenth century.

Copper ores, usually as malachite or chalcopyrites, were worked at the Mary Mine (440347) on the shore south of Tonderghie near Burrow Head;

from a vein near the Waulk Mill, Kirkcowan (332602); on a larger scale in the 270-feet deep Enrick Mine (619549) and between 1908 and 1911 at the Doon of Culreoch (584627) near Gatehouse-of-Fleet; in two shafts on Hestan Island (838503); and in Colvend at a 'copper pit' (868528) east of Glenstocken Sands, and *in* the Piper's Cave (889545) in a 60-feet horizontal shaft and a 20-feet vertical shaft.

The Dalmellington iron mines in Ayrshire were, of course, on a very large scale. In Galloway iron ore was mined at the Coran of Portmark mine (503938) in the hills west of Carsphairn, and in the shafts in the Blue Faulds field of the Auchinleck mine (771526) near Auchencairn. Finding bands of shale stained red or purple because of the diffusion of iron has often resulted in extensive and unsuccessful searches for haematite, for example at Barrhill immediately south of Newton Stewart.

Nickel and arsenic were obtained from the nickel arsenide and iron sulpharsenide ores at Talnotry. There were two shafts near the line of the Old Edinburgh Road from Newton Stewart to New Galloway (at 482717) and another two shafts near the Grey Mare's Tail and the Black Loch respectively (494727) near Murray's Monument. Outside Galloway there are interesting antimony mines at Glendinning (NT 299968) with the remains of the eighteenth-century miners' village of James Town, and at the Knipes (NS 65 10) in upper Nithsdale south-east of New Cumnock.

Galloway, then, is good territory for the amateur collector of mineral specimens and gemstones. Many are difficult to identify in their natural state, but in general any quartz crystal pieces you find attractive and the more obvious items such as black haematite or yellow/orange/brown barytes should be picked up. Many of the best places, spoil heaps, quarries, burns, hill and farm land, road and railway cuttings, are obviously, of course, when you think about it, someone's property, and a genuine attempt should be made to obtain permission before doing any serious collecting. Most of the vertical and many of the horizontal shafts have been filled in, but some could be danger areas, and your enthusiasm should properly be tempered with a sensible degree of caution.

Beaches and shoreline areas can be worthwhile. You might look for, and without a deal of patience and good fortune not find, reddish barytes at Tonderghie, agate and onyx at Monrieth, topaz and agate at Rigg Bay, Garlieston, barytes, jasper, haematite, carnelian, and malachite at Barlocco and Rascarrel, epidote and molybdenite at Almorness, and amethyst, haematite, cairngorm, and pitchblend (uranium oxide) between Sandyhills Bay and Portling Bay. The railway cuttings between the old Gatehouse Station and the Water of Fleet Viaduct might yield yellow/brown iron pyrites, and the road cuttings near Clatteringshaws garnet (reddish/purple alamandine); and at the quarries at Craignair look for tourmaline (brown/black schorl) and at Lotus Hill, Beeswing for calcite, epidote, beryl, fluorspar, and molybdenite. Ramblings on Screel, Buchan Hill and Criffel might produce amethyst, on Pibble Hill cairngorm, on the Clints of Dromore garnet, on Long Fell tourmaline (schorl), and on Knocknairling Hill near New Galloway garnet (brown/red andradite) and tourmaline (blue indicolite).

This all sounds very purposeful. And on the whole hill-walking, discounting the record breakers ticking off all twenty-three summits in Galloway over 2000 feet, is perhaps most enjoyable when you have a reason for doing it, whether on paid vacation employment as a ponyman cum occasional acting auxiliary sheepdog, or exploring landscapes from above, or hunting birds and animals with a camera. It is possible to plan all sorts of day walks and hikes in Galloway either using public transport or a car. Those who prefer to stay in the mountains for a few days at a time will find bothies at Culsharg (415821) north of Glentrool, at Backhill of Bush (481843) east of the Cooran Lane, and at the White Laggan (467774) south of Loch Dee. Whether you plan a genteel walk or abseiling on the Mullwharchar cliffs, it is sensible to remember the simple commonsense rules—use new (not old) maps, preferably at the 1:25000 scale, with details of forestry plantations and tracks, do not rely on out-of-date guidebooks, try not to underestimate the time you will need to cover the distances involved, and particularly in interior areas with their bogs and tarns and lochans, take a compass, and unless you are Supergirl or Superman, leave a note where you are staying of the route you are going to follow.

Before exploring the mountain heartlands there is a lot to be said for trying out some of the most easily accessible climbs. Criffel (957618) is quite marvellous. Perhaps because of the sea in front of it it feels higher than it is at 1868 feet, and it certainly has the best views of the Solway Firth and vistas over to the Cumberland hills. Watch the tide racing in over the mudflats. From New Abbey village find the mill pond and follow the road up to 957654, then over a little footbridge and on to the track south up the hill to Knockendoch and up the ridge to Criffel summit (Douglas's Cairn); or, taking the A710 to Roadside south of Loch Kindar (979638), walk up the Ardwall road and the forest track up to the ridge between Knockendoch and Criffel summit.

Bengairn (770545) is only 1280 feet, but it is a real hill, quite steep, and with fine views over Auchencairn Bay and Hestan Island to the south-east and to Gelston and Carlingwark Loch to the north. Walk up from Auchencairn village taking the Cemetery road passing Bluehill, Auchenleck, Glenhead and Hass. Climb up to Dungarry fort (758536), a rather good Iron Age fort, from the track to Nether Linkins, and up to Bengairn from the old footpath from Hass to Over Linkins. Screel Hill (781553) has, at 1126 feet, almost as good a view, but it does appear to be unapproachably encompassed by plantations. However, there are tracks you can follow through up the hill from the Gelston road just before Potterland Bridge (797552).

Cairnsmore of Fleet (502670) is a 'must do'. From a distance it does look large and dull, but at 2329 feet it is a good climb, although it is difficult not to keep stopping to look across at the stupendous view over the Cree estuary and Wigtown Bay down to Cruggleton and Isle of Whithorn and then across to the Isle of Man, and from the top over to the Merrick and the vast quantities of forestry, but on a clear day also over even to Ailsa Craig off the Ayrshire coast. Approach from Palnure and Cairnsmore Estate and a clear path up Bardrochwood Moor and zig-zags up to the summit. The cairn may be Bronze Age. Good ridge walking. Aeroplane wreckage pieces from both World Wars I and II. Wild goats, foxes, red deer more likely to be seen on the north side. Same return route; or a hard ridge walk to the north, where you might come across a 'Billy Marshall' cave (494679), 30-40 feet long but concealed under a huge boulder on the north slope, down to the Louran Burn and to Corwar and the A712; or along Blairbuies Hill and through firebreak gaps in the forestry plantations to Bargaly Glen for Palnure.

The huge Galloway Hills area is roughly within the rectangle formed by the A714 from Newton Stewart to Bargrennan and the side road to Straiton on the west, the B741 Straiton to Dalmellington on the north, the A713 Dalmellington to New Galloway on the east, and the A712 New Galloway to Newton Stewart on the south. The most popular routes are from the Newton Stewart side; the more exacting hikes to less explored areas from the Straiton and Carsphairn sides.

As a quite tough introduction to the hills there is a lot to be said for starting with Curleywee (454769). Take the road through Minnigaff village and then follow the Penkiln Burn up to Auchinleck Bridge (447705). One way from here is to go up the forest road on the west side of the Penkiln Burn and then up by the Nick of Curleywee to the top ('nick' meaning gap, pass, saddle between ridges). Various boggy pools near the top, and the Five Pound Well is not as promising as it sounds. However, the forestry plantations now make this far less attractive a route than in the old days, and you may prefer instead to continue on the road north-east from Auchinleck Bridge up to Drigmorn and then work up the east side of the Pulnee Burn and up to Curleywee from Bennan Hill. Excellent views from Curleywee, the local 'Matterhorn', even though only 2212 feet, over to Loch Dee and the Merrick and the rough country to the north. Quite wild and, when the mist comes down, on the eerie side, no doubt enhanced by names like the Throat of the Wolf's Slock. Return, possibly after climbing round the saddle to Lamachan, slightly higher at 2349 feet, to Auchinleck Bridge; or, take the track east of Curleywee round the base of the White Hill and east of Loch Dee, over Dargall Lane and down the Glenhead Burn to Loch Trool and to Glentrool village, where, if you had an early start to the day, you might be in time to catch the local bus service to Newton Stewart.

The Merrick range has really five summits, Benyellary 2360 feet and Merrick 2765 feet, tackled from Glentrool; and Kirriereoch 2565 feet, Tarfessock 2282 feet, and Shalloch on Minnoch 2520 feet, best approached from the Straiton road. The Merrick is usually climbed from the Bruce Stone car park at Loch Trool, hence up the west side of the Buchan Burn and past Culsharg bothy, up Benyellary and on to Merrick following the nineteenth-century stone dyke, itself an amazing feature at this height when you think of the toil involved. The north face of the Merrick is steep and is best avoided. The climb can be very wet going in places and quite tiring, and a shorter climb up the Fell of Eschoncan to 1142 feet from the same starting point and with excellent views over Loch Trool would be a much better idea for a first-day-of-the-holiday outing, particularly if children and dogs are there as well. From the top of the Merrick you have before you a positive sea of lochs and peaks, and on a good day over to Ben Lomond and the Perthshire hills and to Arran, Kintyre, Ireland, Man and Cumberland.

Possibly as attractive and enjoyable is to take the track up the Buchan Hill, to 1600 feet if you go to the summit, cross the Gairland Burn and work along the Rig of the Jarkness, and then round to Craiglee, returning by the Trostan Burn. Visible from above at various points on the hills above Loch Neldricken is the 'Murder Hole', a roughly circular lagoon area on an inlet at the north-west end of the loch. An area of water with accumulations of mud and decayed vegetation round the edges, it is curious and odd, but not really especially sinister in spite of the name which is derived from Crockett's *The Raiders*.

Tackling the dramatic rocky ridges from the 2115-feet Craignaw to Craig Neldricken and from the Nick of the Dungeon to Dungeon Hill and to Mullwharchar at 2270 feet requires a very early start, careful planning, and some determination. Only, however, attempt as much as you can cope with at the time and carry enough food. But as this is the land for the golden eagle and buzzard, peregrine falcons and red deer, and does have a real wilderness quality about it, it should be attempted only given the prospect of reasonable weather conditions. There is a case for tackling this area from the north, that is going by car from the A713 along the Loch Doon road to the Castle, and walking along the forest road past Starr and across Gala Lane and south into the forest, then ups and downs by Hoodens Hill and the Lump of the Eglin to Mullwharchar, but this is very hard going indeed, a sair trachle.

From Craignaw and the Dungeon Hill you are looking down on to the remarkable Silver Flow, a lovely name for one of the most famous and most studied floating bogs in Britain. Hardly an attraction for most holidaymakers and not marked on the 1:50000 O.S. map, perhaps to discourage visitors, the Flow is in the area with the Saugh Burn on the east, the Brishie Burn on the south, and the Lochs of the Dungeon on the west. The Flow is a sort of enclosed plateau of 472 acres, with peaty pools up to 20 feet deep, ditches, hummocks and ridges, the whole full to the brim with water, and a growing thing as decaying vegetation marginally heightens the whole each year. It is also a little paradise for botanists, with a profusion of different mosses, bladderwort, butterwort, sundews, white sedges, bog asphodel/myrtle/and rosemary. Magnificent and beautiful, and rather terrifying. Film buffs will be reminded of the sort of screen classic in which the dark villain comes to a sticky and muddy end in just such a place as this. Unless with a Nature Conservancy party, keep well clear, and if in the general area circumvent it on the north side if making for Backhill of Bush.

The least-known hills are the Rhinns of Kells range, from the Coran of Portmark 2042 feet and Meoul 2281 feet, approached from the Garryhorn Burn, and along the ridge to Carlin's Cairn 2650 feet and Corserine 2688 feet; or up the Garroch Burn road for Loch Dungeon, Meikle Millyea 2450 feet, Millfire 2350 feet, and Corserine. There are usually even fewer hikers and climbers on the hills on the other side of the A713, the Moorbrack Hill 2137 feet already mentioned in connection with mineral developments and Cairnsmore of Carsphairn 2614 feet.

Now, gosh, this does all sound rather desperately invigorating and just a bit hearty. Are there no hills for the lazy, who want a short climb with a minimum of walking? Well, indeed there are. And you could start with a small Iron Age hill fort in this area by taking the B7000 from the A702 near Dalry or the B729 from Carsphairn to where it cuts off to the east above High Bridge of Ken, and hence to the bridge over the Water of Ken. A short scramble up the stony hill brings you to Stroanfreggan fort (637920), with very good views along the valley which has important prehistoric and Dark Age sites.

It would be a good idea to make use of the Southern Upland Way in this area to go up Culmark Hill (640897) for a super view of the Glenkens and the hills to the west. Take the B7000 to the side road at Barlaes Cottage (618857) and continue on it to a short distance beyond Butterhole Bridge (641881). The Upland Way goes along this road, past the Marskaig road end, and then cuts up the hill to the left through some trees and then over moorland to the top of the hill. The Way is marked as an old footpath on the O.S. map surveyed in 1850, and is on the line of one of the old drove roads.

Trusty's Hill (588561), west of Gatehouse-of-Fleet, has a splendid view at 225 feet of Fleet Bay, the Cally Estate, the planned town, and the Fleet valley. Take the road on the right at the end of the long straight stretch of the main road west of the Fleet Bridge, and then continue on it up the hill past some very pleasant houses until you see the sign for the footpath to Trusty's Hill. This is a good example of a small Iron Age and Dark Age hill fort, with seventh-century Pictish carvings on the rock face above the entrance on the south side. These are unique in the south-west of Scotland. Note the double disc and Z rod, the dagger and the sea monster. A pleasant walk is to continue west along the now blurred and confusing line of the old footpath to Anwoth, going down through a forest break to the old church.

The Doon Hill (403654) is a good short walk up from the main street in Newton Stewart. Take the lane past the Galloway Arms Hotel, the footpath up the hill above the *Gazette* offices, and continue on the road up the hill with the Douglas Ewart High School on the right—charming views of the hills and woods to the north and north-east—and on to Blairmount Park and up the gentle slope of the hill.

Windy Hill (430554) above Wigtown has a marvellous panorama over the town to Wigtown Sands and Creetown, to Kirkdale and Borgue, and south over Wigtown Bay to the Cumberland and Man hills.

The Hill of Ochiltree (327741) is completely different. Take the B7027 from Challoch on the A714 north of Newton Stewart and continue to the side road at 321708 (to Bargrennan). Walk from here passing Beoch (321717), a mediaeval homestead moat site—the farmhouse may incorporate the walls of an earlier, perhaps a tower-house, structure. You join the Southern Upland Way about half a mile beyond Beoch and take it along the road past Glenruther and then off the road over the Hill of Ochiltree until you rejoin the side road. On the south slope of the hill you cross a dip which is marked on the 1848 O.S. survey as the line of 'The Deil's Dyke', which may have been a fourth/fifth-century linear earthwork running from Loch Ryan and through Penninghame and Minnigaff parishes towards the Solway Firth. It runs across this hill from one side to the other (almost west to east) for about a third of a mile. From the hilltop there are interesting views of the lochs and forests to the north and west.

For a hilltop view of Loch Ryan take the A718 from Stranraer, the B798 to

Leswalt, and then the minor road past the old churchyard and up High Kirkland Hill to stop below the Tor of Craigoch (008646). Quite high at 410 feet, but starting from about 360 feet on the road, this was probably a hill fort. Superb views to the Wig and Cairnryan to the north-east and towards Stranraer to the south. It is easy to forget that ships sailing out from Stranraer for Ireland are in fact going *north* up Loch Ryan before swinging out and around north of Milleur and Corsewall Points.

Now then, what do you do with Aunt Jane and Uncle Fred, averaging 78 and 15 stone, who would like to climb up and down some hills in a car? Well, of course, there are the main roads, such as the A713 from Dalmellington to Carsphairn and the A714 from Barrhill to Bargrennan, which still have, in spite of the forestry, some fine panoramic vistas, but six spectacular little runs you might like to try to test your car brakes and your passengers' nerves are: the same run from Leswalt past the Tor of Craigoch, then continuing to the T junction at NW 978663, by the B738 to Ervie, and back by the B798 to Leswalt, for interesting farming landscapes and seascapes; the triangular run up the hill from Drummore passing the school, left on the B7065 past Kirkmaiden Church and the fort next to it, south to the crossroads at Damnaglaur, and then left down the B7041 passing High Drummore and back into the village; for super views across to Murray's Isles, Ardwall Island and Wigtown Bay, take the tight little side road going off the A75 near the old Kirkdale Bridge at 517531, the road to the right over Barholm Bridge, up the steep winding road which takes you along past Barholm Castle, and then east passing Bardristane and High Auchenlarie before returning to the A75 near Laggan; the minor road west from the A762 at Laurieston through the forest and then down the long hill towards Gatehouse-of-Fleet; the A711 south from Kirkcudbright to Mutehill, the first road on the left going up the hill along the Buckland Burn, crossing the Buckland Bridge and taking the road to the left past High and Low Kirkland to join the B727, and then down the hill into Kirkcudbright; and the road from Shawhead to Glenkiln Reservoir (840784), hence by Speddoch Hill (on O.S. Sheet 78) down to the Cairn Water, west parallel with the Glenesslin Burn past Sundaywell and the side road to Loch Urr, down the road on the west side of Loch Urr and west of Monybuie Flow to Corsock, along the A712 and south on the B794 (signposted for Dalbeattie) to Old Bridge of Urr, then right to Clarebrand and on to Castle-Douglas.

Locals will all have their own favourite viewpoints to add to these. Visitors can easily miss them and can, moreover, on a short weekend visit to Galloway get a very one-sided impression of the area. To travel to, for example, Newton Stewart by the A76 to Dumfries and the A75 by Castle-Douglas is to pass through a predominantly farming landscape; but to take the A713 from Ayr to New Galloway and the A712 via Clatteringshaws is to pass through miles and miles of forest. Forests now blanket some 22% of the land area of Dumfries and Galloway Region, the result mainly of high-density planting in the 1960s and early 1970s. Forestry is now a major industry with a predicted capacity to provide an annual crop of one million cubic metres of timber by 2030. In spite of some small disposals of land under recent government policy in 1984/85, the Forestry Commission has a massively preponderant share of the Galloway forests.

It should be said that there is still a vocal anti-forestry lobby, possibly originally based in part on a natural suspicion of the role of a 'nationalised' industry which the Forestry Commission, founded in 1919, of course is, but more generally on a nostalgia for the old (and equally man-made) bare upland landscapes. Although it might seem at first sight that forests of Sitka spruce in Galloway are about as visually appealing as forests of Sitka spruce in Finland, nevertheless closer examination of the work of the Forestry Commission shows that, after mistakes no doubt in the early years of major expansion, it has gone out of its way to improve both its image and its performance. To persuade people that it is possible to learn to live with and even to love conifers is certainly partly an astutely managed public relations exercise by the Commission, but it does produce real benefits. And if you look at the forests you see many examples of areas where felling and thinning have been done to allow views to emerge again, where dull straight lines have been concealed or masked to provide some variation, where open spaces have been left or rowan and birch and Scots pine planted on little hills and in spaces between the dark walls of spruce, and where drystane dykes have been replaced or repaired. At the same time very elaborate provision has been made to 'open up' forest areas by planning walks and trails, car parks and picnic areas, caravan sites and vacation cabins, offering very good value rough shooting leases, devising road routes such as the Queen's Way and the Raider's Road, opening a Wild Goat Park, a Deer Range and the Galloway Deer Museum on the A712. While it would not be difficult to criticise any or all of these operations, the overall intention is certainly admirable.

Holidaymakers may also enjoy looking at the industry itself by visiting the Kirroughtree Forest Garden Policies and the Fleet Farm Nursery for an impression of the scale of the operation in the millions of trees seeded in beds for future planting, and in spotting some of the work being done in felling and clearing and in preparing stobs and poles and sawlogs. Some horses still work in the forests, but you are more likely to see tractors these days. The post-war Forestry villages at Glentrool and Kendoon are interesting as examples of modern planning. Changing patterns of work and residence and the problem in each case of 'isolation' have resulted in houses being sold off to private buyers.

The main forests include Mabie Forest near New Abbey, occasionally infested with packs of yelling schoolchildren, the Fleet Forest near Gatehouse-of-Fleet, Penninghame Forest north-west of Newton Stewart, Kilsture Forest near Sorbie (including oak, birch, ash), the huge Glentrool Forest of some 50,000-plus acres (including hazel, oak, ash, sycamore, Norway maple), Carrick Forest in the north, Kirroughtree Forest near Minnigaff (including ash, beech, cypress, various eucalyptus trees), Clatteringshaws Forest, Dundeugh Forest, the Garraries Forest east of Lochs Enoch and Neldricken, and Bennan Forest, Cairn Edward Forest, and Garcrogo Forest east of New Galloway. Some of the more interesting varieties of trees are from plantations going back to the 1930s and '40s.

There is probably virtually no 'natural' forest in Galloway, that is in the proper sense of deciduous woodland which has not been planted or coppiced or managed over many hundreds of years. However, there is some very attractive older woodland, often with oak, birch, and alder, and sometimes also beech, hazel, rowan, hawthorn, willow and wych elm. This includes the Wood of Cree, the earlier woods at Caldons, Buchan and Glenhead in Glentrool, Garlies and Knockman Woods in Cumloden Deer Park near Minnigaff, the woods at the edge of the Bennan Forest in the Ken valley, the woodland with oak and holly at the Needle's Eye Reserve, and the Castramont Wood north of Gatehouse-of-Fleet. These older woods have the delights also of masses of ground plants, ferns and mosses, wood sorrel, speedwell, yellow pimpernel, golden rod, wood sage, and many others.

Many estates have eighteenth and nineteenth-century woods and plantations for pleasure and profit in their policies, including exotic importations such as the huge Douglas Fir and Giant Sequoia. Castle Kennedy with its pinetum with two hundred varieties of conifers and its monkey-puzzle trees is perhaps the most impressive. Others of note are Arbigland, Kirkennan, Munches, Cally, Monrieth, Glasserton, and Galloway House at Garlieston, Logan and Ardwell, and Glenlee Park in the Glenkens.

With its mountains and hills, moors and flows, marshes and merses, sand dunes and sea cliffs, Galloway has an immense variety of areas of botanical interest. The mild and relatively frost-free climate along the Solway, and especially in the Rhins of Wigtownshire, makes it possible for many plants to survive at their northern limits and for more exotic sub-tropical importations to flourish in sheltered gardens and woodland. Portland spurge and seakale and elecampane survive, the non-fruiting palm is a not uncommon feature in local gardens, eucalypts do well as far up the Solway as Kippford, bamboo can be found growing wild, rhododendrons become miniature forests in the Lochnaw area. Showpiece gardens include the Logan Botanic Gardens with cabbage palms and tree ferns and giant flax, Castle Kennedy with its radiating avenues and formal gardens, Arbigland, Ardwell, and smaller gardens such as Broughton House in Kirkcudbright with its Japanese theme and Barnhourie Mill. And in many towns and villages—Dalry is a good example—the small house gardens ablaze with colour and imaginative sensibility provide much pleasure to residents and visitors alike.

Other areas of special interest for botanists and ecologists include the merses along the Nith with their sea meadow grass, red fescue, sea milkwort, sea arrowgrass, sedges including chestnut sedge, sea lavender, and yellow marsh cress; the Drum Mains reedbed (984610); Kirkconnel Flow between New Abbey and Dumfries, a raised bog altered by peat cutting and nineteenth-century ditches, with heathers, lichens, and Scots pine; the Ken-Dee marshes at Hensol and Holland Isle and Kenmure Holms, with some unusual plant life including seawort, spignel, gingerbread sedge, and purple small-reed; the Dowalton Loch site, drained in 1863, a farmland area including rocky scrub and wet and dry grassland with a rich variety of plants including marsh and heath spotted orchids, sundew and butterwort, field gentian, quaking grass, yellow sedge, marsh marigold, meadow sweet, bog bean, water plantain, and many others; Kilhern Moss, south-east of New Luce, another eerie peat-bog site, but unusual as being a crater type on top of a hill and therefore possibly a lake 10,000 years ago; the sand dunes at Torrs Warren south-west of Glenluce; and the Mull of Galloway clifftop area with some surprising plants, including yellow vetch and mountain milk-vetch.

Most areas of interest south of the A75 are likely to be on private estate or farm land. Knowing which farm and which farmer is no longer easy, given the number of amalgamations over the last thirty years, with from two or three to as many as eight farms being taken into one unit. Farming is still very much the main industry in Galloway, and farms are more necessarily than ever commercial enterprises. Although some farm wives are happy to take bed and breakfast visitors, and although you may still if you search hard enough find a few smaller and simpler, more traditional farms, by and large farmers have to be businessmen with expertise in devising programmes of integrated management, in coping with the complex financial problems posed by variations in UK government and EEC planning, in implementing scientific breeding schemes and in caring for livestock which require to be protected from a host of diseases and potential maladies, in running

Carsphairn

'Rush Hour Traffic' in Carsphairn, c.1910. Note the carts and street furniture and the shop on the left, and four delightfully overdressed children. The little boy on the right is in a sailor suit. The girl on the left has a hoop.

expensive and complex machinery, and in organising as small a labour force as possible with maximum efficiency, which on at least one estate includes using hand walkie-talkie sets from office to farm labourer on his tractor in the fields.

Although there are area specialities, such as early potatoes in the lighter and warmer soils of the raised beaches in Wigtownshire, and there is a fair acreage of barley, but very little oats, Galloway is essentially livestock farming country with large numbers of dairy cattle (although fewer than formerly) especially in the Rhins of Wigtownshire, beef herds, and hill and moorland sheep, often now in amalgamations of hill sheep and lowland cattle units.

The range of breeds and crosses from Galloways and Ayrshires with Herefords, Friesians, Jerseys, Charollais, Holsteins, Limousin and Highland Cattle is now bewildering to the amateur. Straightforward Galloways are still, however, numerous and popular, with a good export market for high quality stock. West Germany has been a good market in 1982 and 1983. With their thick long black outer 'waterproof' coats and second soft inner layer well able to winter out, and good at searching out food for themselves over large areas of poor-quality grazing marginal land, they are tough and hardy beasts. As well as the plain black Galloways there are also Red Galloways and the recently registered White Galloways, which you may spot on Ardwall or Kirkmabreck; and the Belted Galloways ('Belties' or 'the cows with their liberty bodices on', a naughty phrase from the '20s) and Red Belted Galloways with a snow-white band round their middle. Visitors seem generally to find 'Belties' particularly appealing, but should not stop their cars suddenly on the A75 in Anwoth or Borgue parishes to photograph them if they have a 'cowboy' of a different sort belting down behind them in a juggernaut. There are also 'Beltie' herds in the USA, Canada, Australia, New Zealand, and South America.

The days of farm cheesemaking are probably gone forever, but the creameries at Dalbeattie, Kirkcudbright, Sorbie, Bladnoch, Dunragit, and Stranraer manufacture a wide range of milk-based products, from Scottish Cheddar and UHT milk and high protein powders used for stabilising the whisky/cream mix in liquors and in animal feedstuffs, confectionery and coffee whiteners, to the Feta cheese supplied to Arab countries and to Iran. Feta cheese was originally a goat milk cheese, but the Galloway Creamery Feta is made from cow's milk.

Blackfaces are still the basic sheep stock in Galloway, but there are North Country Cheviots, Bluefaced Leicesters, Charollais sheep and various crosses. Blackface rams in 1983 and 1984 made record prices at Newton Stewart of £17,000 and £14,000, and although these are exceptional, the statistic does help to make the point that the hill sheep you see at Glenquicken, Cuil, Drannandow, Cambret, Claughreid and many other farms are valuable properties.

To understand Galloway it is an experience to spend some time at the sheep or cattle sales in the markets at Castle-Douglas or Newton Stewart. Even the most apprehensive and uncomprehending are still most unlikely to end up the proud but accidental owner of a Beltie! In the summer the Agricultural Shows at Stranraer and Wigtown and Kirkcudbright are great occasions, and another educational and enjoyable experience is to visit Palgowan Open Farm off the Glentrool to Straiton road north of Newton Stewart. Palgowan is a large hill farm with Blackfaces grazing on Benmore, Benyellary, Merrick and Kirriereoch. It has demonstrations of dogs working cattle and sheep, clipping, wool and skin curing, drystane dyking, and craft work in horn.

The drystane dykes are very impressive features of the Galloway landscape, on the roads and lanes and climbing up and over the hills above the A75. Training courses are still provided by the Castle-Douglas training group of the Agricultural Training Board, and the Stewartry of Kirkcudbright Drystane Dyking competition held in alternate years (last in September 1985) at Gatehouse-of-Fleet is a national event to which dykers come from all over Scotland.

Few farms now have hens or ducks or geese. You may still see near Kirkcudbright and Garlieston some of the magnificent Clydesdales, the most charming and gentle of all animals, to seventeen or eighteen or nineteen hands high and with a yard-long face. The Clydesdale is now a popular show horse and is in demand for that purpose for export markets in Canada, the USA, and Australia, just as in the nineteenth century, when it was a great working horse on the Prairies, there was a thriving export trade in the Galloway strain of Clydesdales owned by the Pickens and Sproats and Marshalls and Browns. A few individuals keep one or two goats to sell surplus milk and yoghurt and cheese, and there are milking sheep for sheep's cheese on a farm near Annan. Rare breeds which you may come across include Manx Loghtans at Dunscore, and Shetland cattle, Eriskay ponies and North Ronaldsay and Gotland sheep near Gatehouse-of-Fleet. Although this might seem at first sight to be decorative or hobby farming, this is in fact very practical and important work keeping the older breeds in being as part of the national heritage of the British Isles.

CHAPTER 4

Beasts and Birds

Galloway is one of the best places in the British Isles to see and study wild animals and birds, almost as good for the former as it is internationally known for the latter. Probably the most accessible and visible animals must be the feral goat population at Glentrool and in the Wild Goat Park (492720) on the A712 near Murray's Monument. Many of the extremely attractive and photogenic black/brown/cream coated goats at the latter are now about as wild as a bevy of street photographers. The goats are probably all the descendants of domestic animals allowed to run wild in the nineteenth century. The tenants of 'Drumruck, Murraytoun and Orquhers' north of Gatehouse-of-Fleet, for example, ran 800 goats and 300 sheep under the terms of their 1775 lease. Normally very shy animals which keep clear away from humans, they are spectacular on steep rock faces, especially the formidable billies with their horns up to three feet long. The ones you see near the Water of Fleet Viaduct might well be directly descended from the Drumruck goats. The population is now managed and controlled by the Forestry Commission with the occasional contribution by poachers from an ethnic minority in the West of Scotland.

Red deer were plentiful in mediaeval Galloway, but were probably almost extinct by the end of the eighteenth century. Their survival was largely due to the creation of a number of nineteenth-century deer parks with their own herds, most notably the Galloway Estate park at Cumloden near Newton Stewart, and the encouragement of deer in the mountain hinterland behind. The native strain may have been improved in terms of body weight by the introduction of North American Wapiti deer at Cumloden and possibly with stock from the Duke of Bedford's Woburn estate. By the end of the 1939-1945 War and throughout the 1950s and 1960s most of the 1,500 and 1,700 beasts were running wild. Following an extended programme of necessary culling (262 killed in 1974 and 369 in 1975) the present number is probably about 500, kept as far as possible west of Loch Ken and north of the old Dumfries-Stranraer railway line and including a number also in Wigtownshire. With this stock management history and the relatively soft living in Galloway, it is not surprising that the Galloway red deer are by a considerable margin of up to 40% or 50% body weight the largest in Scotland. Of course the numbers are rather different, as there may be some

Memorial to a practical conservationist, John Murray, gamekeeper to Capt. John Gordon of Kenmure Castle, who died in 1777 after forty-six years' service. In Kells Churchyard, New Galloway. Note powder flask, fishing rod, gun, dog and game bird.

200,000 red deer in the Scottish Highlands and Islands. They are far more impressive when seen in the bare hills or if encountered to their and your own mutual surprise in the woods, but can more easily be seen grazing on grass and heather and lichens and mosses at the 600-acre Red Deer Range on Brockloch Hill (522732) above the A712. It is also interesting to note that a red deer farm has recently been established on a 90-acre holding at Barnhourie, near Sandyhills, and that this may eventually have 200 hinds plus followers.

Driving along the A712 through the forests at night can be a bit nerve-racking, seeing not pink elephants or wild men of the woods or our

Galloway headless ghosts (which prefer anyway the fat good land to the south), but the bright eyes of red deer and the ill-defined shapes around them. They are definitely a hazard, but you are far more likely to hit roe deer at their regular crossing places, and the little roe deer bucks at 30 inches at the shoulder and 40 to 60 lbs are tough little brutes who can easily knock in the side of the average British car. There are enormous numbers of roe deer all over Galloway in scrub and woodland areas, but they are extremely wary of humans and usually have plenty warning of anyone approaching through trees and undergrowth, so they are not all that easy to spot. With foxy red summer and grey/brown winter coats they are charming little creatures, but Bambi is unfortunately very destructive, eating the shoots and buds and twigs of small trees, and has to be kept down. The 'high seats' or wooden platforms you see in some forestry plantations are used for shooting roe deer. If you do not see them, you may well hear them yapping or barking to each other from May to September, the doe naturally being more talkative than the buck except during the rutting season, or see plenty evidence of their tracks and droppings, or note the trees with their bark rubbed away by bucks rubbing their antlers from about 7 to 22 inches up above the ground, or be puzzled by the weird pattern of single or concentric circles or rings made round a bush or a shrub tree during rutting.

The old estate parks held some exotic varieties including Muntjac deer from the East Indies, Chinese Water deer, and a few Sika deer from Japan or Formosa, a smaller version of ordinary red deer; you might come across fallow deer in the Cumloden Park and Wood of Cree area and in Dumfriesshire in the area between the River Annan and the Forest of Ae. The fallow deer vary in colour from red/brown with white spots to black/grey or cream or a whiteish brown, and are about three feet high at the shoulder with stags up to 200 lbs. Between Newton Stewart and Creetown it is not easy to be certain which variety you are seeing.

Foxes are very common indeed in woodland, scrub and forest and hilly areas. Indeed afforestation has coincided with something of a fox population explosion for farms close to large forests, with particular problems near Carsphairn and in Upper Nithsdale. Annual kills in Forestry Commission properties can be very substantial (1,354 foxes in one year in all South of Scotland forests, for example). There is nothing perhaps quite so magical as watching unobserved a large dog fox at work moving across country. Again you very often catch a fox in car headlights at night.

Red squirrels, stoat, weasel, brown hares and blue or mountain hares are fairly common. So unfortunately are mink, and they might become a real menace. Badgers are plentiful, but, of course, rarely seen by anyone. Otters

"And Angels . . ." A McConchie photograph of a group of little Kirkcudbright girls, c.1895, very much in the style of so many Hornel paintings.

are not scarce, but are almost as elusive. The two lively sculptures of otters by Penny Wheatley are worth looking for, one on a rock in a pool in the Black Water of Dee on the Raiders Road from the A712 to the A762, and the other as a monument to Gavin Maxwell, of the Elrig and Monrieth family, on the headland between Monrieth Bay and Kirkmaiden Bay. Wild cats in the strict and proper sense, that is not merely feral domestic cats, have been reported in the Dundrennan area and in Laurieston Forest.

Extinct animals include reindeer, wild ox, brown bear, elk, wolverine, lynx, polecat, wolves (as late probably as the sixteenth century) and boar. Actually a pair of wild boar were imported to Ardwall in 1969, had a litter of piglets, and then all escaped in 1970. This engendered some considerable excitement and alarm amongst adjacent proprietors, pig farmers, the Forestry Commission and the Department of Agriculture. However, all were killed in the first round-up except one, later christened 'Fred', and he remained at large for some time. When at last shot he was reputed to be five feet long and to weigh 274 lbs. Apart from this excellent true story there are, however, unfortunately no loch monsters, no mermaids, and no escaped puma stories, so clearly there is plenty of scope for initiative in the local Tourist Board offices.

Grass snakes are probably rarer than adders, which seem to be common on rough and hill ground and in the forest areas. The adder or northern viper is about 18 to 20 inches long, has a zigzag body-decorated pattern and has a V or diamond marking on the head. The skin is sloughed twice a year, and skin colour and the colour of the markings vary at different stages of the life cycle. You are most likely to see young or baby adders basking in the sun in the high summer to soak in ultra violet rays. At least one beach access path over rocky ground seems to have a number every year. You may well hear somebody complaining about a 'plague' of adders, but this is not necessarily statistically impressive evidence and rather relates to the real possibility of seeing a large number in a small area in a limited time period. Adders hibernate in an earth burrow or under boulders in scree, often in a cluster, until February or March, and later in the year travel if not as a Marxist collective, at least together and more or less at the same time to summer feeding grounds. These might be several hundred yards away, and there they will have dens in old trees or grass tussocks or in rocky banks. They eat mice and shrews and voles and nesting birds.

Adders are very shy, hide and hiss furiously, but only bite for self-preservation. Inquisitive small terriers are vulnerable and can die from bites. On the other hand it is doubtful if the number of humans who have died from adder bites in Scotland over the last hundred years has reached double figures. However, bites should be attended to at once—any dramatics with pen knives or Count Dracula acts are unnecessary, but you are anyway infinitely more likely to be bitten by a dog, a cat, a child or a parrot, or all four, than by an adder. Bee stings are statistically more dangerous.

There are plenty of lesser animals for predators, of whom birds are, of course, the most professional killers. Frogs, newts, lizards, and toads, including the rare natterjack toad in the Southerness to Caerlaverock area, are the most noteworthy.

Birds are a consuming interest for many who live in Galloway, and to the flocks of ornithologists in cars and coaches who come here all the year round, but perhaps especially in the autumn and winter months from September to March. There is always something of interest from birds which live on or visit salt marshes or dunes or sea cliffs or pebble beaches to birds which prefer moorland and mountain and freshwater lochs and streams. With Scottish Wildlife Trust, Royal Society for the Protection of Birds (RSPB), and National Nature Reserves, and a network of minor and side roads providing quite easy access by car or on foot, observation safaris in comfort are easy to plan. And there are simply enormous numbers of geese and waders, and a remarkably high proportion of some British birds, with perhaps one-fifth of British peregrine falcons and a considerable percentage of the world population of barnacle geese wintering and roosting in the Solway area.

Given the difficulties in identifying size and shape and colour markings from the silhouettes of birds against the sky in often only fleeting glimpses, experts will often admit to uncertainty; amateur enthusiasts may prefer the luxury of seeing what they want to, but in any case will have done their homework on habitat and feeding characteristics and swimming and flight peculiarities and calls and songs by reading some of the excellent field guides published by Collins, Hamlyn, Mitchell Beazley and Macmillan. Birds are mostly very efficient food gatherers, and it greatly enhances understanding and enjoyment to know what they are doing. Watch, for example, that charming little killer the oyster catcher stalking and taking cockles on a receding tide. It gets its beak into the partly open shell as the cockle is filtering water through its feeding tube, severs its muscles so that it is helpless, and then takes it to a stony surface to smash the shell open. What admirable economy of effort and elegance!

Very few suggestions are offered here about the numbers of particular bird populations, as although there are an ample number of reliable reports available, and especially for the more gregarious varieties, these are constantly changing, and the data in many specialised and local studies of only a few years ago are now inevitably and substantially out-of-line with present figures. This may be because of increases in numbers, as with the barnacle geese in the Solway and birds of prey in the forest areas, or in the other direction whether from local reasons, such as excessive shooting by wildfowling parties from continental Europe and England, or from climatic and other variations hundreds of miles away. The pressure of just too many ornithologists at the same times and places is probably not yet a major problem, although whether all farmers would agree with that assessment is another matter. There is also, of course, and perfectly understandably, an anti-bird lobby amongst some farmers whose fields are the feeding ground of geese; but land reclamation by farmers could in the next decades become more of a problem. However, there is no need for pessimism in such a rich and large area with such a variety of habitats.

The salt marsh and inter-tidal stretches in the Nith estuary and the northern Solway between Carse Sands at Kirkbean and Blackshaw Bank and Priestside Bank at Cummertrees constitute one of the best areas in the British Isles for wintering geese and ducks and waders. The most important part is the National Nature Reserve, opened in 1957, from Caerlaverock to the Lochar Water, and the overlapping Wildlife Trust Reserve at East Park farm (NY 051656) (O.S. sheets 84 and 85). The latter, which in summer has sheep and cattle grazing, in winter is pasture for geese. It has an excellent observatory and tower and hides. Take the B725 from Dumfries, passing Glencaple and Caerlaverock Castle, and the side road at NY 030668 to East Park. Walking on these public roads and on the track south of Caerlaverock Castle is interesting.

Huge numbers of barnacle geese, increasing from 3,000 in the 1950s to 8,000 plus in the mid-1980s, fly in during September or October from Spitzbergen via Bear Island, some 1,500 to 1,800 miles north. They are very gregarious and in a field can seem as noisy as a kennel full of dogs abandoned while their owners are on holiday. There are also large numbers of pinkfooted geese from Iceland and Greenland; greylags and Greenland whitefronts; and occasional rarities such as Baikal geese from eastern Russia and Western bean geese; and also Bewick's swans from northern Russia and Finland, and whooper swans from Iceland. Good numbers of golden plover, oyster catcher, curlew, dunlin, pintail, scaup, knot, widgeon, redshank, teal, ringed plover, beetailed godwit . . . plus hen harriers, merlins, peregrine falcons and kestrels.

For more of the same, and certainly more greylags, pinkfoots, and barnacle geese, continue on the B725 to NY 105678, turn right south to Priestside and then follow the road parallel with Priestside Bank and on to Cummertrees. Hence either by car on to Powfoot for the rocky Powfoot and Howgarth Scars, or walk down the track from Cummertrees.

For a brief stop and walk if spending the day in Dumfries, take the B725 to Glencaple Quay (994686), and walk along towards Storr Point on the road. Time permitting, the walk up the side road at NY 003666 passing Dovecotwell, north past Greenmill, and back passing Muirpark to Glencaple has excellent views of the Solway and Lochar Water towards Cockpool, and a good variety of bird life.

A good part of these rich rations continues on the west side of the Nith. Taking the A710 from Dumfries to New Abbey, you pass more winter pasture used by geese and swans, with Bewick and whooper swans sometimes near Islesteps (965728) beside the little Cargen Pow burn. Continue passing Kirkconnel Flow and New Abbey, stopping at the end of the public side road at 978641 east of Loch Kindar to walk down past Overton to Burnfoot (988636), looking across east to Blackshaw Bank and south to the Carse Sands.

At Kirkbean take the minor road to Carsethorn for access to Carse Sands and the stretch past Hogus Point, Barron Point and Black Craigs to Southerness Point, a mix of rocky foreshore and scars, sand dunes, and pasture ground behind. The side road from Carsethorn passing Nethermill, Gillhead, Moor, East Preston and Loaningfoot to Southerness is very pleasant. Look for greylag, pinkfooted and barnacle geese, whooper swans, widgeon, pintail, scaup, knot, lapwing, turnstone, redshank, bar-tailed godwit, oyster catchers, scoter, merganser, great crested grebes, red-throated divers, purple sandpipers, greenshanks, stonechats, short-eared owls, little terns and hen harriers.

The A710 from Caulkerbush to Sandyhills has splendid views (for car passengers only, not drivers) from on high (910558) over Mersehead Sands and towards Southwick Water and Preston Merse. Greylag and pinkfooted geese, widgeon, pintail, shoveler, scaup, redshank, oyster catchers. . . .

Again on the A710 walk down the side road at 881547 and hence footpaths for Portling Bay and Port O' Warren. There are cormorants, fulmar, razorbills, and house martens in cliff-nesting sites.

The richly varied area between Colvend and Auchencairn includes the twenty-acre National Trust for Scotland bird sanctuary of Rough Island (843532) and a small nature reserve at the little Glen Isle peninsula (833547) opposite Kippford, four other promontories at Almorness Point, Girvellan Point, Torrs Point and Balcary Point, and the Rough Firth estuary, Orchardton Bay, and Auchencairn Bay. Continue on the A710 for roads cutting off for Rockcliffe and Kippford, which are linked by a footpath; and the A710 to Dalbeattie and the A711 from Dalbeattie to Palnackie and Auchencairn. With salt marsh, inlets and a mud estuary which almost dries out at low water, look for scaup, widgeon, merganser, shelduck, common terns, oyster catchers, redshanks, curlew, greylag geese, and herring gulls.

Hestan Island (839502) is likely to have terns, oyster catchers, ringed plover, rock pipit, fulmars, guillemots, greater and lesser black-backed gulls and herring gulls.

Take the side road, by car or on foot, from Auchencairn (799515) to Balcary, and the excellent Balcary Heughs cliffpath walk round the Point to look for cormorants, guillemot, razorbills, fulmar, and kittiwakes.

More of the same passing Orroland Bay, Port Mary, Abbey Head, Netherlaw Point, Balmae Ha'en, and Torrs Point, but access problems make this a very difficult area. The delightful little up and down hill road at 772486 passing Heart Moss, Upper Rerrick and Fagra before coming down into Dundrennan village above the Abbey can be rewarding.

Kirkcudbright Bay, mainly mud estuary and some salt marsh, is less outstanding ornithologically. Take the A711 to Mutehill (687486) and the side road out to The Lake (681473), and from there walk out the roadway *cum* track passing the Lifeboat Station. You are likely to see widgeon, lapwing, golden plover and redshank.

From Kirkcudbright itself take the A711 to Tongland Bridge and the A762 towards the Low Bridge of Tarf (685541). Pleasant walking along the main road here and across the bridge, looking for herons, dippers, kingfishers, green sandpipers and greenshanks. . . . It is also possible to walk along the east bank of the Dee from 690522 to Tongland Bridge.

Take the A755 from Kirkcudbright across the river and the B727 along into Borgue parish as far as 647475 for the side roads to Ross Bay and Brighouse Bay. Meikle Ross, looking over to Little Ross Island, has fulmar, razorbills, shags, kittiwakes, guillemot, and cormorants.

On the A75 west of Gatehouse-of-Fleet, Skyreburn Bay, Mossyard Bay, Ravenshall Point, and Carsluith with a mixture of rocky shore, mud estuary and scrub and woodland are probably less interesting for birds than the moorland and hill ground behind. Variously terns, greater blackbacked gulls, oyster catchers, scoter, red-throated divers, and stonechats, whitethroats, goldfinches, linnets, and yellowhammers. . . .

Wigtown Bay, the area more or less from Creetown on the east to Jultock Point near Innerwell on the west, is a vast area of intertidal sand, salt marsh, and inks, and with the reclaimed Moss of Cree between Carty and Wigtown. Access is difficult, and walking on the inks on the west side can be dangerous. The best car route is the A714 from Newton Stewart to 423627 and the side road by Carty Port along the Moss of Cree to Wigtown. Walk down to Wigtown Harbour (438546) and over the bridge at Bladnoch (421541), and then turn left passing the Creamery along the River Bladnoch to the old quay (427538). The numbers of wintering geese have declined, but are still substantial. Look for greylag and pinkfooted geese, some Bewick's and whooper swans, pintail, shelduck, shoveler, oyster catchers, redshanks, curlew, black-headed gulls, widgeon, merganser, golden plover, bar-tailed godwits, snipe, teal, greenshanks, scoter, lapwing, skylarks, merlin, hen harriers, and sparrow hawks. . . .

The sea cliffs at Burrow Head are likely to have cormorants, shags, kittiwakes, razorbills, and perhaps a view of shearwaters and skuas. The A747 from Monrieth to Auchenmalg has numerous stopping places and a variety of different types of shoreline. Look for terns, curlews, sandpipers, golden plover, and perhaps peregrine falcons. On the other side of Luce Bay the sand dunes and foreshore are largely inaccessible from Ringdoo Point to the stretch north of Clayshant. You may see greylags and Greenland whitefronts in the Dunragit and West Freugh areas.

The Scar Rocks (263345 and 259333), visible in Luce Bay to the south, are very interesting indeed. The seabird population there seems to have greatly increased over the last fifty years. Big Scar is about 100 yards long and about 50 feet high, and also has a stack on the west side. There are gannets, kittiwakes, guillemot, black guillemot, cormorants, shags, razorbills, herring gulls, and possibly rock pipits, fulmar, and terns and peregrine falcons.

The A716 from Sandhead along the west shore of Luce Bay, passing Chapel Rossan Bay, New England Bay, Terally Bay, and Kilstay Bay to Drummore, and the side road from the B7041 to Maryport Bay (143344) are very interesting, and have numerous good stopping places. Look for terns, curlew, sandpipers, possibly great northern divers and peregrine falcons, and perhaps corn buntings.

The B7041 and the minor road past West and East Tarbet takes you to the Mull of Galloway and its excellent seabird colonies nesting in holes and ledges and crevices: fulmar, cormorants, shags, kittiwakes, razorbills, guillemot and black guillemot, herring and greater and lesser blackbacked gulls, perhaps a few puffins, and possibly jackdaws in the same area.

There are various good watching points on the west coast of the Rhins from Clonyard Bay, Port Logan, Ardwell Bay, Port of Spittal Bay and Portpatrick to Killantrigan and Corsewall Lighthouses. A good idea for more cliff scenery and seabird colonies would be to tackle the first stretch of the Southern Upland Way from Portpatrick (Inner) Harbour and Portpatrick Hotel to Port Mora, Port Kale, Portmaggie and Black Head and Killantrigan Lighthouse, and hence inland to the A764 at 000574.

Loch Ryan from The Wig at Kirkcolm to Leffnol Point and Cairnryan is easily accessible, with numerous stopping points on the A718 and the A77. Look for widgeon, scaup, merganser, eider, possibly a few greylag and Brent geese, great crested grebes, oyster catchers, blacknecked and Slavonian grebes and golden plover.

Away from the coast Galloway is again fortunate in the richness and variety of its bird life on moorland and farmland, forest and hill ground. Changes in land use have certainly meant that some birds, for example corn buntings and corncrakes, are now scarce, but of course birds that enjoy wooded habitats have flourished mightily of late.

Rather special features include blackheaded gulls at Loch Moan and Loch Macaterick; ravens nesting on the moorland north-west of Corsemalzie, off the B7005 from Bladnoch to Luce Bay; enormous numbers of rooks roosting in conifer woods at Auchenreoch near Crocketford; heronries at Machermore near Newton Stewart and at Dalskairth in Troqueer parish south-west of Dumfries; and the ornamental golden pheasants and Lady Amherst's pheasants from China and Burma in Kirroughtree Forest and at Bargaly and Talnotry, presumably descendants of the Duke of Bedford's decorative stock on Cairnsmore estate many years ago.

Another feature is the recently opened Bird Garden at the Fordbank Hotel near Wigtown. This has seven hundred birds from Australia, Malaysia, Vietnam and Africa ... including exotic pheasants, parakeets and lovebirds.

The White and Black Lochs at Lochinch are an important wintering area for wildfowl, greylag geese (and feral greylags), shoveler and goldeneye and tufted duck. The lochs are private, and the side roads off the A75 at 097605 and 108597 are not really satisfactory for viewing. The side road at 101603 to Loch Magillie and Soulseat Loch and back by Mahaar and Mark to the A75 is a most enjoyable short drive or walk. Expect to see widgeon and mallard.

Castle Loch, Mochrum (286537) is noted for its breeding colony of freshwater cormorants, but numbers have declined. The side road from the B7005 actually passes Mochrum Loch, the Black Loch and Fell Loch, not the Castle Loch. Look also for greylag geese, mergansers, dunlin, terns and grebes.

The Scottish Wildlife Trust reserve at Dowalton (406468), with marsh and scrub and meadow land, has a good variety of winter and summer birds. As with many reserves, access is only by special arrangement. There are whooper swans, bitterns, mallards, widgeon, peregrine falcons, hen harriers, kestrels and sparrowhawks: and blackcap, water rail, sedge warblers, whitethroat, and willow warbler.

The huge area from Cairnsmore of Fleet to the Rhinns of Kells, or from Newton Stewart to New Galloway and Carsphairn and Straiton, with the conifer forests and some older woods of oak and birch and willow and alder, and hills and mountains, and streams and lochs and marshes, has now a vast array of bird life. Access is by main roads, side roads, forest roads and walking trails. Look for wood warblers, redstarts, woodpeckers, woodcock, sedge and willow warblers, redpolls, bullfinches, willow-tits, longtailed tits: black grouse and red grouse, goldcrest, chaffinches, crossbills, nightjars, tree pipits, pied flycatchers, grey wagtails, grasshopper warblers, ring ousels, whinchats, stonechats, dippers, golden plover, goosanders, curlew, dunlin, barn owls and tawny owls and long-eared and short-eared owls, blackthroated divers, buzzards, peregrine falcons, sparrowhawks, hen harriers, merlin, kestrels, ravens, golden eagles, and possibly some snow buntings in the winter.

The RSPB 524-acre reserve at the Wood of Cree on the east bank of the river north of Newton Stewart has a rich mixture of oak and birch woodland and reed and marsh and pool areas. Birds include sedge and teal warblers, dippers and grey wagtails, pied flycatchers, tawny owls, woodpeckers, willow tits, treecreepers, wood warblers, redstarts and sparrowhawks.

Loch Ken and the marshes, fields, woods and hills around it from New Galloway to Parton and Crossmichael constitute a very rich area for wintering wildfowl and breeding birds. There are many good viewing points on the A713 and the A762 on the east and west sides of Loch Ken; and on the A713 from Castle-Douglas to Townhead of Greenlaw, the B795 to Glenlochar, and the side road on the west side of the River Dee/Loch Ken north to Bridgestone, Livingston, the Mains of Duchrae farm road end, and west by Craig to the A762 north of Laurieston. There are important RSPB reserves, one at the Kenmure Holms marsh south of New Galloway, and the other at the marshy bays and oak wood south of the Loch Ken Viaduct near Hensol. Look for greylag geese, Greenland whitefronted geese, pinkfooted geese, bean geese, goosanders, mergansers, goldeneye, tufted ducks, pintail, mallard, widgeon, shoveler, gadwall, smew; hen harriers, peregrine falcons, sparrow hawks, buzzards; a large barn owl breeding population; swifts, swallows, sedge warblers, willow tits, pied flycatchers, and grasshopper warblers.

The 1300-acre Threave marshes/Threave Island/Kelton Mains farm reserve north of the A75 is another important winter feeding and roosting place for wildfowl. Viewing points on the A75 to Bridge of Dee, the side road at 733601 north passing Lodge Island and Threave Mains to Glenlochar, and on the B795 to Townhead of Greenlaw. Greylag geese and Greenland whitefronted geese, pinkfooted and bean geese, and whooper swans and Bewick's swans.

For Carlingwark Loch and the marshes take the B736 road at the north end of the loch or the side road at the south-west of the loch beyond the old village of Buchan and south to Mid Kelton and Gelston. Make the rectangle by taking the very pleasant walk or drive along the B727 at the Gelston end and the A75. Look for greylag geese, Greenland whitefronted geese, bean geese, whooper swans, goldeneye, tufted ducks, goosanders, smew, pochards, spotted cranes, and water rails.

To the east along the A75 note Auchenreoch Loch and take the side road at 831727 passing Auchengibbert and turn south-east along the south end of Milton Loch to Milton on the Old Military Road. Look for greylag geese, widgeon, teal, bearded tits. Then continue south to the road junction north of Kirkgunzeon at 862678 and take the road running east passing Drumcoltran to come down to the A711 at Beeswing. Then take the road south-east from there passing Loch Arthur to New Abbey. You can reasonably expect to see grebes and smew, and may hope to spot corncrakes and corn buntings.

CHAPTER 5

Hunters and Farmers

Discovering Galloway in the sense of looking for the visible remains of the cultures and evidence of the settlements of northern European hunters and farmers and warriors and their descendants over some 9000 years provides both the rewards and pleasures of discovery and the excitement of the hunt, whether in search of stone circles and cup and ring marked rock surfaces and other *erotica neolithica* or for early castles and tower houses or for corn kilns and mill lades. Galloway shared the evolving series of cultures variously referred to as Mesolithic and Neolithic and Bronze Age and Iron Age and common to Scotland, Ireland, Wales, England and much of northern Europe. Without going into excessive detail it is worth remembering that these cultures almost certainly coexisted across the traditional and conveniently neat but misleading time periods often awarded to them: and that many sites and structures (hut circles or farmhouses or enclosures with ritual or defensive purposes) may have been used by peoples of different cultures for similar *or* different purposes.

The first thoroughly modern men and women, as compared to man-like creatures or *similitudines homines* of 250,000 to 200,000 B.C., were living in southern Britain some 40,000 to 30,000 years ago. While it is just possible that the first people in Galloway were here experiencing some sort of Eskimo existence at an earlier time, it is more likely that it was after the north of England was free of ice about 13,000 years ago that the first men and women in Galloway arrived as members of hunting parties visiting as summer migrants (in a sense, as tourists). The ice sheet over Galloway had melted away towards 8000 B.C., and a damp and warm climate followed with great forests and heavy dense vegetation.

During the 8th and 7th millennia nomadic settlers, motivated not by population pressure nor by the need to find new food sources but rather by man's sense of adventure and the urge to explore and discover new lands, moved from Cumberland and possibly from Antrim and Derry in Ireland into Galloway and Ayrshire. They established encampments and gathering sites along the coast from the Nith and Urr and Dee estuaries to Wigtown Bay and Luce Bay and Loch Ryan and north to Ballantrae and Girvan. This does not mean that the sites located and examined provide evidence of continuous Mesolithic settlement over 4000 years to 3000 B.C. or later, a length of time so extraordinary that it is difficult to comprehend. Indeed most of the camps represent only the settlements of a few months or years of little groups of five or ten people.

Nothing will ever be known of their language or beliefs, but it does seem likely that the total number of people involved was small. Although some estimates of the size of the Mesolithic population of Scotland seem ridiculously low and hardly sufficient to constitute a viable breeding group, it probably nevertheless is true that the whole population of Galloway about 5000 B.C. was not greatly different from the total number of players and spectators at a modern Southern Counties Football Association match between Tarff Rovers and St Cuthbert Wanderers.

These hunters and fishers and food gatherers were permanent residents, but followed an essentially nomadic life, perhaps covering a wide geographical area along the coast and up the river valleys during each year or over every few years. Their camps were all either at the coast or along the line of the river systems and lochs which provided the only practicable access through the great forests of oak and deciduous woodland and also security for escape from wild animals. Some camps may have been essentially transitory hunting bases, others industrial sites with chipping floors for turning beach pebble flints into scrapers and blades and arrows and axes, and others more long-term stopping places with lightly built huts set into scooped hollows, bottomed and revetted with stones, roofed with branches and rushes, and adjacent to fire areas with hearths.

Excavation and chance finds of hammer stones and bone or antler barbs and pins and prongs and axes and fish spears for hunting and fishing give a picture of a society where to survive meant developing finely tuned skills and expertise. The red deer antler harpoon found in the bed of the River Dee at Cumstoun in 1895 and now in the Stewartry Museum in Kirkcudbright is a good example of their technology. The camouflaged pit traps with pointed stakes set below found in Mye plantation on the west side of Luce Bay possibly belong to this period, or are evidence of old hunting skills still in use in the Neolithic world. Bones found on various Mesolithic sites include bear, lynx, lemming, deer, wolf and wild boar, with all kinds of birds and fish and molluscs.

This may sound simple and straightforward, even idyllic, but in reality life was nasty, brutish and almost certainly short. It is an almost impossible exercise to imagine what their camps were really like, and it is made more difficult by the fact that the sea level was at different times below the present level and up to 25 or 30 feet above it. Anyway, visiting the sites of scooped hollows is less exciting than reading about them.

The early 7th millennium camp with a charcoal hearth at Redkirk Point south-west of Gretna is an example of a beach site subsequently covered by the sea. Barsalloch (343422) and Low Clone (333453) on Luce Bay near Port William are important excavated early 5th millennium sites at the top of the old cliffs occupied at a period when the sea covered the present foreshore and A747 road area. Barsalloch was a small camping settlement; Low Clone seems to have been a more substantial camp with a scooped area of 45 by 15 feet with house shelters and a working area from which some 1,600 flints were recovered. Other coastal sites with probable or possible evidence of Mesolithic activity include, from east to west, Borron Point, Tallowquhairn, Powillimount and Maxwellfield, Gillfoot, Cowcorse, the Mote of Mark near Rockcliffe, Hestan Island, Mossyard, Isle of Whithorn, Monrieth, Airlour, Gillespie, Auchenmalg, Stairhaven, Kilfillan, Luce Sands in general including Torrs Warren, Aird east of Stranraer, Low Balyett, Kirkmabreck near Ardwell, Balgown, Terally, Grennan, Drummore, the Mull of Galloway, Portankill, and Downan, Ballantrae and Girvan in Ayrshire.

A large number of inland Mesolithic lochside and river terrace sites with flint waste areas and some hearths have been located far into the northern hinterland of the Stewartry. There is no reason why these should be significantly later than the 5th millennium coastal sites. The main areas identified are along the Black Water of Dee and Clatteringshaws Loch and Loch Grannoch, along the Water of Ken including Stroangassel and Stroanfreggan, the Water of Deugh to Carsphairn, round Loch Doon and along the River Doon further north and perhaps on a route towards the Ayrshire coast. There seems every reason to suppose that further investigation of the Cree and Urr and Nith valleys will produce further evidence of hunting and camping sites.

Both on inland and coastal walks look out for old rabbit warrens (or 'bunny banks' as the children call them), mole hills, and eroded terraces and slopes for possible chance finds.

Mesolithic sites are not even remotely spectacular, but the remains of the buildings and monuments of Neolithic Galloway are exciting and impressive. From these alone it is clear just how fundamental a revolution the first farming folk settling in Galloway after about 4200 to 4000 B.C. achieved over the following centuries through the development of an agricultural economy. It seems also from descriptions in the Statistical Account of Scotland (1791-99) and in nineteenth-century journals that until the Agricultural Revolution of the late eighteenth and early nineteenth centuries there had indeed been many more fine cairns and circles still to be seen.

The Neolithic period and the 'Bronze Age' are perhaps best seen as one period (4200-800 B.C.) of the growth and development of a mixed farming economy which contained within it a series of overlapping cultures involving probable changes in ritual and belief and more identifiable changes in pottery styles and techniques variously associated with Beaker people (about 2000 B.C.) and Food Vessel people. Bronze and copper goods, tools and weapons (axes, spearheads, daggers, rapiers) were introduced from about 2000 B.C. by travelling metalworkers and merchants carrying their stock with them. The hoard of twelve rapiers found at Camp Hill 'fort' at Drumcoltran near Kirkgunzeon and the mixed bag found at Eschonchan Fell at Glentrool were probably examples of such stock collections. The availability of metal tools probably did not involve any fundamental changes in ordinary life, although it perhaps eventually did mark changes towards a more warlike society organised for defence and aggression towards the end of the period.

The number of North European farmers crossing the Solway and establishing settlements along the Galloway coastline was almost certainly very small. Probably the new people fused ultimately with the old nomadic folk to form a larger (and healthier) gene pool. Although further colonisation from outside may have taken place, the traditional view of a series of wholesale immigrations by 'peoples' now seems less likely than a pattern of slow indigenous population growth with the gradual settlement of upland and hill areas and the occasional appearance of new ideas and new people. Estimates of population size would be unwise overall, but it might be reasonable to allow for twenty to fifty persons for each of the major cairn and ritual sites which had spread by 3000 to 2000 B.C. into the hinterland from the Mull of Galloway to the hills above New Luce and Carsphairn. The average lifespan was quite probably twenty-five to thirty years, and a man or woman of fifty was then very old. There is no way to know whether their language or languages belonged to a pre-Indo-European group or not, but it is quite likely that any new people appearing over the centuries might have had very different linguistic traditions from the original settlers.

The key to this Neolithic world and what made a 'civilised' life possible was the control of the environment through clearing woodland using stone axes, bringing land under cultivation with cereal crops, and grazing cattle and sheep and pigs and goats. Over the centuries fields were cleared and settlements established in upland areas to 700 and even 900 feet, in places where in a less favourable climate today mixed farming would be difficult and certainly not financially viable. Although it is possible to hazard a guess at the line of their regular routeways, it would be a romantic illusion to imagine that in taking the tracks, for example, from Claughreid to California and Cambret, or from Cauldside over Cambtet Moor to Glenquicken, or from Drannandow past the Napper's Cottage to 'The Thieves', the walker was following lines necessarily older than mediaeval ways or pack routes. But it is possible.

Although considerable quantities of Neolithic material have turned up from the Luce Sands and elsewhere, few individual houses or farms have been located with any degree of certainty. There are many hut circles, for example on Irelandton Moor north-west of Twynholm and Cairnmon Fell on the west side of the Rhins from Sandhead; but hut circles are only rings with circular stony banks marking the foundations of the walls whose upper parts were of turf or wood, and similar houses were built and occupied in Iron Age and mediaeval Galloway. It is also quite possible that Neolithic farmhouses were on the same sites as the later farm complexes such as Mossyard or Newton or Claughreid.

So it is rather from their public buildings and ceremonial sites and ritual monuments that it is possible to see something of the Neolithic world. The most important are probably the public buildings, the cairns or communal tombs which were used as burial places and centres of activity for communities over periods of 1500 or even 2000 years during which burial customs might change and the cairn itself evolve, change in shape and grow enormously in size. Many are on sites with splendid views and may themselves have been visible from a distance when complete in terms of height and possibly covered with glittering white pebbles.

It is not convincing to see them as evidence of a particular type of society, communistic or hierarchical or tribal or whatever. The larger cairns in Galloway could have been built readily enough by an extended family group of ten to twenty or thirty people, or by a larger 'sub-tribal' unit acting as a controlled labour force under the direction of a 'chieftain' or a 'priest'. No outside 'builder/architect' figure with any special engineering skills need have been involved.

Equally, although there is no doubt that the investment of time and labour and loving attention in building and maintaining these structures shows that religious belief and ceremonial observance relating to death and after-death were at the very centre of Neolithic life, nevertheless their existence provides very little information about the nature of these beliefs. The cairns are, after all, technological masterpieces, not exercises in theology or philosophy. The significance of changes in burial customs from inhumation (and possibly excarnation, that is, laying out dead bodies on platforms to rot and placing only the bones in the tombs) to cremation and the use of cinerary urns is not really clear. Did this have a religious

Cairnholy II Chambered Cairn showing capstone and entrance with portal stones. When in use largely covered with smaller stones.

significance related to fire rituals or was this rather a matter of custom and convenience? At a guess the cairn builders may have believed in the power of an Earth Mother Goddess and/or in the sun and the moon as gods and goddesses and observed him/her/them for good or bad omens. Did they also see their ancestors and the more recently dead, buried with objects from their lives, as gods, or were they merely obsessed with caring for their 'spirits' or 'souls' in an afterlife? Were there also auxiliary 'tribal' deities tied to localities (sea, water, trees), or did they have totems expressing a group identity such as eagles or dogs or birds? Is the term the 'Eagle Cairn' at Carndryne, north-west of the Mull of Galloway, significant or is it merely and more probably just a placename coincidence?

There are all kinds of cairns, large and small and long and round, to be seen in Galloway, from the 'showpiece' long cairns Cairnholy I and II (517539 and 518541) to the grass-covered stony mounds casually visible from the road, such as the virtually linear cemetery along the line of the B7079 into Minnigaff off the A75 and the cairns beside the B735 towards Kirkcowan, to the enormous number on hill and moorland up to 750 and 950 feet (many now lost inside forestry plantations). New examples are still being recorded.

As a result of excavations at Mid Gleniron I and II (187610 and 188609),

Lochhill (968651) and Slewcairn (924614) it is now possible to understand just how complex can be the structural history of the largest of these, the long cairns, of which usually only a depleted and final version is visible. While there is no reason why their development should be uniform, it now seems possible that many began about 4000 or 3800 B.C. with wooden or stone mortuary structures and a simple round cairn; and then went through various stages from a larger round cairn with additional chambers to become finally a long rectangular cairn (Cairnholy I and II are respectively 150 and 70 feet long) with an impressive semicircular end with a facade of boulders or pillars and dry stone walling facing and partially enclosing an area used for ceremonial activity including ritual fires. The contents of the commonly four or five chambers must have been cleared out many times during the hundreds of years of usage. There are other interesting long cairns at Drannandow (408713) and Boreland (405690).

The 'passage grave' group of cairns are generally round rather than long, with again a varying number of chambers, and have entrance passages from one end running from the exterior into a burial chamber. Look for examples, often difficult to find, at Cairnderry (316799), the White Cairn of Bargrennan (352783), Sheuchan Cairn (338838), the King's Cairn, Kirriemore (377854), the Caves of Kilhern (198644), Cairn Kenny (174752), and the Druid's Grave (338944).

There are also a very large number of round cairns from twenty to fifty to a hundred feet in diameter, more often than not probably having box-like cist burials rather than enclosing chambers, for example on Bardennoch Hill south of Carsphairn and on the moorland west of New Luce from Auchmantle to Cairnscarrow and Cairnerzean Fell; circular cremation cemeteries enclosed by thick turf-covered banks, for example at Bargatton (686626); individual stone cists found placed in the ground without a covering cairn, for example at Redbrae (392557) and Glenquicken (508582); and 'cairnfields' with dozens of five to ten to twenty-feet diameter stony mounds usually grass-covered, very difficult to distinguish from field clearance heaps or boundary markers, and more convincing if adjacent to large cairns or stone circles, as for example at Cauldside (529571). Many areas with large numbers of these small cairns have been located, including Meikle Auchenfad (950682), Glaisters (888655), Cornharrow (661929), Holm of Dalquhairn (645006), Stroanfreggan (647934), Corseglass Hill (646857), Glenshimmeroch (644880), Craigengillan (628949), Bardennoch (572908), Knockreoch (575863), and Bargrennan Burn (335800).

Many visitors will find the stone circles and standing stones in their often moorland settings most evocative expressions of the hidden mysteries of the ancient world. Although the earliest British henges with wood or stone circles date back to 3000 or 2900 B.C., the small circles in Galloway may not necessarily be earlier than 2000 to 1500 B.C. The lost circles, such as those in Kirkbean parish and the two missing circles at Glenquicken, would make a richer group, but what is left still constitutes a fascinating gallery of religious art.

Although primarily sanctuaries and areas for ritual and ceremony, it is also possible that they served as focal points for occasional gatherings of the farmers and herdsmen and fishermen living in a particular locality. It seems very probable that some of the ceremonies were related to burying the dead and caring for the spirits of ancestors, as in a number of examples, such as Cauldside and High Auchenlarie and Glenquicken, the circles were part of larger complexes with cairns or cists nearby or even inside the main ritual area. Did the circles also, like the miniature versions carved in 'cup and ring markings', provide a means of expressing through ritual the beliefs and identities and history of a 'people' or a 'tribal' sub-group? Did they provide an opportunity to appease the gods and acquire some security against the terrible forces of pain and evil and illness and disease and disaster encountered in the short, uncertain and uncomfortable progress through this life? Did the ritual visions of life and death (the unfolding of dreams) performed through dancing and acting round and through the circles and alignments include drug-induced hallucinations? Take the children round them 'Ring A Ring O' Roses' and you are probably closer to understanding what the circles were than by reading some of the quite extraordinary and sometimes fanciful 'scientific' theories developed about prehistoric science and mathematics.

It is clear that the people erecting these circles had some basic technological skills in moving and raising large stones, and it seems likely that they had a rudimentary and essentially empirical interest in watching and trying to remember some of the movements of the sun and the moon, and perhaps had worked out some sort of way of calculating roughly the usual times of spring and summer for basic farming needs. It might be sensible, however, to observe with a good deal of cautious scepticism the 'scientific' attempts to explain these monuments as being solar and lunar observatories (and even computers) to track the very complex eighteen-year cycle of revolutions of the moon and to predict lunar eclipses and to calculate exactly and precisely the winter and summer solstices. This does require the time and the facilities to record and analyse complex data and information over many years, combined with the development of mathematical (especially geometrical) and statistical skills of a high order. These were also, you may choose or not to believe, employed in laying out not just circles, but ellipses, 'egg-shaped circles', and concentric circles set out to different centres, all on the basis of a supposed standard unit, the megalithic yard (2.72 feet or 0.829 m.), used uniformly throughout the British Isles and south through France and to the Mediterranean. The more elaborately 'accurate' and detailed the measurements and alignments sought, the more dubious it becomes, and more particularly when applied to the simple and bare moorland sites such as Cauldside and Glenquicken. Visitors should use their common sense and make up their own minds.

The most interesting Galloway circles are the Stones of Torhouse (383565), a clinically neat line-up of nineteen granite boulders with the largest stones at the east-south-east and a group of three stones in the centre, Glenquicken (509582), a charming little twenty-eight boulder circle with a larger stone five feet nine inches high in the centre, and Claughreid (517560) with nine stones and a central boulder. The emphasis on the centre area has something in common with the Grampian recumbent stone circles, with their three stones at the south-west angle, such as Sunhoney, Midmar Church, and the Nine Stanes in Garrol Wood near Banchory. Other local circles are the Twelve Apostles (947794), Cauldside (529571) with ten tiny stones beside a ten feet high and sixty-three feet diameter cairn, the Holm of Daltallochan (553942) with thirteen stones, and a possible circle with four remaining stones at High Auchenlarie (539534).

Look for standing stones in relation to circles, for example one south-east of the Holm of Daltallochan circle (553942) and three stones in a row on the crest of a hillock east of the Stones of Torhouse (384565); as markers adjacent to cairns, for example the holed stone five feet high at Crows (365558) beside the denuded large round White Cairn; reused, although possibly in their original positions, in dykes, for example in the south wall opposite Bladnoch village (424542) and on the west side of the road from Whithorn to Portyerrock (467398). And other examples at Dalarran Holm (639791), Park of Tongland (700561), Loch Mannoch (663609), Bagbie (498564) with a cairn, four stones and another single standing stone to the south, The Thieves, Drannandow (404716) with two stones inside a bank of earth and stones, Boreland, Kirkcowan (352581), near Longcastle (382481), the Wren's Egg (361420) with two stones, Milton Hill (362416), Drumtroddan (364443) with three stones over ten feet high, the Carlin Stone near Elrig Loch (326497), and Glentirrow (146625).

The miniature version of the circles and standing stones is the series of cup and ring markings sculptured by chipping and rubbing techniques on rock surfaces and stones and boulders found at over a hundred sites in Galloway,

High Banks, Kirkcudbright. An amazing cup and ring marked rock surface discovered in 1911. Small deep cups massed round concentric circles and cups. Casts may be seen outside the Stewartry Museum in Kirkcudbright.

which with mid-Argyll has probably the best examples in Scotland. Rerrick, Kirkcudbright, Anwoth and Kirkmabreck parishes in the Stewartry and the Whithorn to Port William area in the Machars have the main concentrations. They date from the late Neolithic period from about 2000 B.C. onwards, possibly for five hundred years or possibly for a thousand. Confirmation of the earlier dating is provided in the location of cup and ring markings on rock surfaces near circles and cairns (High Auchenlarie, Cairnharrow and Cauldside), in the same area as standing stones and circles (Balcraig, Drumtroddan and Cauldside), on the stones used in chambered tombs (Cairnholy I, Cairnderry) and on the slab covers of cists, and on portable stones placed inside chambered tombs presumably towards the end of their period of usage (Cairnholy I) or found nearby.

Cups are roughly circular or oval hollows up to six or seven inches in diameter: rings are grooves as concentric circles (up to eight or nine in number) round the cup and up to twenty-five inches in diameter. Other straight and curved lines, irregularly placed cups and clusters of cups, spirals, dumb-bells and rectangles make up a variety of possible patterns and designs. Were they coloured or 'painted' originally to make them stand out more dramatically? To see them more clearly today, use powder or chalk (and sheep droppings help for photographic purposes!).

E.A. Hornel, who had casts (now outside the museum in Kirkcudbright) made of the superb High Banks group, and Sir Herbert Maxwell of Monrieth, who had Balcraig and Drumtroddan placed in State care, were among those fascinated by these exotica.

Although it will never be possible to understand what they mean, there is little doubt that they were intended as statements to parallel those made in the stone circles and cairns, whether in the ritual performed for an earth goddess or in the adoration of the sun and moon. There may have been scope for creativity and originality in developing local styles, with High Banks as one such remarkable vision (of cairns and circles and cairnfields?). There is, however, surely no need to accept the idea of a megalithic inch (as one to forty in relation to the supposed megalithic yard, that is 2.07 cm.), and there is no need either to assume that other than the best and clearest examples are complete statements. Many markings, after all, may easily have been only practice work or 'doodles'. Enjoy them and look for more in stone dykes and drains and on rock outcrops in the moors and hills.

Note the examples in the museums at Kirkcudbright and Whithorn and in a private collection at Kirkdale House, and look for the rock outcrop sites, usually difficult to find, at Newlaw Hill (733488), High Banks (709489), Grange (687471), Clauchendolly (643472), Tongue Croft (603483), Cairnharrow (540568), Cauldside or Cambret Moor (a boulder at 529571), Mossyard (545514), Knock (364402), Balcraig (374440 and 376445) and Drumtroddan (363447).

CHAPTER 6

Warriors and Peacemakers

There is a uniformity during the long period from the eighth century B.C. to the fourteenth century A.D. which may be surprising. The farmers and the poor folk in Galloway ('Welsh' or 'Irish' or 'English' or 'Norse') lived their lives as best they could using methods and tools that probably changed little over the centuries; religious specialists offered a diversity of deities and then uniformity under one, but the transfer to Christianity was probably a slow and uneven process lasting from the third to the thirteenth century or later; and a succession of warrior aristocracies with special military expertise exercised power locally without the inconvenience of effective interference from any centralised authority, whether from rulers in Cumbria or Northumbria or Scotland or England. Wars and raids and conflicts and tensions, with occasional interludes of peace, were the norm. Security lay behind fortifications, hill forts, promontory forts, stockaded farmhouses, crannogs, earthwork and stone castles, sometimes in a succession of buildings on the same site over hundreds of years.

By between 800 and 700 B.C. farmers had become warriors and builders of defensive structures (including some hill 'vitrified' forts) as the result of a combination of pressures derived from internal population growth, wetter and colder climatic conditions which allowed peat bogs to cover areas previously worked and occupied, *and* because of the arrival of new settlers from South Britain. Possibly by 700 B.C. and certainly over the next six or seven centuries Celtic 'Iron Age' immigrants, whether at first as refugees or broken tribes or latterly as whole bands and tribes, established themselves as the new masters. Whether this involved hundreds or rather thousands of people and to what extent the old population was enslaved or absorbed is not clear. Although P Celtic (ancestral and akin to Welsh) was the dominant language of the Galloway tribes over at least a thousand years into the sixth century A.D., there is no reason why pockets of pre-Indo-European language groups should not have survived in the hills and forests and hidden valleys for several centuries.

The 'hegemonies' or 'federations' (perhaps rather grandiose terms for very loose alliances of bands and sub-tribal groups) of tribes in Galloway were referred to in Roman Britain as Novantae, those in Dumfriesshire and the Upper Ward of Lanarkshire as Selgovae, and those in Ayrshire as

Damnonii. The Brigantes in Cumbria and the north of England may well have held parts of south-east Dumfriesshire.

It is possible to put together a composite view of Novantae and Selgovae from Roman literary sources dealing with Celtic society in Gaul and Britain, from Irish and Welsh vernacular literature and oral tradition, from local folklore, from chance finds of hoards and from the results of excavations of crannogs and forts. They were magnificent savages, men to whom war was a game and an art and a science, men who charged into battle mad from drugs and with hair stiffened straight with lime and to the sound of war horns and trumpets; and women who fought alongside the men in local war groups, perhaps the first gaggle of emerging feminists, 'Boudiccas' from Balmaclellan and 'Boadicias' from Borgue.

They were patrons and customers of artists and craftsmen in iron and engraved and moulded bronze and gold from all over the Celtic world as far away as Austria and Germany and of local workshops producing simpler everyday items. Look in national museum collections for bowls, flagons and drinking cups, chariot fittings and cauldron chains, helmets, bronze shields, iron swords and decorated sword hilts and scabbards in bronze, bone combs, enamelled jewellery, bronze hand mirrors and plaques, and torcs or neck rings. Treasures found in Galloway include a gold torc from High Drummore, the Plunton armlet, a bronze mirror and crescent-shaped plaque from Balmaclellan, and from near Castle-Douglas the Torrs pony cap and drinking horn terminals and the Carlingwark hoard with a huge cauldron and tools and implements used by farmers. There may be a role here for the use, with the permission of landowners and tenants, of metal detectors to work round partially or fully drained lochs and springs and wells in the hope of locating other votive deposits.

To place treasured goods in watery graves was to offer them to the gods associated with those places. To understand this is a step towards following the logic behind the location of Christian holy wells and churches—the early Church followed the simple and wise expedient of taking over pagan sanctuaries—and towards glimpsing the meaning of the fears still lurking in seventeenth and eighteenth and nineteenth-century Galloway. Celtic religion was strange, sometimes unpleasant and even truly evil, although at least there was an element of choice. The Druids, the religious men and diviners and philosophers at the centre of Celtic culture and mythology, worked for and through a panoply of gods. There were deities associated with particular places, with sacred underground sites as paths from and to the underworld, with sacred woods (perhaps Holywood near Dumfries), with streams and rivers and pools and lochs and wells, including healing springs and wells. Andrew Symson, in his *Description of Galloway* (1684), describes how local people still resorted to and left offerings at the White Loch of Mochrum near Monrieth, the Rumbling Well north of Buittle Kirk, Kissickton Well near Meikle Ross in Borgue parish, the Gout Well of Larg near Minnigaff, the Laird's Croft Well in Kirkcolm parish, and the Muntluck Well 'in the midst of a little bog' in Kirkmaiden parish.

Then there were the gods and goddesses of war and the monster gods consuming bodies and spirits and encouraging torture, such as divining by studying the death throes of ritual victims, and human sacrifice, for example 'the wicker man' filled with living men and consumed with fire on Anglesey.

One of the most important deities was the great horned or antlered god, and associated with him were the cult animals venerated by tribal groups, the horse, the wolf, the bear, the stag, the raven, the eagle, the dog, the serpent. The horse may have been important in the Stewartry, as a horse's head was found under the altar of the old pre-Reformation church at Rerrick south of Dundrennan, a marvellous piece of oneupmanship for the old beliefs, and headless horses are prominent in local folklore.

The cult of hunting and collecting human heads, taking severed heads in battle and bringing them home tied across a saddle or round a horse's neck, and nailing up heads on forts and houses or in trophy rooms in sanctuaries, was a way of capturing forever the spirits and powers of your enemies. Local tales and traditions of headless ghosts of men and women, sometimes endeavouring to catch up with the heads floating through the air in front of them, headless pipers and headless horses are associated with Kirkdale Glen, Cardoness, the Buckland Burn near Kirkcudbright, Barnbarroch in Kirkinner parish, Piltanton near the Luce Sands, and Tynron Doon above Tynron near Moniaive where heads rolled down the hill to land in St Bride's Well. The persistence of these tales suggests just how much fear and terror was engendered by this cult. Look for the stone heads from Collin and possibly Dunscore at Dumfries Museum, on the old church at Glencairn near Moniaive, and the ?sixteenth-century heads on the doorway at Barholm Castle above Kirkdale Glen; and for springs and wells and fort and settlement sites for possible paranormal experiences to lend a new significance to those old and wise phrases 'heads will roll' and 'keep it under your hat'.

Primitive and vile though they may have been, at a more mundane level the Celtic tribesmen were sensible and practical. They made their own iron tools and weapons using wood-fired kilns for smelting, for example at Genoch Sands near Glenluce; and they were competent and probably quite efficient farmers. Their main wealth and status lay in cattle and horses, but their livestock also included sheep (wool for spinning and weaving) and pigs; they also planted flax and perhaps large areas of early forms of barley and beared wheat (emmer). It is clear, also, from their farmhouses and crannogs and forts that they had very considerable expertise as practical builders and engineers. The standard Iron Age building was the round house. You may see the remains of sites inside single or double palisaded oval enclosures or stockaded farmhouses, or inside forts, or in undefended enclosures and platform sites on river terraces and adjacent to forts. A kraallike structure, it had a heavy thatched roof and walls of wattle and daub with timber posts and rafters. Apart from the forts, the most obvious sites of these now are the crannogs. These were artificial (sometimes partly natural) sixty to one hundred-foot diameter platforms for farmhouses set into bogs or lochs with a base of timber logs and brushwood and earth and boulders. They often had underwater wooden or stone causeways towards the shore, 'harbour' landing places of timber, and sometimes 'outside' enclosures on the land opposite the crannog. The farmhouse with wooden floors offered a fair degree of comfort and security without the expense of fortification. Some now remain as grassy mounds in fields of drained and cultivated water areas; others are still visible as little islands in lochs, or appear only in very dry summers. Some fifty locations in Galloway include Loch Arthur, Lochrutton, the excavated crannog in Milton Loch, Carlingwark Loch, and the important group on the site of Dowalton Loch and in Ravenstone Loch. Crannogs continued in use into the seventeenth century, and some (Loch Urr, Lochinvar and Lochnaw) were mediaeval castle sites.

The vast number, over one hundred and thirty, of promontory and hill forts and miscellaneous Iron Age defensive earthworks in Galloway is the clearest possible expression of the insecurity inherent in Celtic society. The pressures creating the need for sub-tribal and local neighbourhood populations to build forts as temporary or semi-permanent communal refuges were both internal—slave and cattle raiding, head hunting and nomadic warfare—and also, especially towards the end of the first century B.C. and in the first two centuries A.D., the external problems arising from the expansion of Roman power and Roman slave trading. Quite probably also most local groups themselves regarded raiding as an essential part of their existence, so at least some of the forts may be seen as offensive as well as defensive in intent.

The oppida, the hill fort tribal centres or 'towns', such as the thirty-nine acre Eildon Hill North near Melrose or the smaller eighteen-acre Burnswark Hill (NY 185786) near Lockerbie, are absent in Galloway. The Novantae may have been less politically sophisticated and integrated, although the difficulties of cross-country communications in Galloway may also be a relevant factor.

The hill forts (about seventy in the Stewartry and sixteen in Wigtownshire) and promontory forts (about ten and thirty) include some large sites, such as the nine-acre Moyle fort (848576) near Barnbarroch and the eight-acre Giant's Dyke fort on Barstobric Hill (687606) in the north of Tongland parish. The Mull of Galloway (143307) *may* have been an even larger fortress if the lines of ditches and banks at East and West Tarbet at the north end of the promontory are boundaries of a defensive nature.

But the great majority of the forts are small, some even minute, single or double-ditched and banked. The more interesting or spectacular include the Doon (657488) above the Dee estuary south-west of Kirkcudbright, with huge banks and ditches and an annexe at the east corner perhaps imitating Roman military planning; the large inner promontory at the Isle of Whithorn (480360); the DOE promontory fort at Barsalloch (347412) south of Port William; Kemp's Walk (NW 975598) with triple banks and ditches, south-west of Leswalt; and Dunman (097334) on the headland north-west of the Mull of Galloway. Note the heavy concentration near the Mull and near Burrow Head.

The excavated rectangular earthwork at Rispain (429399) is perhaps best described as a first century B.C./first century A.D. defended homestead rather than as a fort, although the ditch and bank are impressive. Others, such as Trowdate 'Mote' or 'Rath' (758690), are difficult to classify.

There are several vitrified forts, that is forts where the stone walls laced with vertical and horizontal timber beams have been burnt at temperatures of 1000 to 1200 degrees Centigrade, turning the rocks into streams of molten 'glass'. Whether this was deliberate as an exercise for ritual purposes (the cleansing of a 'defiled' fort) or a stage in the development of specialised stone-walled fortifications is another matter. Immense quantities of timber and brushwood would have to be used in strong wind conditions to produce this fusing effect. Examples include the Mote of Mark (844540), Castlegower (793589), Mochrum Hill (720745), Edgarton Mote (673630), Trusty's Hill (588561) and the Doon of May (295515).

An example of still more exotic military engineering is the chevaux de frise, pointed stones set into the ground on flat or rough ground as a formidable obstacle to cavalry and infantry, at the Fell of Barhullion (374418). Compare the better examples at Cademuir Hill near Peebles and at Dreva above Broughton near Biggar.

By the first century B.C. and the first century A.D. stone-walled forts had evolved in the north and west of Scotland into the specialised military architecture of brochs, circular/oval towers with double wall thicknesses and intra-mural stairways, and, larger in internal area, the D-shaped galleried duns with some similar features. There are examples in Galloway at Ardwell (067446), Teroy (099641) and Stairhaven (209533). The fort at Crummag Head has also been suggested as another possible broch. Castle Haven (594483) to the east in Borgue parish is a heavily restored galleried dun. All sorts of theories have been advanced to explain the presence of these brochs in the south-west. The idea of a sort of alliance between Novantae and the northern tribes against the Roman Empire towards the end of the first century A.D. sounds plausible, with the brochs being the result of co-operation and technical advice and assistance from outside military personnel. They are unlikely to have been bases colonised from the north. However, there is probably no reason why local men travelling on the seaways to Mull and Tiree and Lewis or even to the Orkneys and Caithness should not have seen brochs and brought back ideas for taking stone-walled forts in Galloway a stage further in the hope of providing some more effective protection against Roman slave gatherers.

Local wisdom used to be that Gallovidians had remained free and unconquered, apart from the orderly tyranny of Rome. This was always a sweet myth, for even without the modern evidence of direct rule and occupation Galloway was anyway far too near to the Roman military province in the north of England and to Roman routes north through Dumfriesshire to have been free from slave traders hunting out men, women and children to supply the hungry slave markets of the Empire.

After the invasion of South Britain in 43 A.D. the area roughly north of a line from the Severn to the Humber was finally taken under Roman control in 71 and north Wales was added by 78. Gaius Julius Agricola's campaign in southern and central Scotland between 78 and 82 and north through Perthshire and Aberdeenshire in 83-84 was part of a grand strategy to conquer all of Britannia (England, Wales and Scotland), and possibly Ireland as well. Seen in this context, the Agricolan advance and Flavian consolidation after 85 begins to look like a logical and efficient way of establishing land routes north through Annandale with forts or marching camps at *Birrens* (BLATOBVLGIVM on O.S. Sheet 85) east of Ecclefechan and at *Milton* south-east of Beattock and through Nithsdale from *Ward Law* (UXELLUM?) near Caerlaverock to *Dalswinton,* and west towards the coast facing Ireland by cross-country routes towards *Glenlochar* near Castle-Douglas and *Gatehouse* and further north from *Castledykes* in Clydesdale to *Loudon Hill* and probably towards *Irvine* and *Girvan* in

Ayrshire. The powerful Roman navy could move heavy supplies and carry out advance surveys and reconnaissance work. The fort at Glenlochar with no less than seven temporary camps adjacent should have been a base for advancing north up the Dee valley towards Ayrshire and west by the Gatehouse fortlet to a large unlocated base on the east bank of the Cree between Creetown and Minnigaff. Roman Wigtownshire, however, is still a mystery, although it would be surprising if there had not been naval bases between Garlieston and Port William and at Rerigonium between Stranraer and Innermessan on Loch Ryan. Whether there was a landward route from the Cree towards the Luce valley and Loch Ryan parallel to the A75, or south-west by Longcastle to Luce Bay and by Luce Sands over to Loch Ryan is still open to speculation. The evidence for a marching camp at Girvan is interesting and makes the Stranraer connection seem certain.

The Roman occupation of Galloway falls into two phases. The first lasted from about 80 to between 105 and 117, when a Brigantian revolt, possibly in alliance with Selgovae and Novantae and other North British tribes, forced a retreat to the line between the Solway and the Tyne. At this time Glenlochar and Dalswinton were destroyed by fire. Hadrian's Wall was built in the 120s as a linear barrier to control the movement of people and goods and cattle and as a symbol of power and military strength, but it is important to remember that it was not a boundary marking the end of the area under Roman control, neither an 'Iron Curtain' nor a 'Maginot Line'.

The second phase in Galloway lasted from about 139 to between 180 and 196, coinciding with the reoccupation of the Scottish Lowlands and the building of the Antonine Wall and their abandonment in the late 190s. New fortlets and stations in this period included *Carzield, Barburgh Mill, Durisdeer* and *Crawford*. Glenlochar was occupied again, but not Gatehouse.

The third and fourth centuries continued to see Roman fleets in the Solway out of Skinburness and Maryport, and Roman patrols far north and west of Hadrian's Wall, with Birrens used as an outpost for the surveillance certainly of east Dumfriesshire up to 367, when the Wall for the first time became the real frontier. The Novantae and Selgovae may well have been organised as client principalities or buffer states with a mixture of subsidies, political missions and occasional punitive raids. The Novantae may still have been troublesome at times, judging by the fortifications along the Cumbrian coast south of Bowness and Maryport to St Bees Head.

What remains to be seen of the Roman era in Galloway above ground has very little impact compared to studying aerial photographs, and in particular those taken of Glenlochar and Gatehouse in 1949 by Dr J.K.S.St. Joseph of the University of Cambridge. These and subsequent work have revolutionised our understanding of this period. In some instances aerial photographs showing hollows and inequalities on the surface make clear what is either only partly visible or has hitherto gone unrecognised. But the more fundamental discoveries, as at Glenlochar, have been made through observing crop marks and differences in the growth of vegetation. Grasses and crops do less well on the lines of old walling and ramparts and roads, whereas growth is richer above ditches and pits where the earth holds moisture better, so these show up as bands and lines and marks, especially in dry summer seasons.

The marching camps (734645) near to Glenlochar fort were temporary structures with single earthwork banks and ditches, professionally laid out and with cooking pits and latrines. Each may represent halts lasting for one or for several nights. The thirty-one-acre camp at 739642 south-east of the fort was large enough for a legion (5000 infantry) plus cavalry and auxiliaries. It had an annexe for holding prisoners and slaves and the huge wagon train of ox-carts travelling with the army.

There are few traces left now to make out Glenlochar fort site (735645) on and to the south of the B795. It was excavated in 1952. At just over eight acres it provided accommodation for one thousand men, cavalry and infantry, on patrol duties on the route west and working in conjunction with the Solway fleet. The whole area between the Nith and the Dee and the Cree must surely have been controlled by such a large force. The multiple defences of three ditches on the north and west were strengthened on the vulnerable south-east angle by an extra ditch and nineteen large pits for obstacles or structures of some sort. The fort faced west across the river. It had a regular street system with a headquarters building and six and twelve barracks. There were really three forts, as Glenlochar was rebuilt twice in the Antonine period on the same site. A large defended annexe with triple ditches on the north-east included wagon park and storage areas. Another north-west annexe included a courtyard building close to the river which may have been a posting service rest-house, a suggestion with fascinating implications and making the concept of a fort on the Cree seem even more likely.

The Gatehouse fortlet (595574) in a field north of the town slots neatly into this picture as a staging or convoy post for one hundred men. Like Glenlochar it was located on the east bank of the adjacent river and is on level ground beside a good crossing place. It was excavated in 1960 and 1961. The overall area including the outer of the two ditches is two acres, 190 by 162 feet, but the space inside the defences is only 0.7 of an acre. Into this space is crammed a street from the central north-east gate to the south-west gate almost opposite, two barrack blocks, buildings for maintenance and storage,

The Roman Fortlet north of Gatehouse-of-Fleet discovered through aerial photography in 1949. On the east bank of the Fleet guarding a crossing point (Cambridge University Collection: copyright reserved).

a granary, an oven and a water tank. It seems to have been occupied only for a short time during the first-century Flavian period. Without the aerial photograph it is almost impossible to see any indication of the presence of the fort.

It is instructive to compare Gatehouse with the fortlet north of Durisdeer (NS 903049) which is set on a hillock between two burns and guards the road north from Dalswinton and Carronbridge to Crawford. It is quite exceptionally well preserved, with clear banks and ditches still visible.

Also in Dumfriesshire and three miles north of Birrens fort (NY 218753), the two Roman practice camps north and south of the Selgovae hill fort of Burnswark are of outstanding interest. The camps and the engineering and siege training works (NY 185787) with three 'artillery' emplacements for spring-operated catapult type machines to fire lead bullets are a spectacular demonstration of professional expertise in the art of war.

The Roman roads running north through Annandale and Nithsdale are well known and are marked on the O.S. 1:50000 maps. Watch towers and signal stations with stacks of straw and beacons prepared with logs were placed at varying intervals. The routes, however, going east to west through Galloway are less obvious. It seems probable that sections of the road from the Nith (and from the harbour at Caerlaverock?) coincided with the eighteenth-century 'Old Military Road' from Lochfoot towards Milton and with the farm road to West Glenarm, with the line thereafter cross country towards Glenlochar to cross the Dee at Culvennan. The line south-west to Gatehouse is less clear, but was well north of the A75, and nearer the Fleet valley north of the Barlay Burn (631594 to 622588) and on by Fleuchlarg. Did the route west from Gatehouse coincide in part with the Corse of Slakes road into Kirkmabreck parish? North of Glenlochar and Dalry, was the Roman way on the line of the mediaeval pack route west of Polmaddie running north on the west side of Bardennoch Hill? Was the route to the sea from Glenlochar south-east to Balcary rather than by the Dee to Tongland and Kirkcudbright?

Caches and casual finds of third and fourth-century Roman coins, for example at Balgreggan quarry in Stoneykirk parish and in Stranraer, are evidence of trade and commercial activity spreading from Carlisle along the Solway coast and possibly continuing after the disintegration of Roman power in Britain at the end of the fourth century or about 410. This complements the evidence for the existence of a partly Romanised and literate Christian British population in the Whithorn area and in the Rhins in the fourth and fifth centuries, probably linked to other groups in Man and Ulster and north Wales.

The garrisons along Hadrian's Wall, Syrians, Thracians, Spanish, French, Africans, Britons and the civilians in Carlisle in the third and fourth centuries supported many gods, the old Roman Jupiter and Juno and Minerva and Mars and Mercury, the local Celtic deities 'adopted' as Brigantia and Maponia, and latterly new religions from the east including Mithraism from Persia and Christianity from Judaea, the last popular with officials and merchants and urban elites. The regional capital, Carlisle, was also the headquarters of Christian bishops who were responsible for a diocese extending throughout the tribal lands of the Brigantes and the Selgovae and probably also the Novantae in Galloway.

Evidence of their success is found in the cemeteries with west-east orientated long cist burials without grave goods at Terally and Curghie and High Clanyard in Kirkmaiden parish and at Whithorn below the east end of the mediaeval priory and above earlier Roman cremation burials; in the fourth-century pottery at Whithorn from Alexandria, with Antioch and Rome the most important early Christian cities; and in the number of early, possibly fifth and sixth-century, simple circular ditched and banked enclosures for chapel and cemetery, including possibly Kirkbride (561562) on the Skyre Burn beside a holy well (possibly a pagan Celtic place).

The most impressive evidence, however, which really establishes the importance of Whithorn and Kirkmaiden/Stoneykirk as the earliest centres of Christianity in Scotland, is the group of inscribed stones now in the Priory Museum at Whithorn and at Kirkmadrine church (080483) south-west of Sandhead. These are memorials of about 420 to 450 inscribed in simple capital letters and in Latin with the Romanised personal names of clerics and laymen—Latinus and Barrovadus on the stone at Whithorn: Viventius and Mavorius ('praecipui sacerdoti', that is holy and chief priests) and Florentius at Kirkmadrine, where they were found in 1861 being used as gateposts. The original site in the Kirkmadrine area is unknown, but somewhere between Sandhead and Chapel Rossan seems likely. Another, now lost, stone was found at Low Curghie near Drummore as a memorial to Ventidius, so there is almost certainly another early site nearby.

It does therefore seem probable that St. Ninian (or Nynia) came from Carlisle to Whithorn as a 'bishop' to serve an already established Christian community, and indeed it is possible that in 396 or 397 he was not the first bishop and certainly not the first priest to work there. St Ninian and St. Patrick of Ireland were probably both priests drawn from the Romano-British ruling elite in the Carlisle area, which reinforces the key importance of the Solway and Irish Sea routes at this crucial period of history. Priests and missionaries went out from Carlisle, and very likely from Whithorn as well, over to Ulster and north into central Scotland via the Tweed and Clyde valleys.

Perhaps in the same orderly way this elite attempted to maintain a system of political alliances among the tribal leaders or 'princes' in Cumbria and Dumfries and Galloway under the 'protection' of war leaders or 'kings' in Carlisle. Certainly the historical figure King Urien of Rheged seems to have ruled in the 570s and 580s an area including Galloway, Dumfriesshire, Carrick and northern Cumbria. Trade contacts still continued between 450 and 700 with the Mediterranean and south-west France, as is shown by the pottery and glass and bronze brooch moulds found at the Mote of Mark. But the overall impression of the fifth and sixth centuries is still rather of disharmony, unrest and war between Christians and pagans, including from the last quarter of the sixth century invading Angles from Northumbria. Irish invaders (referred to as the Cruithne) had settled in the Rhins of Wigtownshire in the second half of the fifth and in the sixth century, introducing new K or Q Celtic or Gaelic placenames.

In these dark times the old hill and promontory forts were needed again, and even strengthened with additional banks and ditches, as for example at Trusty's Hill fort and at Campbelton fort (658539) south-west of Twynholm and opposite the older Doon hill fort to the north. At least one, the Mote of Mark, may not have been developed as a fort until about 450. There may also have been defensive enclosures imitating Roman rectangular earthworks: the Watch Knowe (743864) at the north end of Craigmuie Moor, rectangular with rounded corners and double ditches, is a possible example.

Joseph Train, the Excise officer at Newton Stewart and Castle-Douglas who supplied Sir Walter Scott with antiquarian reports and objects, had a theory that there was a linear earthwork, called the Deil's Dyke, the equivalent of a Roman frontier wall, running all the way from Loch Ryan via Maberry and Ochiltree and Drannandow and Craignelder on to Tynron and Penpont and south to Hightae and on to the Solway. This was almost certainly wishful thinking, but the idea of some sort of turf bank defining boundaries in much more limited areas is quite feasible. The other Deil's Dyke in Nithsdale south of Sanquhar is an example of either a late Iron Age or mediaeval earthwork bank for some such purpose or to mark out a hunting forest area. The Galloway turf banks, *if* there were such stretches in some areas, could be either British sixth century or Anglian eighth century (compare Offa's Dyke on the western border of Mercia as a political concept) or indeed mediaeval.

Meanwhile although British, that is Welsh-speaking, missionaries still continued their work, for example St. Constantine in the Urr valley in the 570s, the overall impression is that in the second half of the sixth century and in the seventh century the church in Galloway changed radically under the impact of the marvellous fervour and enthusiasm and saintly scholarship and craftsmanship of the Irish Celtic monastic church. Even major centres such as Whithorn became monasteries, probably in the seventh century, and others were established at Hoddam and Applegarth in Annandale and Staplegorton in Eskdale. St. Finnian may have founded a monastery at a lost site in the Elrig area of Wigtownshire, with perhaps a chapel or oratory on the shore at Chapel Finian (278489). The picture is however very incomplete because no large monastic enclosure of the Irish type, as at Iona or Clonmacnois, has yet been identified in Galloway. It is just possible that the St. Peter's Stone in the Priory Museum was a cross marking the edge of the monastic precinct area, but more probably it was located at an oratory on the hill between Whithorn and Isle of Whithorn. And there must surely have been a Celtic monastic foundation in the Dee valley between Kirkcudbright and Kelton Hill before the association of the Northumbrian St.Cuthbert, who died in 687, with Kirkcudbright.

For clues to Celtic church locations look for Annat/Annait placenames, for example Annat Hill (384465) south of Camford near Longcastle; for

objects such as the seventh-century Celtic bell from Monybuie in the upper
Urr valley and the little holy oil flask from Barr of Spottes near Haugh of Urr;
and look for early chapel and oratory sites, for example the Irish-type timber
oratory on Ardwall Island and the possibly sixth-century chapel under the
east end of Whithorn Priory; for isolated retreats and hermitages, such as St.
Ninian's Cave used either by St. Ninian or more probably by his successors at
Whithorn, the island in Castle Loch, Mochrum used from Elrig monastery,
and more sensationally the Scar Rocks in Luce Bay which would have
seemed an even more attractive solitary location; for pilgrimage centres, with
St. Ninian's shrine at Whithorn popular probably as early as the sixth
century; and for holy wells, with the Wells of the Rees (229723) the only really
spectacular example.

The pagan hordes of English tribes invading Britain probably reached
Galloway about the 580s or 590s and established their dominance in
south-west Scotland by the middle of the seventh century. The marriage of
Rhienmelth, the grand-daughter of King Urien of Rheged, to Osui of
Northumbria about 632 might be a pointer to a key stage in the recognition of
Anglian political supremacy. In the absence of any special skills shown in
military architecture, there are very few obvious signs of which fortified
strengths they occupied. The siege and burning of the consequently vitrified
Mote of Mark belongs to the late seventh century, but whether as the result of
an attack by 'natives' on Angles or vice versa would be guesswork. Some
episode in the long struggle between the Picts of northern and eastern
Scotland and the Angles, culminating in the battle of Nechtansmere in 685,
may be marked by the Pictish symbols on Trusty's Hill fort, either as a
memorial to a Pictish leader killed in taking an Anglian stronghold or, less
probably, as a monument to record a peace treaty or a marriage settlement.

Anglian control in Galloway was perhaps essentially colonial. It did not
involve the migration of a tribe or a people, but rather the introduction of a
new ruling elite of landowners or governors. The local population remained
basically Welsh and Irish speaking, but the language of their new masters,
Northumbrian English, probably became at least temporarily dominant in
some areas over the next three hundred years. Although the Northumbrian
period lasted into the late ninth or early tenth century, and well after the
collapse of Northumbria itself, there is very little evidence, apart from the
Anglian crosses, of their presence. Some Anglo-Saxon coinage has been
found, for example coins of Eanred (808-841) in Luce Sands.

The remarkable Anglian crosses, mainly ninth and tenth century, belong
especially to the Machars of Wigtownshire and came almost certainly from a

workshop at Whithorn. After the conversion of the leaders of Northumbria to Christianity in the 630s, and no doubt years of evangelisation and consolidation, Anglian clergy dominated the church in Galloway by the 710s or 730s. Their eighth and ninth-century bishops at Whithorn included men with names such as Pecthelm and Pectwine. The penetration of this control into the smaller churches is suggested by the stone chapel and the stone with the Anglian name Cudgar found at Ardwall Island. In the 880s Whithorn may have become a refuge for Northumbrian monks bringing their treasures with them to escape the Vikings: their books, so the legend goes, included the Lindisfarne Gospels, and during a crossing in a storm from Cumberland to Galloway the great book was swept off their boat, only to be washed up the following morning at the Isle of Whithorn.

Of the crosses, the fantastic Ruthwell Cross is unique, important on a European scale as one of the finest examples of 'Dark Age' art and propaganda combining Roman figure sculpture with a long runic poem and vine scroll decoration. It is usually described as late seventh or early eighth century.

The more commonplace but still very pleasing ninth and tenth-century Anglian crosses, with interlacing on the shaft and a disc head and with bosses or pierced spaces between the arms of the cross, can be studied in the splendid collection in Whithorn Priory Museum, probably only a few yards from where they were carved. These have been assembled over the years from all over the southern Machars including St. Ninian's Cave and Monrieth. They were probably mostly monuments in memory of particular individuals. The sheer number of them and the diversity of locations in which they have been found suggest a great many small church sites in eastern Wigtownshire. It is not easy, however, to be sure of their original positions. The very well-preserved Monrieth Cross in the Priory Museum was in fact taken to Monrieth House in the nineteenth century from its original location at the Court or Castle Hill of Moure (382433), which is some three hundred yards north of the Old Place of Dowies (381430). There is another good tenth-century cross now inside Kirkinner church, a second Kirkinner cross at Knockgray, Carsphairn, and shafts at Wigtown church. There are other tenth and eleventh-century crosses and slabs from Kilmorie (at Corsewall House, Kirkcolm), Drummore, Sinniness, Craignarget and Glenluce in Wigtownshire, and Minnigaff old church. The very small simple crosses from Ardwall Island (at Ardwall House), and at Anwoth and Kirkclaugh probably belong to the eleventh or twelfth century. The Craignarget stone with swastikas and the Kilmorie cross, probably defaced by pagan Norse raiders adding a human figure, are a reminder of the

86 *Discovering Galloway*

The Anglian tenth-century cross formerly at Monrieth House and now in the Whithorn Priory Museum. Very clear interlacing and disc head bosses.

complex cultural traditions and styles crossing and clashing in Galloway in those grim years.

Very simple wayside crosses along pack routes or at fording places are difficult to date, but tenth/eleventh century or later seems possible for the examples from High Auchenlarie (at Kirkdale House), Stroanfreggan (at Hastings Hall, Moniaive), from Dalshangan (in Broughton House garden, Kirkcudbright), at Daltallochan and on Bardennoch Hill, and for the Glaik and Liddesdale crosses (in Stranraer Museum). What images these conjure up of travellers and pilgrims traversing the hills and glens, fearful always of the demons and pagans never very far away.

In spite of this rich heritage of sculptured stones, the tenth and eleventh centuries saw chaos and confusion reign in Galloway. York in 867 and Carlisle about 875/880 had fallen to pagan Danes who settled in eastern Dumfriesshire in numbers and possibly as far west as the eastern Stewartry. Placenames such as Tinwald and Torthorwald and the pagan influence seen in crosses from Wamphray and Closeburn and Glencairn come from them. After the collapse of Northumbria, Anglian 'governors' and landed men and churchmen may still have maintained some order in Galloway into the 900s or even the 920s, but they were eventually overwhelmed by new invaders from the north and the west, the Gall-Ghaidhil or 'foreign Gaels', partly pagan and partly Christian, men from the Hebrides and Kintyre and from Ireland and Man. National and notional boundaries changed between Britons of Strathclyde and Scots and Picts and Danes and Norsemen with alarming rapidity, but Galloway was securely part of the new North Sea empire from Norway and Iceland and Greenland to the Faroes and Shetlands and Orkneys to Man and eastern Ireland and Cumberland through most of the tenth and eleventh centuries.

Within Galloway a new hybrid elite of warriors and farmers and traders emerged, probably more Gaelic than Norse and perhaps during the eleventh century anyway more Christian than pagan. There are few clues and fewer hard facts about what sort of people they were. The double-headed sword and pin and bead and glass linen smoother found in a pagan burial in St. Cuthbert's churchyard in Kirkcudbright might be those of an early tenth-century mercenary employed to protect the settlement and church there against raiding Vikings, or might even be evidence of an 'urban' Norse trading centre. The trade silver and coins from York and Mercia and Carolingian France and Arabic Baghdad found at Talnotry (near Murray's Monument) are probably a trader's hoard of about 920 to 930.

The sagas offer some vital information. Njal's Saga mentions that the Icelander Kari Solmundarsson passed the winter in 1014 with 'earl Malcolm' at Hvitsborg, that is at Whithorn or at a fortified camp nearby; and the Orkneyinga Saga has Earl Thorfinn of Orkney using Gaddgeddler, that is Galloway, as a base to raid into England. So it seems that by 1000 the Gaelic-Norse hegemony had stabilised into an 'earldom' of Galloway which lasted to the end of the century. For individual landholdings one of the very few suggestions is that the churches held in the 1170s by Iona—Kirkcormack, Kelton, Barncrosh (Tongland) and St. Andrews (Balmaghie)—might correspond to the area ruled by one family.

No traces of ship burials or long houses have been identified in Galloway. The good farm land of Sorbie, Kirkinner, Eggerness, Whithorn, Glasserton,

Sinniness, Borgue or Kirkcudbright may still contain secrets to be discovered.

Direct evidence of Viking reoccupation or development of fortifications or 'borgs' hardly exists. Forts in the southern Rhins ought to be possible locations for bases or strong points, and the Old Fort at Dinnans (478402) near Whithorn, Castle Haven, which was reoccupied in the ninth century, perhaps the Doon (657488) above the Dee estuary, and the curious Green Island promontory 'fort' (838716) in Milton Loch.

But Galwedia or Gallwitheia at the end of the eleventh century seems a very strange place, with a polyglot collection of peoples and languages—Welsh and Irish, Northumbrian English, Danish, Norse, Gaelic and, of course, Latin as the language of the Church which was still in the 1090s fighting pagans and paganism in a very dangerous and unstable world.

CHAPTER 7

Castles, Country Houses and Coo Palaces

Allowing for the exaggeration likely in Christian propaganda versions of history, the enthralling descriptions by English ecclesiastical chroniclers and annalists of the Galwithienses campaigning and plundering in Northumberland and Cumberland still clearly show that Galweia or Gallowithia in the twelfth and early thirteenth centuries retained many peculiar customs and pagan traditions and enthusiasms. They were seen as separate and different folk as the routine, probably stereotyped, entries by clerks in charters show with the references to French, English, Scots and Gallovidians *(Francis et Anglis et Scottis et Galwensibus).* Their customs included selling female captives as slaves to Ireland for payment in cattle; somewhat informal 'marriage' relationships allowing for easy 'divorces' through which wives could be sold and/or husbands changed on a monthly basis; blood brotherhood with the dead by drinking watered human blood; a distinctly pagan hostility to the Church, not just in looting but in desecration, decapitating clergy, placing human heads on altars, and eating flesh in Lent; and the sort of savage frolics (tossing infants up into the air and spitting them on their spears) associated with the Gall-Ghaidhel.

Galloway, although within the overlordship of the kings of Scotland, was a large and in practice virtually autonomous province extending east into Nithsdale and north into Clydesdale and Carrick. Its ruler Fergus (from before 1138 to 1160) was referred to as *princeps,* and even as *rex.* It presented special problems and dangers for Alexander I (1107-1124), David I (1124-1153), Malcolm IV (1153-1165) and William I (1165-1214) because it was so close to the expanding frontiers of the Anglo-Norman kings of England, *and* to Argyll and the Hebrides still (until 1266) under the kings of Norway, and to the Norse kingdom of Man.

It is important to see the development of modern Galloway in the twelfth and thirteenth centuries within this context of the rivalries of ambitious dynasties and families. 'National' territories and frontiers (as indeed local boundaries) within the British Isles were still fluid. It was still possible that Strathclyde and Lothian and Galloway and Cumbria and Northumbria would merge into a permanent political unity, as certainly Malcolm III (1058-1093) and his sons intended. William II of England had captured Carlisle in 1092 and established a frontier line south of the Solway; David I retook Carlisle in 1136 and restored 'Scottish' control of Cumberland and Westmorland; but Malcolm IV had to surrender the northern counties to Henry II in 1157, and although not formalised until 1237, this effectively marked the 'Border' for the next five hundred and fifty years.

A stable and secure Galloway was especially important for David I whose 'capital' was in Carlisle rather than Edinburgh or Dunfermline. In turn a powerful Scottish king effectively in control in Cumberland and Westmorland had the opportunity to establish a new centralised royal authority and to reduce the independence of Galloway. This became part of a slow and gradual programme of virtuous modernisation and reform and improvement through the introduction by ruthless men of elements of the new feudal order into central and local government, in land tenure and in the Church. The key to making this new order possible and permanent was the introduction of a landholding elite of men expert in war and castle-building, loyal to their oath to their lord, men hungry for land and power whether from Normandy, Brittany, Gascony or Flanders via Northamptonshire or Yorkshire or Cumberland. The land grants they received, whether for old estates or for amalgamations or subdivisions of existing units, were based on knight service. David I's charter granting Annandale to Robert de Brus in 1123/24 for ten knights' service was probably the first great feudal holding in the south-west. Other great tenants further west, Balliols and de Morevilles, followed and in turn probably granted holdings for one knight or in fractional fees of $\frac{1}{2}, \frac{1}{4}, \frac{1}{8}$ knight service or sergeanty service for a mounted archer or spearman.

The part played by Fergus, Uhtred (1160-1174), Gilbert (1174-1185), Roland (1185-1200) and Alan of Galloway (1200-1235) is complex. Roland and Alan were great feudal lords with extensive holdings in Scotland, England and Ireland; Fergus and Uhtred were perhaps much more Gallovidians first and supporters of the new order second. Fergus is particularly interesting. He, and Ulric and Duvenald who were both killed, had been leaders of David I's army at the Battle of the Standard in 1138; and he was related by marriage to David I (both he and Alexander I married illegitimate daughters, Elizabeth and Sibylla, of Henry I), so it is not surprising to find him as a patron of the new order in the Church and introducing Anglo-Normans. On the other hand his daughter Affreca married Olaf, the Norse King of Man, and their son Godred was King of Man from 1144 to 1154, and in 1160 he led a rebellion against Malcolm IV. After three campaigns he was forced to surrender and retired to Holyrood Abbey where he died in 1161. Uhtred continued to introduce feudal elements, and married Gunnild, daughter of Waldof, lord of Allerdale in

Westmorland. However, after the failure of William I's attempt to retake Cumberland and his capture in 1174, Uhtred and his brother Gilbert drove out the 'English and French' and destroyed their defences and castles *(munitiones et castella)*. Gilbert, who represented the old Celtic-Norse traditions at their worst, had Uhtred killed in excruciating circumstances at the Isle beside Kirkcudbright (probably at Palace Isle in Loch Fergus, but possibly St. Mary's Isle or Inch Island south of St. Mary's Isle). After Gilbert's death in 1185 Roland defeated Gillepatrick and Gillecolium in two campaigns and brought in many new Anglo-Normans so that the whole process of castle-building took on a new momentum. Roland acquired estates in Northamptonshire and Yorkshire through his marriage to Elena de Moreville. Alan is an even more extraordinary figure: one of the great magnates on whose advice King John signed Magna Carta, he also intervened in succession problems in Man and raided and plundered in the Hebrides. He married three times, to a daughter of Reginald, Lord of the Isles, to Margaret, daughter of Earl David of Huntingdon, and to Rohais, daughter of Hugh de Lacy, Lord of Ulster. On his death Galloway was divided between his three daughters, Elena, married to the Earl of Winchester, Christina, married to the Earl of Albemarle, and Devorgilla, married to John Balliol.

The marriage alliances suggest just how Galloway was changing. The old Celtic-Norse rulers were gradually replaced by men from Cumberland and Yorkshire, de Morevilles, Balliols, de Vaux, de Campania, de Berkeley, de Veteripont, Gospatrick fitz Orme, David fitz Terri, de Bek and de la Zouch and others taking their names from their estates, de Culwenne, de Twyname, de Suthayk, de Kyrcudbrith and de Kirkdale. English peasants in varying degrees of free and 'unfree' settled with their lords, for example at the Inglestons in Kelton and Borgue and Kirkgunzeon parishes.

The early charters have many Celtic witnesses with marvellous names such as Gillecatfar and Gillecrist mac Gillewinnin, and also have references to the lands of Celtic figures such as Gilleker and Gillecolum; but there are fewer after 1185. In Wigtownshire, however, the Celtic 'clans' persisted through the thirteenth and well into the fourteenth century, as the list of men aiding John Balliol taken at Wigtown in 1296 shows. It included Gillenef McGillherf, Gillcryst McEthe, Duncan McGillauenan, Cuthbert McEuri, Kelman McKelli and Auchmacath McGilmotha. Goodness knows what they did to their enemies in battle, but their names are enough to frighten most people!

The new order was achieved only after rebellions and slaughter and devastation and almost 'racial' war, especially in 1174-1185, with conservative opposition to change persisting far longer in the Machars and Rhins of Wigtownshire. After Alan's death another rising in 1235 was led by his bastard son Thomas of Galloway and was only suppressed after the intervention of Alexander II. And in a famous episode in 1247 the Earl of Winchester had to flee from his castle (Wigtown or Cruggleton?). The depth of this hostility is also suggested by atrocities against the new clergy. In 1235 the prior and sacrist of Tongland were killed in their church and the Cistercian abbot of Dundrennan was murdered by a kilted figure (no doubt in the Marxist jargon of the 1980s a 'freedom fighter') on this or on another occasion. In the Scottish Wars of Independence post-1286 Galloway anti-Scottish separatism and conservatism were used by Edward I to attract support, and he even brought the eighty-eight-year-old Thomas of Galloway from imprisonment in Barnard Castle with a special charter of liberties and freedoms for Galloway. In the west the MacCanns and the McDowalls were especially persistent supporters of Edward I, and indeed in general in the war years up to 1314 Galloway was pro John Balliol and anti Robert I. Galloway was nearly devastated by castle sieges, including the famous siege of Caerlaverock Castle in 1300, and battles and engagements such as those at the Cree in 1300 and at Glentrool in 1307. Edward I's itinerary for 1300 is very interesting and well documented and included the well-known 'dinner, bed and breakfast' stop at Girthon near Gatehouse-of-Fleet.

Galloway is one of the best areas in Britain to see the physical evidence of early mediaeval castles and fortified sites. Old hill and promontory forts, such as Tynron Doon and Dunskey near Portpatrick, were still used in the Middle Ages, and others, for example Boreland of Borgue and Kirkclaugh, were developed for motte castle-building. Some of the first castles may have been ringworks or ring mottes, that is simple ditch, bank and palisade defences, now difficult to distinguish from later mediaeval structures. There are possible examples at Duchrae (664696), Pulcree (593583), and Bombie (715505). Fergus and Uhtred had their main strongholds at the 'palitium' on Palace Isle (698511) at the north end of the now drained Loch Fergus, potentially a most important site but very difficult to make much of now, and at Cruggleton (485428), which has the complete sequence of motte, courtyard castle and tower house.

The typical early castle is the motte (preferably not 'mote', a very different lady as Dickens and Mayhew enthusiasts will recall). Mottes are super fun for the family, exciting to climb (try Druchtag or Kirkclaugh on a wet day), often in spectacular places, far more impressive from the top than you would think possible from below, and often the site of wooden castle structures from the early twelfth century until the building of a stone tower house in the sixteenth century. The earliest Galloway mottes date from the 1130s or 1140s (Lincluden, Troqueer, Buittle, Urr, Cruggleton); many were heightened and improved or only constructed post-1185; others may very well belong to the thirteenth century or even later. Most were built by the new Anglo-Normans, with the classical castle-church-village grouping still clear at Druchtag near Mochrum, Minnigaff, Balmaclellan, Dalry and Twynholm; others may well have been the work of Celtic-Norse imitators following the latest fashion in military architecture. One possible example is Castle Ban (NW 966678).

There are over fifty mottes in Galloway, with clusters near and in Dumfries, along the river valleys of the Urr and the Dee and the Fleet, and on the sea coast, including the line of probably post-1185 mottes in the Rhins. It is striking how few there are in the Machars. Most are straightforward castles built as bases to establish and maintain dominance over new land holdings, permanent castles and strongpoints. It is possible that those in more remote locations, such as Machars Hill (470652) and Skaith (382662), might have been rather hunting lodges for the Balliols and other great tenants to use on visits to their deer forests and vast sporting estates.

The motte of Urr, over five acres in extent, is one of the largest and finest in Scotland. Most are very much smaller, but even the least impressive may have been a surprisingly sophisticated and complex structure. The castle mound itself, an artificial (but often partly natural) series of layers of earth and small stones, was mostly circular or oval, sometimes the classical Christmas pudding shape, sometimes rectangular, sometimes terraced, sometimes little more than a platform above marsh and swamp and stream below; ranging in height above the surrounding ditch from ten to thirty or forty feet, and perhaps heightened on several occasions over the decades; and with a deep and wide ditch, dry or wet, round the base. Some had a bailey or courtyard, defended by an outer ditch and stockade, with space for barns, stables, kitchens, perhaps a hall or a chapel, and huts or houses for retainers. It is just possible that some had timber beams laid round the sides of the mound, so that they looked more like a static tank than a grassy hillock as seen today.

On top of the mound, or built into it, was a wooden blockhouse or tower, possibly crenellated and perhaps with external fighting platforms if the illustrations in the Bayeux Tapestry are an accurate guide, and perhaps also buildings of wattle and daub. There would be a timber stockade round the edge of the motte, perhaps with small towers or turrets along the inside.

The classical Christmas pudding-shaped motte par excellence at Parton beside the old railway line north of Castle-Douglas.

Access to the top of the mound was likely to be by a flying bridge over the ditch from the counterscarp, or by steps up the side of the motte from a bridge over the ditch at the base. Excavations at Urr and Sorbie have confirmed elements variously of this interpretation.

Good examples, mostly visible from the road, include Lincluden (967779), Urr (815647), Maxwelton (817896), Lochrinnie (728871), Dalry (618813), Balmaclellan (653793), Kirkland Parton (696697), Kirkcormack (717574), Twynholm (663542), Boreland of Borgue (646517), Barmagachan (613494), Cally (606556), Boreland Anwoth (585550), Kirkclaugh (534521), Minnigaff (410664), Druchtag or Boghouse (349497), Balgreggan (096505) and Innermessan (084633).

Sorbie (451469) is a good example of a motte in a marshy swampy area. It is not surprising to find islands in lochs in use as strongpoints carrying, variously, wooden and stone buildings and halls from the twelfth to the sixteenth centuries. Loch Urr (763845 island, 759843 promontory) and Lochrutton (898729 and 900731) are examples of crannogs and promontories on the mainland opposite operating as the equivalents of motte and bailey castles. Other island sites with mediaeval halls and structures include Stable Isle, Loch Fergus (697507), Lochinvar (658853),

Lochmaberry (285751), Castle Loch, Mochrum (293541), and Lochnaw (NW993632); and in addition later tower houses such as Craigcaffie (088641) seem to have been built in very 'wet' locations.

There is another and difficult to identify category of very miscellaneous twelfth to sixteenth-century earthworks, oval or roughly rectangular enclosures with water-filled ditches for security against men and wild animals, and possibly even for fishpond breeding and storage. These include the episcopal palace site at Penninghame Hall (409605); and moated manor or homestead moat or fortified farmhouse sites at Palace Yard, Enrick (614544), Auchenfranco (893724), The Ditch, Boreland of Gelston (783572), Crogo (758774), the enormous Fortalice of Greenlaw 'island' on the bank of the Dee (741636), Camphill, Whinnyliggate (717519), Meikle Spyland (714518), Clownstane, Bombie (708502), Brockloch (707517), Dunrod (699459), Queen's Hill or Fellend (689590), Plunton (605507), the Old Place of Broughton (456452) and Crows (368557). Dunrod and Crows are close to old church and possible deserted village sites. Mediaeval halls have been found at Ardwall Island (573495) and Hestan Island (839503). And the Cistercian abbeys at Holm Cultram in Cumberland and Dundrennan had twelfth-century and later granges in Kirkgunzeon parish, quite probably fortified and defended by men-at-arms. The former might have been located around the site of the fine sixteenth-century tower house at Drumcoltran.

Deserted mediaeval villages have proved a subject of absorbing interest in England, but in Galloway settlements were not so much in villages round a castle or a church, although there are examples such as Dunrod and Kirkcormack, but rather in tiny hamlets and clusters of houses, in groups of buildings as fermtouns and in separate farms. Some were deserted by the fifteenth and sixteenth centuries, and of course there are others, such as the Clachan of Penninghame (413612), only abandoned towards the end of the nineteenth century. The eighteenth and nineteenth-century deserted mining villages, for example Woodhead (532936), generally have much more substantial remains. Look for evidence of mediaeval sunken roadways and tracks, the sites of stone-walled houses (many would have had only turf and mud huts), the sites of mills indicated by the remains of lades, kilns for drying grain, boundary ditches for the village precinct, and (less likely in Galloway) dovecot and windmill and rabbit pillow mounds. Polmaddy (590878), still occupied in the sixteenth and seventeenth centuries, with mill and lade, smithy, inn, kilns, fields and a mediaeval bridle track, is especially fascinating. Other sites, often with little or virtually no physical evidence surviving, include Kirkconnel near Springkell (NY

248755), Tynron (812934), Terregles (943767), East Preston (968564), Kirkconnel near New Abbey (977680), Galtway (707487), Cruives of Cree (377708), Old Feys (372652), Airylick Mochrum (309498) and Braid Hill (259600).

The only example of cultivation terraces at Blairs Hill (466612) behind Pulwhat Bridge mill above the A75 (six terraces about forty-four to fifty-six yards long and nine to eleven feet wide) may be associated with the Cistercian hospital of Crithe for pilgrims crossing the Cree en route to St. Ninian's shrine at Whithorn.

The Dundrennan—Kirkcarswell—Rerrick—Dunrod area is good for indications of the ridge and furrow lines of mediaeval strip field farming (runrig), especially clear in sharp evening sunshine.

Mediaeval boundaries between estates and properties followed burns and lanes, such as the Dufpole or Kirkgunzeon Lane, and were also marked by dykes, cairns, crosses marked on trees, and by stone crosses.

To most people, however, 'mediaeval' means the massive stone walls of courtyard castles and walled towns and abbeys and churches. War and military architecture in the thirteenth century became increasingly elaborate and scientific, and Galloway had four formidable castles with great curtain walls and flanking towers built between the 1230s and the 1300s at Wigtown (438550), Kirkcudbright Castledykes (677509), Buittle (819616) and Cruggleton (485428), the last two developed from mottes. Buittle was built by the Balliols, but who built the others and when (1230s? 1260s? 1290s?) is by no means clear. Roger de Quinci, the Earl of Winchester, might have built Kirkcudbright and/or Wigtown and Cruggleton, or Kirkcudbright and Wigtown might have been royal castles, as was the 'new' castle at Dumfries Castledykes (976746) post-1185. Kirkcudbright and Cruggleton have been excavated. Later thirteenth and fourteenth-century pottery from the English Midlands and south-west France was found at Kirkcudbright. But at all these sites only fragments under earth and grass are left, although it is possible to get some idea of the scale of Kirkcudbright Castle from the mounds and bumps at Castledykes. Edward I lived here for about ten days in July 1300 with his army, and some of his fleet of ninety-five ships based at Skinburness must have been in the Dee estuary. For a better idea of these castles visit the Brus strongholds at Loch Doon (now at 484950) and Lochmaben (NY 088811) and the splendid Caerlaverock Castle (NY 025656).

It is scarcely possible now to imagine Dumfries, or Kirkcudbright consisting of the old High Street between the river Dee on one side and the creek or swamp on the other, or Wigtown (closer? to the castle and the harbour than the present town square) as mediaeval defended towns. Whithorn with its long main street still retains some of the feel of a compact defensible unit. It seems very probable that the development of towns in the south-west goes back to the period of rapid change and growth under William I between 1185 and the 1200s. New towns at Ayr (1197) and Dumfries (1186) were intended as first, secure bases and centres for the sheriffdoms which would isolate and help to pacify Galloway, and second, as places with walls and defences which would keep lawless elements out and provide conditions suitable for the growth of trade in surplus agricultural produce, perhaps influenced directly or indirectly in time by the success of the Cistercian sheep ranching on their granges, and in manufactured goods. The names of some of the first merchants have survived, for example Erkin of Kirkcudbright trading to Ireland from Roger de Quinci's lands. There are also a few record references to early ports, for example Hur (between the Dub O' Hass at Dalbeattie and Palnackie on the Urr) from Holm Cultram material c.1185.

The earliest evidence for the existence of urban settlements and/*or* the granting of a charter includes Dumfries in 1186, almost certainly with defences which could still be refortified in the Jacobite rebellion year of 1715; Annan by the 1190s; Lochmaben by 1290; Staplegorton by c.1285; Urr (below the motte) by 1262; Buittle in 1324-1325; Kirkcudbright by 1237 or 1288, probably with water defences and walls still in use in 1547 and still standing in the 1590s; Wigtown by the 1260s or 1292; and Whithorn, an ecclesiastical burgh in 1325, but almost certainly much earlier. Innermessan (084634), north of Stranraer on the ridge and plateau north and east of the motte, and which still had streets and lairds' houses in the later sixteenth century, might conceivably have its origins in the late twelfth or thirteenth century, although there is no evidence to support this suggestion.

Towns offered some degree of security, but the vast majority of the people continued to live in farms and dispersed settlements in rural areas. In the long term the programme of modernisation or 'Normanisation' in religious affairs supported by the Scottish kings and the lords of Galloway (no doubt from a mixture of piety and self-interest) was far more important in eradicating pagan ways and traditions and in establishing new conventions in the rules of war and the conduct of peace. In part, of course, the reforms were only a matter of new fashions and customs in religious observance, for example during Lent or in conducting the mass exclusively in Latin. However, it also meant the introduction of a new ecclesiastical aristocracy of Anglo-Norman secular clergy and religious replacing the

Celtic 'scolastici' or 'scollofthes' whom Ailred describes at the church of St. Cuthbert in Kirkcudbright as late as 1164.

More fundamentally it meant the imposition of a new practical centralised disciplined structure of church government, international and local. As part of a new fairly uniform system of territorial dioceses, rather akin to royal sheriffdoms, the bishopric at Whithorn was resored with the election in 1128 and consecration in 1133 of Gilla-Aldan. Although he must have been one of the old Celtic or 'Culdee' clergy, his successors from bishop Christian (1154-1186) onwards were probably part of the new order; and from about 1175 Premonstratensian canons consitituted the chapter of Whithorn. Like the bishops of Orkney and the Isles under the archbishops of Trondheim, so the bishops of Galloway were under and consistently loyal to the archbishops of York until 1472, and indeed in the twelfth and thirteenth centuries frequently acted as suffragan bishop in York. The wars between the kings of Scotland and England in the two centuries thoroughly disrupted these relations.

Even more permanent, and in many instances surviving until well after the Reformation, the system of parishes in the Stewartry and in Wigtownshire staffed by secular clergy emerged at this time in districts defined by the estates held by the Anglo-Norman lords and knights. It is by no means clear how this worked in practice, or whether there were enough priests to fill all the charges or where they came from, but it does seem to have been the responsibility of the new landowners to endow and maintain churches beside their castles (Minnigaff, Cruggleton for example) or on older religious sites. The parishes in the Statistical Accounts of the 1790s are often later (before or after the Reformation) amalgamations of smaller parish units, for example Sorbie from Great and Little Sorby, Kirkmadrine and Cruggleton; Glasserton from Kirkmaiden and Glasserton; Kirkcudbright from Dunrod, Galtway and Kirkcudbright; Borgue from Senwick, Kirkandrews and Borgue; and Kelton from Gelston, Kirkcormack and Kelton.

The work of the monastic and religious orders in Galloway was probably even more important in the twelfth and thirteenth centuries and still is an outstanding part of the architectural and spiritual heritage of the south-west. The houses of these supranational organisations, founded and supported by both the kings of Scotland and the lords of Galloway from the time of David I and Fergus through their grants of land and of the revenues of parish churches, served a wide range of different purposes and uses. All in their various ways helped by example to make local peace and progress possible and all were busy practical orderly communities designed (often in

France, as at Citeaux and Premontré) as centres for prayer and worship and contemplation. It is possible that some, for example the Augustinian foundation at St. Mary's Isle, may have been established on the site of earlier Culdee religious centres.

Of the monastic orders, the Cluniac Benedictines who specialised in elaborate ritual and music and services perhaps had least to offer Galloway, and their only house in the south-west was the abbey founded at Crossraguel near Maybole in Ayrshire in 1214-1216. The Cistercian monks (generally laymen not priests) were the most successful in Galloway with abbeys at Dundrennan, founded in 1142 by David I and/or Fergus and colonised from Rievaulx, 'the mother of mercy', in Yorkshire; a doubtful house at Soulseat, founded about 1148 by St. Malachy of Armagh, which lasted only a few years; at Glenluce founded in 1191-1192 by Roland; and at Sweetheart founded in 1273 by Devorgilla de Balliol. The special importance of the Cistercians and their lay brothers lay in their dynamic creative work in land use and management, draining swamps and turning wastes into profitable farmland and sheep ranches. If at all possible get hold of Walter Daniel's life of Ailred, abbot of Rievaulx between 1147 and 1167, a truly good and great man, who visited Dundrennan and Kirkcudbright in 1165 and gives us a marvellous description of the twelfth-century world of faith and miracles. The architecture of Dundrennan in particular reflects accurately the early ideals of austerity and simplicity so valued by the great St. Bernard of Clairvaux, just as Melrose and Sweetheart for all their merits do represent degenerate Cistercianism.

The Augustinians and Premonstratensians were regular clergy, that is priests able to assist in parish church services and missionary and evangelical work and to act as clerks and chaplains to great lords and their ladies. In spite of the number of grants of the revenues of parish churches assigned to Holyrood Abbey by Fergus and Uhtred only one Augustinian house, St. Mary's Isle near Kirkcudbright, dependent on Holyrood, was founded in Galloway. It dates from some time before 1220. Its precise location is uncertain, but may have been on the same site as the later (and now demolished) St. Mary's Isle House. Four of the six Premonstratensian houses in Scotland were in Galloway. The first, colonised directly from Premontré, was at Soulseat (101587) on the manor of Inch, which belonged to the bishop of Galloway, about 1175 or earlier and probably on the site of the earlier Cistercian monastery. The most important, however, was Whithorn cathedral priory, established about 1175 or earlier and colonised from Soulseat. The others were Tongland (698539) near Kirkcudbright, founded in 1218 by Alan of Galloway and colonised from Cockersand, and

Holywood (955796) near Dumfries established before 1225 and colonised from Soulseat.

Smaller and later houses include a Benedictine nunnery at Lincluden founded by Uhtred before 1174 and suppressed in 1389; the Cistercian nunnery of St. Evoca on the west bank of the Dee between Kirkeoch and Lower Nunton (possibly at Nunmill 659488), founded before 1423; the hospital of Crithe on the river Cree, founded before 1306 and dependent on Dundrennan abbey (possibly at Spittal north of Creetown); Franciscan houses in Dumfries established between 1234 and 1266 and in Kirkcudbright in 1455; a Dominican house in Wigtown founded in 1267 or before 1287; and the collegiate church at Lincluden founded by Archibald Douglas about 1389 and incorporating the hospital between Lincluden and Holywood established in 1372.

The universal values and the perfection and order sought in the religious life in these houses is still perfectly expressed in the remains of the buildings still to be seen at Dundrennan, Glenluce and Sweetheart, each with its church laid out on one side of the cloister and the dorter range with the chapter house, the frater range with dining room or refectory and kitchen, and the cellarer's or laybrothers' range making up the sides of the rectangle. The outstanding feature at Sweetheart is the remarkable enclosure wall marking the outer precinct, which although not essentially defensive, nevertheless suggests that the security usually guaranteed within was one of the most important aspects of monastic life.

Another way of seeking inner peace and perfection and of expressing penance for ordinary or even exceptionally wicked demonstrations of human fallibility was to go on pilgrimage. Whithorn was, of course, a major pilgrimage centre for commoners and for kings from Robert I to James IV alike. Pilgrims arrived by sea from Ireland and the Highlands through Portpatrick and Kirkcolm, from Lanarkshire and the Lothians by Dalry and Wigtown, from Ayrshire by Barrhill, the Wells of the Rees, Laggangairn and Kirkcowan, and from Wales and the north of England by Isle of Whithorn. As well as St. Ninian's shrine at the east end of the priory church, there is also the important cave retreat on Port Castle Bay south-west of Whithorn which may have been used by Ninian himself and certainly by his immediate followers.

The remains of mediaeval parish churches in Galloway are meagre and disappointing. Buittle and Cruggleton are the best, and the site and fragments of the old church at Southwick up the Back Burn and of the presbytery at Senwick are interesting. However, the scarcity of old churches is more than balanced by the extraordinary richness and variety of late mediaeval military architecture, if that is not too grandiose a term for the later fourteenth to mid-seventeenth-century tower houses of greater and lesser families—Stewarts, McCullochs, Hannays, Hays, Browns, Kennedys, Agnews, McLellans, McDowalls and Gordons. The importance they attached to defensive measures and to security as opposed to comfort in their fortified houses is a reflection of a number of problems—the chronic weakness of Scottish central government; the overthrow and collapse of the Douglas lordship of Galloway in 1455 which left a power vacuum not filled by any single family or 'clan'; and the persistent hostility between Scotland and England in the fifteenth and sixteenth centuries with occasional intervals in which peace was declared. Although only eastern Galloway was generally in any danger from cross-Border raiding, the effect of the relative weakness of Scotland (Dumfries, for example, was taken by English forces in 1536, 1542, 1547-1548 and 1570, and Kirkcudbright successfully stood off an assault on the town by Sir Thomas Carleton's detachment from the English army of invasion in 1547) must have increased the feeling of vulnerability. Good men and true in Galloway, of course, such as Leonard Robertson of Kirkcudbright and his 'men of weir and marrinaris' in the 1570s, took a suitable revenge on the English.

More fundamentally, within Galloway the competing ambition and greed of the various families and the decidedly rough company of their followers, who behaved rather like football supporters today, produced not total anarchy but rather a perennial atmosphere of doubt and uncertainty in the face of violence. Young heiresses were kidnapped and married off to obtain possession of their lands; barns were fired, crops stolen and cattle rustled; and ironically a good deal of time and money spent in disputes before courts of law. Neighbours were, as in international relations, usually enemies—McDowalls, McKies and Hannays in 1526; the Hannays of Sorbie and the Murrays of Broughton in the 1590s and 1600s in a series of feuds involving Kennedys, Dunbars and Stewarts of Garlies; and McCullochs and Gordons as late as the 1660s and 1690s. And family disputes might become confused with quarrels between Catholics and Protestants in the sixteenth century, and between Presbyterians and Episcopalians in the seventeenth century.

So, as in Ireland, earlier mediaeval castle sites continued in occupation with a series of new buildings until a tower house was built adjacent to a motte, as at Sorbie, or even inside a motte, as at Myrton. Alternative concepts found little favour in Scotland, although Morton Castle (891992) is a fine example of a later fourteenth-century hall house.

The Castle of Park with a complex of eighteenth and nineteenth-century farm buildings around it—in some respects closer to the original concept than the beautifully restored freestanding tower house as seen today.

Most towers are seen now as buildings standing in isolation, but a tower house was originally part of a complex of farm buildings, barns, stables and retainers' quarters inside a courtyard area with a stone barmkin wall, and sometimes an outer ditched enclosure for cattle and horses. Towers were usually random rubble stonework with perhaps rough cast or harling. Earlier towers were mostly rectangular, three or four storeys high, with defence conducted from the top with projecting timber war-heads or stone corbelling with machicolation and, after about 1500, from the ground floor using small inverted keyhole or dumb-bell gunports for hand guns. A four or five-storey wing was sometimes added.

Sixteenth-century towers were more likely to be built on the L plan. Doorways in early towers were often at first-floor level, with access by ladder or external stair; in later towers the doors were on the ground floor, and in L-plan towers usually in the re-entrant angle. The walls were honeycombed with a labyrinth of passages and mural chambers, with a wheel stair either in the wall thickness in a corner or in the wing of L-plan towers. In the later sixteenth and seventeenth centuries decorative and even frivolous pepperpot turrets and crenellations and machicolation and cape-houses as lookout points and gunports were added to display the status of the occupants. Cardoness, Carsluith and Park, all on the line of the A75, show how the tower house evolved from the middle of the fifteenth to the end of the seventeenth century.

Threave Castle, the largest tower house in Galloway, is quite exceptional in that it was a major castle in the full sense of the term, built by Archibald the Grim after 1369 as the central strength of his lordship. The remarkable artillery curtain wall with three circular corner towers with slits for hand guns and long and cross-bows is now thought to have been built in 1446/1447.

A wide variety of tower-house architecture can be seen at Hillis (912726), Drumcoltran (869683), Orchardton (816551), Barscobe (659806), Earlston (612840), Plunton (605507), Rusco (584604), Cardoness (591553), Barholm (520529), Carsluith (494541), Garlies (422691), Castle Stewart (379690), Sorbie (451470), Isle of Whithorn (476365), Dowies (381430), Myrton (360432), Mochrum (308541), Carscreugh (223598), Park (188571), Castle Kennedy (111609), Craigcaffie (088641), Stranraer (061608), Corsewall (NW 991714), Lochnaw (NW 991628) and Dunskey (003533).

Meanwhile, although monks and friars and priests had carried on their duties fairly well in spite of great difficulties and with meagre resources, there had been a Scottish Reformation in 1560. Compared to events in England, it was not a violent upheaval and did not involve any great popular hostility to the old Church or its clergy or even its buildings. Violence and religious mania were largely confined to the seventeenth-century struggle, a disgusting spectacle of waste, slaughter, sorrow and grief, between varieties of Episcopalian and Presbyterian Protestantism that were almost equally evangelical, fanatical, intolerant and totalitarian. No doubt many decent and sensible folk managed to live quiet lives by agreeing to conform to the prevalent fashions in the Presbyterian (1638 to 1660 and after 1689) and Episcopalian (1600 to 1689) periods of dominance.

A strong folk tradition or memory of the role played by the Covenanters, or more properly 'conventiclers'—that is, the more extreme element who supported Presbyterian ministers ousted from their charges and who also opposed Episcopalian repression with sporadic guerilla warfare, ambushes and assassinations, in particular during the 'Killing Time' between 1685 and 1688—is even now an important part of life in Ayrshire, Lanarkshire, Dumfriesshire and Galloway. The subject has to be approached with some delicacy of sentiment because the people who believe most sincerely in the romantic, sentimentalised nineteenth-century picture of these years are in general the nicest and best and most socially conservative Gallovidians you will encounter. It has to be pointed out, however, that many good people just do not fully appreciate the enormous differences between then and now and the extent of the bigotry and arrogance of all parties in an era when religion did not mean love, charity, tenderness, tolerance or benevolence, but the imposition of certainties of righteousness by doctrinaire intellectuals and busybodies. The world then was still seen as a battleground between God and the Devil or Anti-Christ, with God and the angels on one side regularly intervening in everyday matters and, on the other, Satan trying to steal the souls of men and recognised variously as the Pope, bishops, the Episcopalian or the Presbyterian church, kings, witches and enchanters, demon spirits, heretics in all guises and lunatics. Rival versions of Christianity were seen not just as unfortunate errors, but as the worship of Satan. It is therefore worth remembering that the surprisingly stock phrases and sentiments you read on monuments and churchyard stones may be essentially propaganda, at best oversimplified statements of opinion and at worst twisted distortions of history. The heirs of the Covenanters were not to be found in the—on the whole—decent and moderate established Church of Scotland in the eighteenth and nineteenth centuries, but in groups such as the Cameronians and the Macmillanites who remained outside it. If in doubt on the fanaticism of the seventeenth-century Episcopalian and Presbyterian churches, ask yourself why so many poor women were executed as witches by strangulation and burning ('worried at ane stake till they be dead and thereafter their bodies to be burnt to ashes'). Was it really necessary to burn Agnes Comenes, Janet McGowane, Jean Tomson, Margaret Clark, Janet McKendrig, Agnes Clerk, Janet Corsone, Helen Moorhead and Janet Callan at the Whitesands in Dumfries on 13th April 1659, or Janet Macmurdoch from Airds near Crossmichael and Elspeth Thomson from Glenshinnoch in Rerrick parish in Dumfries on 18th May 1671, or Elspeth McEwen from Cubbox in Balmaclellan parish at Kirkcudbright on August 24th 1698? Isn't it high time monuments were put up to these martyrs to the religious mania of their judges, jurors, elders and ministers and accusers?

Well, tolerance *was* an eighteenth-century invention, a triumph of expediency over the religious principles of Covenanters, Episcopalians and Presbyterians alike and part of a welcome retreat from the supernatural world and towards control of the environment through improvements in agriculture and technology and education. Until the eighteenth century, life was probably seen essentially in terms of the passage of the soul through a bleak and brutal and transitory existence. Men and women made certain basic assumptions about the placing of the boundaries between the physical and the spiritual world on the whole quite alien to modern readers. It had been assumed, for example, that the material environment responded to man's moral behaviour and that unusual happenings (eclipses, earthquakes, lightning) in the natural world were portents of judgements to come. But during the eighteenth century life became easier and quieter, and men and women developed a healthier preoccupation with problems and conditions with which we are more familiar today: improvements, bad debts, wages, parliamentary elections, taxes, fraud, bankruptcies and unemployment.

Of course there were still local events and national occasions which engendered excitement and even violence. The reactions to the 1715 rebellion are fascinating, for not only was the south-west in general notably anti-Jacobite, but Dumfries burgh, in particular, responded by refortifying its mediaeval ditches and defences and by arming its citizenry with the contemporary equivalent of 'Dad's Army' weaponry. The 1745, in spite of an unwelcome visit by BPC's army, passed by very quietly, perhaps an indication of the new good sense of the people in general.

The 1723/1724 Levellers' Rising, Galloway's very own and not very successful proletarian revolution, was essentially a violent and ultimately unavailing peasant reaction centred on the Dee Valley parishes against changes in land tenancies and enclosures. Throwing down dykes and killing cattle and meeting in unlawful assemblies was about the extent of it, although it may also have been mixed up with echoes of the traditional Covenanting antipathy to established authority.

And smuggling in the eighteenth and early nineteenth centuries, indulged in all along the coastline, but especially in Colvend and Southwick parish, in the Port William to Whithorn area, and in the southern Rhins, has left a wonderful collection of tales, half-legend and half-fact, of deeds of daring if not of nobility in importing wines and luxury goods from the duty-free Isle of Man for local use or in transit to Edinburgh and Ayr. Widely accepted in Galloway society as acceptable and even admirable in their behaviour, the farmers and seamen and landowners and ministers who allowed their sturdy greed to overcome their better scruples demonstrated that splendid commitment to the free enterprise economy and the suspicion and resentment of central government interference which has remained a characteristic of the area and its people.

Welsh and Gaelic had probably survived at least to the end of the sixteenth century in Kells and the Forest of Buchan and in the Rhins of Wigtownshire, but long before the seventeenth century the language of Galloway was Scots, that is northern English, no doubt becoming standardised through the pervasive influence of the King James translation of the Bible into English. Far less is known about the rich Galloway dialects than about the Buchan of the north-east of Scotland. Fortunately there is John Mactaggart's marvellously mischievous yet serious study of the words and phrases and games and gossip of his native parish of Borgue with the title *The Scottish Gallovidian Encyclopaedia* (1824). Visitors to Galloway should try to make a point of taking home with them some of his words—belly-timmer, bochles, cutty-glies, flaipers, gill-pies, spankers, troggers, and hundreds more. Recent research by Professor Riach of St. John's University of Newfoundland has also shown the importance of the Irish influence on local words and has brought together some fascinating examples of how different means are used from Stranraer to Dumfries to describe something; for example a slatternly woman is a clart, slitter, scutt, huggery or tudderie. So noo ye ken!

By the end of the seventeenth century it is possible to read the names of quite ordinary people in the 1684 parish lists of lairds, farm tenants, cottars, servants and others—for example Jon., Pa., Margrat and Ardrew McLellan, Anthon Steuart, Barbarie Kinnell, Margrat Clellan, Margrat McCeldrah, William Culloch, Janet Clellan, Margrat Coning, Gilbert Gordon, and Janet Maxwell at Cairletone in Glasserton parish, with their cottars Hendrie Malhensh, Euphanie Jardine, Jon. Gilkesone, Christian Coning and Janet Maxuell. And throughout the eighteenth century the birth and marriage lists kept in parish church records variously become available, and from 1841 the census enumeration books which give person by person details of the inhabitants of farms and clachans and villages and closes in the towns.

From the 1790s to the 1840s a new element was added with the settlement of large numbers of Protestant and Catholic Irish from the nine counties of Ulster, often moving from desperate poverty to conditions that were not much better in the 'Little Irelands' of Newton Stewart, Whithorn and Stranraer or in the poorest and most makeshift rural housing. Immigration and natural population growth more than balanced emigration to North America, Australia and New Zealand, and most rural parishes reached their population maximum in 1841 or 1851, with, for example in 1851, 855 people in Carsphairn parish, 2681 in Kirkmaiden parish and 2946 in Mochrum parish. All the same, the pattern of abandoning marginal hill and moor ground and of rural depopulation in general was already well under way before the first Ordnance Survey maps were prepared in the late 1840s. These included many examples of deserted farms and ancillary structures, for example on General Sir William Stewart's deer park on Cumloden estate near Newton Stewart.

One almost forgotten element was the traveller-gypsy population wandering in bands and extended family groups throughout eighteenth and nineteenth-century Galloway, dealing in horses, making household utensils of wood and tin and copper, selling horn spoons, smoothing irons and kettles, and regarded with a good deal of disfavour and no doubt partly justified suspicion of nefarious activities by 'respectable' locals. The most famous Galloway gypsy 'king' was Billy Marshall (c.1671-1792), perhaps a composite figure made up from two or three historical Marshall 'princes'. If there was only the one Billy Marshall, then he had a truly remarkable life, surviving adventures and polygamy (sixteen or seventeen wives) on a 'James Bond' scale. Andrew McCormick's *The Tinkler-Gypsies of Galloway* (1906) is still worth looking at, especially in the original edition which has excellent photographs of contemporary Marshalls, Campbells and Stewarts.

Many fine traditions and customs have disappeared and are now all but forgotten. The old way in western Galloway of bringing in the New Year with bonfires and processions and exotic ceremonies was one of the most interesting. It was one of the many casualties of the Great War years, when perhaps the loss of so many of the best of the young men knocked the heart and spirit out of whole communities and presented clerical moralists who disapproved of the old ways with their opportunity to prevent their revival. Parades with flute and drum bands were very popular in Creetown and Whithorn and in Newton Stewart, where the 'Belzies Band' of youths in a state of high excitement went from the 'Angle' to the Brewery and back to Creebridge and up into Minnigaff to visit the bonfire there. In Newton Stewart and Creetown the marchers carried flaming torches, and blazing tar barrels (latterly tar and paraffin) were carried mounted on long poles on their shoulders and on hand carts. In Minnigaff the centrepiece was a great bonfire on the Green, fuelled with wood from the Earl of Galloway's estate, but in the early nineteenth century made up by collecting the bones of dead animals over the previous twelve months and older animal bones dug up in the fields and stored during the year in a little hut on the Green. In Kirkcudbright and Whithorn a tradition of collective vandalism spreading mischief and disorder at the end of the old year was maintained by taking garden gates, fences and water barrels and strewing them around the streets to be retrieved by their owners the following day. Best of all was the tradition of dressing up—in Kirkcudbright as the 'Busked Boys', two boys starkly in white to one with a blackened face and dark clothes to represent not Ethiopian minstrels but real figures of darkness, who went round the houses collecting tributes of oaten cakes, supple scones and whangs of

Galloway tinkler-gypsies at the Doon near Kirkcudbright, c.1900. One of a series of 'ethnic' McConchie photographs. Note the small horse-drawn caravan and the formidable, heavily built gipsy woman looking directly at the camera. She is in a number of photographs and was clearly a professional, that is she was paid for her appearances.

indigestible skimmed-milk cheese; and in Newton Stewart as part of a wild masquerade of 'guys' and 'guisers' and 'belzies' with black faces, carrying huge sticks and in fantastic dresses.

The more visible aspects of life are more straightforward. For example much of the present Galloway landscape is still dominated by the work of the eighteenth and early nineteenth-century landowners who developed their estates with their new imposed patterns of fields geometrically divided and ditched and dyked. The increased income from rentals and direct farming went into more improvements (draining, liming, planting woodland), the development of new roads and better port and harbour facilities, small-scale industrial development (tanneries, breweries, grain and woollen and cotton mills), and planned villages and towns. The gracious country houses, some even today sufficiently compact to be occupied as estate headquarters and working farmhouses, were the most important expression of the prosperity, optimism and security of the new order. The best were laid out with avenues, bridges, gardens, orchards, orangeries, deer parks, heronries, icehouses, artificial lakes and fishponds and waterworks, bagnios, arbours, wildernesses and follies. A few (Craichlaw, Cassencarrie) incorporated older towers, but most were built on new sites. Some (Physgill, Logan) have had their Victorian and Edwardian excrescences removed and have recovered something of their original modest elegance; others (Ravenstone, Barnbarroch, Castlewigg) are lost houses. Few, except those now serving as hotels, are open to the public. It would be perverse in these days of international gangs of housethieves to mention which have Ramsays and Raeburns and Angelica Kaufmanns! Houses of particular interest and merit include Greenlaw (754644), Barwhinnock (656549), Cally (600549), Ardwall (581547), Kirkdale (514533), Kirroughtree (422660), Galloway House (478452), Physgill (428367), Logan (096428), and Lochryan (064687).

Parallel or slightly later improvements include the solid farmhouses, stables and barns still to be seen in many parts of Galloway. The twentieth-century coo palaces and silo towers rising up to the sky like great twelfth-century keeps are a reflection of the new but perhaps in the long term slightly precarious affluence of the local farming community.

The planned villages and towns are an outstanding part of the appeal of the south-west, with the contrast between the Georgian elegance on a small scale of the High Street in Kirkcudbright and the manses of the established church clergy as against the rich, and often deliciously vulgar, variety of pink, purple, yellow, brown, blue, cream, and white painted stone walls and door and window surrounds and grey/blue slate roofed houses (thank goodness not the polite black and white monotony in *such* good taste of so many East Coast conservation villages!). Note in particular Kirkpatrick-Durham founded before 1783 by the Rev. Dr. David Lamont, Gatehouse-of-Fleet after 1770 by James Murray of Broughton, Garlieston about 1760 by Lord Garlies, later the 7th Earl of Galloway, Castle-Douglas in 1791 by William Douglas, Port William about 1775 by Sir William Maxwell of Monrieth, and Port Logan in 1818 by Colonel Andrew McDowall. The little nineteenth-century estate villages at Beeswing, Parton and Castle Kennedy and the modern Forestry village at Glentrool make an interesting contrast.

The old tradition of thatched cottages, tollhouses and outhouses shown in photographs from the 1900s and 1910s has unfortunately gone, as has the occupational category of 'thatcher' included in the mid-nineteenth-century census enumeration books. One suggestion for future developments in Galloway which would be very worthwhile both in educational terms and as a tourist attraction is the idea of a 'folk museum' where over the years reconstructions could be attempted of Neolithic ritual sites, Iron Age huts,

A unique picture of a small thatched cottage near the Fell Quarries, Creetown, taken by Hunter of Newton Stewart, c.1900. The roof is in good condition, so probably the house was still lived in when photographed. The 'Sunday best' clothes are fascinating. Note the family Bible held by the old lady.

mediaeval kilns or motte castles, corn kilns, dovecots, thatched houses, perhaps even a grain mill; and incorporating a visitor centre selling local crafts and Galloway books such as Sir Walter Scott's *Guy Mannering* (1815) and *Old Mortality* (1816), S.R. Crockett's *The Raiders* (1893), C.H. Dick's *Highways and Byways in Galloway and Carrick* (1916), and reprints of some scarcer and more obscure works.

CHAPTER 8

Dumfries and Oot—East

Many visitors and most Gallovidians will have an opportunity of passing some time in Dumfries, the 'Queen of the South'. For as far west as Gatehouse-of-Fleet and east to Ruthwell, Dumfries is the regional centre for major shopping expeditions and business purposes. Creetown, Newton Stewart and the Machars and Dalry and the Glenkens look about 50% to Dumfries and 50% to Ayr, and Stranraer and the Rhins almost entirely to Ayr and Glasgow rather than Dumfries and Edinburgh.

Dumfries used to be essentially a quiet and indeed rather serene country market town, distinctively Lowland and Scottish. Well, its football team is still languishing, like Stranraer, in Division II of the Scottish League, but today's Dumfries is much more urban, busier, noisier, all no doubt in a sense a positive achievement, but in some danger, if any more buildings are knocked down and new roads cut, of losing a good deal of its most appealing qualities. It is certainly even more difficult now to envisage mediaeval Dumfries as a defensible town on the hilly ridge roughly above the line of the present Irish Street from Townhead motte towards St. Michael's Church. This was a strong site, with the Nith and its several fording places below on the west, the Millburn to the south, and bogs and morasses close to the town ditches and stockades on the east and the barrier of the Lochar Moss further out, and only vulnerable to attack from the north. Some of the cluster of mottes—Townhead, Lincluden, Castledykes, Troqueer and Kirkland—in and around Dumfries belong to the 1130s or 1150s, and it may well be that there was an established settlement by the 1160s. However, the developments of the 1170s and 1180s, the church of St. Michael, the chapel dedicated to St. Thomas of Canterbury, and the new castle of 1185 at Castledykes, culminated in the creation of the burgh by William the Lion about or by 1186. Appropriately, Dumfries is celebrating its octocentenary in 1986.

It has a rich history of success in trade, commerce, shipping and shipbuilding, and of vigorous defence in wars and engagements against the English as late as 1570, and in civil wars and disturbances during the seventeenth century, and notably in 1715 when the townsfolk were digging ditches, erecting palisades and fortifying the gates against the Jacobite rebels. The last traces of these earthwork defences were removed in 1837, by which time Dumfries had been for many years a centre of culture, civilisation and entertainment, of theatres, libraries, schools and academies for the surrounding countryside.

The obvious starting place for a Dumfries perambulation (leave your car behind) is at the bus terminal precinct on the Whitesands, once the venue of great cattle and horse markets. The bustling Friars Vennel, going up the hill from the ford now obscured by the caul, takes you to the Burns Statue and the site of the Franciscan thirteenth-century house. 'Ye Olde Friars Vault' at the corner of Brewery Street is a potential hazard as a stopping point before you have started! The red sandstone frontage along the east bank of the Nith, 'the Dock', from the caul to Dockfoot Park, was used in the days of sailing vessels by the smaller boats working in the coastal trade. There are amazing scenes every few years when high spring tides coincide with the river in flood and the Nith goes over its banks and into the shops along the Whitesands and at the foot of the Vennel. Devorgilla's Bridge is actually a stone bridge of about 1450 on the site of a 1260/1280 wooden bridge. At the west end visit the old *Bridge House* built in 1662 for James Birkmyre, a barrelmaker in Dumfries, now a Museum annexe dealing with the life of the town. Note the corner boulders for some protection against heavy wagon wheels. The *Town Mills* (1781), three storey and attics, and crowstepped gables, will in the years ahead become a major tourist attraction as a Burns Interpretation Centre.

Climb up Church Street hill to the *Burgh Museum*, a friendly treasure house of local history and archaeology with a vast range of material from cinerary urns to Celtic heads and Roman altar stones and early bicycles. The spectacular windmill tower (1797) is an observatory with a wonderful camera obscura which must have seemed almost like magic in 1836 with the image reflected on to a table of the town laid out below, a sort of early 'Candid Camera'. Don't miss the 'Old Mortality' group outside commemorating Robert Paterson, the Balmaclellan stonemason and businessman, who also prepared and cut the propaganda tombstones of the Covenanting 'martyrs'. Paterson, who died in 1801, was a model for 'Old Mortality' by Sir Walter Scott, who used the information and stories sent to him by Joseph Train, the Excise officer in Newton Stewart. The group here, and the statue at Balmaclellan, were by John Corrie of Lochrutton in 1840.

Go down the Pilgrim Way or the Suspension Brae to the Suspension Bridge (1875) and turn right along the river front and left up the hill to St. Michael's Church and Churchyard. The church (1746) is exceedingly pleasant externally and has worthwhile interior details; the yard contains a

'Old Mortality' or Robert Paterson and his exhausted pony. The delightful group by John Corrie in 1840 outside Dumfries Museum.

fascinating collection of memorial stones, for example for Margaret Walls and James Ewart of Mulloch (1739) against the south wall of the church, and the monument on the cholera burial mound for victims of the epidemic of September to November 1832 in which 421 died in Dumfries (and another 127 in Maxwelltown). Note the extraordinary Burns Mausoleum (1815) by Turnerelli for Robert Burns (1759-1796). It is a wholly delightful shining temple in white marble, sweet and gay, but whether in spirit or in essence, in the detailed representation of the poet, it really does justice to the robustness and vitality and social and political relevance of his life and work is another matter.

Cross the road to the north to Burns Street for *Burns House.* Burns held the tenancy of Ellisland farm from June 1788 to November 1791, but obtained a position as Excise officer in the Dumfries Third or Tobacco Division in September 1789 and was promoted to the Dumfries Port Division in February 1792. He lived in Dumfries first from 1791 in a flat in a tenement in the Stinkin Vennel, now Bank Street, and then in this quite impressively genteel house in what was the Mill Vennel from 1793 until his death in 1796. The Burns House museum is lively, scholarly, and most enjoyable even for those from the north of Scotland or England who would be as likely to enter a haggis-throwing competition as to attend a Burns Supper. Continue past Pickfords Stores and the car park, and turn left into Nith Place. The splendid Royal British Legion building was erected in 1753 by the Town Clerk, Mr Malcolm.

Turn right into Irish Street, still a good mixture of large houses and hotels with some elegant and even amusing touches and painted doorways and window surrounds. Cross over Bank Street and continue to Friars Vennel, and then turn right up to the High Street and along to the right passing Woolworths. The Hole i' the Wa' Inn opposite has some Burns interest. The early eighteenth-century Midsteeple in the centre of the High Street which replaced an earlier tolbooth was used as a courthouse and prison until 1867. The Trades House (1804) opposite is impressive. Continue on High Street beyond English Street to the *Globe Inn,* the favourite Burns howff, past Gashouse Close and nearly opposite Assembly Street—the narrow passage is quite atmospheric and a staggering contrast to the all-too-twentieth century main thoroughfare.

Work down English Street (some good closes to explore) and down Queen Street to the unique Theatre Royal (1792), still in use as a theatre. Return to English Street, turn left into Loreburn Street passing K.S. Dobie and Son Grain Merchants, left into Great King Street passing the Post Office and right along Queensberry Street, now one of the better places for browsing and even buying.

(Turning right into Academy Street takes you to Catherine Street for the Regional Library on the site of one of the original bogs or swamps; to Lovers Walk for the lively Radio Solway which has early morning and lunchtime slots on local news, places and people and some longer programmes such as the excellent 'Auchencairn Connection'; and along Lovers Walk for British Rail Dumfries, a rather splendid Victorian (1860) station with the stationmaster's house above the booking hall, and the admirably sumptuous Station Hotel; and along the Edinburgh Road, a continuation of Academy Street, for the Gracefield Arts Centre, an art gallery with some superb local paintings and occasional exhibitions.)

On Academy Street the present Academy building dates only from 1897; the Moat Brae annexe above the Stake Ford may have been the site of the Townhead motte. Church Crescent towards the town centre has the old 'Trustee Savings Bank' on the west side with the first-floor recess statue of the Rev. Henry Duncan of Ruthwell. Turn left into Irving Street with the pleasantly composed Congregational Church on the left, left into George Street with the Moat Brae Nursing Home on the right and St. George's Church of Scotland with its red sandstone pillars on the left. Castle Street, north-west and south-east off George Street, laid out after 1793, is one of the best parts of the growing town, with excellent doorways and windows with first-floor balconies. The houses are now nearly all legal offices, medical or dental surgeries, or insurance company premises. Turn right from Castle

Street into Buccleuch Street, a right old mixture of architectural styles. The former Methodist Church with its four columns has balance and poise, but the three-storey Clydesdale Bank (1892) by James Thomson is an incredible fun piece. The south side of the street is rather too heavily Victorian Baronial; the north side is much more pleasing, if somewhat mixed. Hence back to Whitesands.

The country and coast to the south-east of Dumfries should not be missed. Bus services from Whitesands take you to Glencaple and to Collin and Annan on the A75; by car take the B725 from St. Michael's Church. *Never*, incidentally, attempt walking to the A75 unless there is a proper footpath—the heavy lorries going at speed are literally killers anywhere from Stranraer to Annan. The park at Castledykes has the 'old castle', a small motte at the river bank (976747) and the 'new castle' of 1185, which was developed as a stone castle in the late thirteenth century (977747), and the site of the Chapel of Our Lady. Don't be misled, however, as it is almost impossible to distinguish between the remains of mediaeval earthworks and nineteenth-century landscaping. The Crichton Royal Hospital, a campus-like conglomerate of buildings including a massive church, was begun in 1835 as a mental hospital. The original intention had been to establish a new university, but this plan, like earlier ventures in the 1690s and the 1720s, failed.

Follow the roads Burns must have known intimately to the ports and harbours on the Nith. Walk down to Kingholm Quay (974736), which with Laghall Quay opposite downriver (973732) was developed in the early nineteenth century and took medium-sized sailing vessels. Nothing remains of the main shipbuilding area and quay at Kelton (990784), which with Glencaple (994687) was used by larger ships trading to North America, the West Indies and the Baltic.

Park at Glencaple and walk along the B725, passing the site of St. Columba's Well and Chapel (998675), skirting or exploring the saltmarsh and foreshore of Caerlaverock Nature Reserve which extends from the Nith to the Lochar Water. *Caerlaverock Castle* (NY 025656) is one of the great castles of Scotland and with its rose-red stonework and water-encompassed setting a dramatic and romantic composition. This area was of great strategic importance over the centuries, as the presence of a Selgovae hill fort and a Roman fort on Ward Law above suggests. The large trapezoidal basin just south of Caerlaverock Castle with banks on the east, north and west and open to the sea towards the firth may have been the dock of a Roman port. There are actually two castles, the great castle proper built before the mid-1270s and, two hundred yards south-east, the earlier 'castle in the march', which was also a stone castle, rectangular, with a moat, but probably built on a substructure of piles.

The unusual triangle of Caerlaverock, so aptly described by Walter of Exeter in his account of the siege by Edward I in 1300 as 'shaped like a shield' and with three sides round it and a tower at each corner, one a double one, is determined by the rock platform levelled off with clay on which it sits. The concentric double moats, up to forty feet wide and with water up to four feet deep, with banks heightened in the sixteenth century for protection against artillery, may have been filled with sea water from the thirteenth to the seventeenth centuries. The present woodland screen area between the castle and the firth is largely a nineteenth-century change in the balance between land and sea. Previously the castle was on the edge of waterlogged marshes and quicksands and could be approached only from the north.

Much of the western gatehouse tower, the lower sections of the curtain wall and perhaps some of Murdoch's tower at the south-west belong to the thirteenth century. But the architectural history of the castle is immensely complex, with five major sieges, the last in 1640, and rebuilding in 1335, 1357, at the end of the fourteenth century, and in 1593. Its first builders and occupants are unknown, but it was held mostly by the Maxwells, the Wardens of the West March after the Douglases, from the early fourteenth century. The remains of four timber drawbridges have been found, and these were in use from about 1277 to the demolition of the defences of the castle in 1640. Don't miss the exquisite Renaissance range of 1634, a lovely rare humanist object in an era of stark religious fanaticism. The delicately carved scenes are from Greek and Roman mythology.

For the contrast visit *Lochmaben Castle* (NY 088811) on the promontory at the south end of the Castle Loch, first a timber 'pele' possibly planned by Master James of St. George for Edward I in 1299, and then the huge stone castle of 1363 to 1376. The scale is still suggested by the massive inner curtain wall and the water-filled ditches and defences. The earlier Bruce castle was the very large motte on the town golf course (NY 081822).

If at all possible get to Ruthwell Church (NY100682). Careful map reading and landscape interpretation is required on these roads. Collect the key at the cottage on the B724. Inside you see the *Ruthwell Cross,* and it is a truly mind-bending experience to encounter this eighteen-feet-high preaching cross in the annexe to the parish church specially built to exhibit it in 1887. It is one of the most important monuments of mid-eighth-century Western Europe. Typically, the General Assembly of the Church of Scotland ordered that it be cast down and destroyed in 1643.

Caerlaverock Castle. A classic R. W. Billings print from *The Baronial and Ecclesiastical Antiquities of Scotland* (1845-1852) showing the great gatehouse and the south-west corner tower behind.

Fortunately the enlightened parish minister, Dr Duncan, had it restored in 1823 from pieces collected in the churchyard. The figure sculpture is masterly, the best in the West for this period, from the aggressive young heroic Christ (with moustache in the Germanic tradition) on the Cross to Mary Magdalene washing His feet, the Annunciation, the Flight from Egypt, and St. Paul and St. Anthony; the vine scroll with birds and beasts is superb; and the margins have inscriptions in Latin from the Vulgate and runes with text from *The Dream of the Rood*. The work is Anglian, but, like the Bewcastle Cross in Cumbria, may owe much to surviving skills and traditions from the Romano-British civilisation of the kingdom of Rheged.

Ruthwell village to the south has the cottage museum where the Rev. Dr. Henry Duncan founded the first 'savings bank' or penny bank scheme in 1810, self-help and practical Christian endeavour at their best.

CHAPTER 9

Terregles, Kirkpatrick-Irongray, Lochrutton and Up North

The hinterland west and north of Dumfries is full of interest. Start by taking the A709 passing Torthorwald Castle—splendid views back to the south and west, and a unique example of a restored cruck-framed and gabled cottage (NY 033785). Walkers can take the Lockerbie bus service from Whitesands, but should not walk on the main road where all too many car drivers give the impression of being determined to get to Lochmaben Hospital by one means or another. Take the minor road north of the village passing Tinwald Shaws to Tinwald, where again there are good vistas from the site of the motte east of the church (NY 003815). The wartime Tinwald Downs Aerodrome (now Dumfries Trading Estate) to the south of Tinwald and east of Heathhall was a base for hundreds of planes. The Dumfries and Galloway Aviation Museum at the old control tower, open on Sundays in summer, includes a Spitfire from the 312 Czech Squadron which crashed at Loch Doon in 1941.

The minor roads through Kirkton take you past the site of Carzield Roman fort (969817). Continue by the minor road by West Gallaberry (963826), which has a unique nineteenth-century horse mill still with machinery, a large rack and pinion wheel and shafts and yokes for three horses, in working order. Continue north-west to Dalswinton. The Roman forts (932842) are near the Dumfries-Glasgow railway line. Dalswinton Lake (943844) was the site of one of the first experiments in steam navigation when Patrick Miller and William Symington tried out a boat with a steam engine in 1788. On board were Henry Brougham, the painter Alexander Nasmyth, and Robert Burns.

After Auldgirth (912866) turn south onto the A76 passing Friars Carse and *Ellisland* (930838), where Burns tilled the fields and planned improvements during his brief and unsuccessful tenancy between 1788 and 1791. It was here that in 1789 he wrote 'Tam o' Shanter' as a witch-story for inclusion in Francis Grose's *Antiquities of Scotland* (1791). At 930831 take the road on the east running closer to the Nith and passing Cowhill and Killylung. Turn west beside the old Moniaive railway line to pass the site of the Premonstratensian Holywood Abbey (956796), where mediaeval pottery and tile fragments turn up in field ploughing. Continue over the crossroads and onto the B729 for East Cluden Mill (943794), a superb late eighteenth and nineteenth-century grain mill with two water-wheels powering five pairs of stones; and for the Twelve Apostles (947794), a circle of eleven big stones, of which five are now upright, in the fields between Kilness farm and New Bridge.

From New Bridge take the A76 towards Dumfries. In the Lochside estate follow the DOE signs for *Lincluden College* (967779) on the banks of the Cluden Water just above the junction with the Nith. In spite of the modern surroundings, there is still a feeling of peace and sanctuary such as pilgrims en route to Whithorn or political refugees (including Queen Margaret of Anjou, the wife of Henry IV of England in 1460) may have known. The motte, oval with a small top area, could only have been in use as a castle for some thirty years, as it cannot have been occupied after the foundation of the Benedictine nunnery for twenty-five sisters about 1164. In about 1400 the nuns were expelled for 'insolence' and 'irregularities' (sounds like a good scandal), and Archibald the Grim, the third Earl of Douglas, established a collegiate foundation for a provost and twelve secular canons, to which a hospital or residence for twenty-four bedesmen was subsequently added.

The layout of the College buildings round a central cloister (there was also a western range providing additional accommodation) probably follows that of the nunnery. The fifteenth-century church is a quite delightful example of rich decorated architecture with a profusion of heraldic material on chancel windows and corbels. Note in the quire the piscina and triple sedilia, the over-elaborate tomb of Margaret, the daughter of Richard III and wife of the fourth Earl of Douglas, with rich heraldic work, and the pulpitum or rood screen at the west end with fine but worn carving including scenes from the life of Christ. The range of domestic buildings to the north provided lodgings and rooms for the provost and canons. The sixteenth-century floral and herb 'knot garden' laid out east of the College is remarkable. Are the terraces on this motte at least partly an extension of delights and walks above the main garden?

For a real country drive take the Terregles road in Maxwelltown just west of the junction of the A76 and the A75. The old (mediaeval?) village of Terregles (942767), street paving of which was still visible in 1844, was north-west of Terreglestown farm. The site of Terregles Brick and Tile Works and kiln was to the west at 936767. 'Friars Island' to the south at 943761 on the Cargen Water sounds interesting. For Terregles Church and Queir (930770) take the road south towards Kirkland. Terregles church, built in 1814 on a much older site, contains sections of woodwork from the choir stalls at Lincluden and, in stark Victorian contrast, the 'Angel of the

Resurrection' by Birnie Philip. The late sixteenth-century post-Reformation Queir, west of the nave, was built as a Maxwell mortuary chapel, perhaps to contain the monument to Edward Maxwell with a figure in a doublet, and with a plumed hat and a sword, dated 1568. The Queir was restored in 1875. The churchyard has good examples of eighteenth-century calligraphy. Continue on the road south from the church taking the road west by Collochan, and west to the road junction north of Beltonhill, and then north passing Seeside with the Iron Age hill fort on Beacon Hill above to join the Dumfries-Terregles road east of the Grove Hospital. The circuit is also an excellent walk with vistas and woods in either direction.

To explore the picturesque scenery of Kirkpatrick-Irongray continue north passing Ingleston to the west and Gateside to the east and on to the road west of Irongray Bridge. Hallhill and Ingleston 'motes' are hill forts rather than mediaeval castle sites. Irongray Church (915796) close to the Cluden Water was built in 1803 and extended in 1872 when two Norman-style doors were added. Note the churchyard stones for Bessie Edgar, 1707, and James Anderson, 1733, with figure sculpture; and the gravestone of Helen Walker who was the prototype for Scott's Jeanie Deans in *The Heart of Midlothian*. Conventicle enthusiasts will want to visit the Martyrs' Monument at Hallhill and the stone 'tables and seats' on Skeoch Hill (859790) which may have been used as 'Communion Tables'. The old track west of the manse running to the south of Hall Hill takes you by Horsebog Loch (898791), a swampy site suggesting Celtic Iron Age possibilities.

Take the road south from Routin Bridge towards Shawhead. The area near Barnsoul is fascinating, with an Iron Age palisaded enclosure, McNaughton's Fort (873778), the horseshoe-shaped Angel Chapel ritual site (874776) and the Angel Well (873777). Just before the complex crossroads in Shawhead village take the road north-west to Glenkiln Reservoir (842778) for one of the most extraordinary groups of modern sculpture in the United Kingdom. Although a private collection, the works by Epstein, Renoir, Rodin and Moore are a public spectacle laid out along the hill and water sides. The Rodin *John the Baptist* is magnificent, and amongst the examples of Henry Moore's strange concepts the *Metal Standing Figure* (1950) and the *King and Queen* (1952/1953) are outstanding. Although many viewers will still be unsympathetic to modern sculpture, the *King and Queen* does have something of the hieratic dignity and enigmatic quality of Romanesque carving. The open-air setting is far more friendly to them than most gallery interiors could be. For an excellent

E

motor run, more sculpture and superb views, continue north by Marglolly Bridge and Sheddochhill, the Cairn Water and Gordieston, and then either to Dunscore and the B729 to Dumfries or west along the Glenesslin Burn and south-west by Glaisters to Corsock and Castle-Douglas. Walkers can best reach this area by taking the Moniaive bus service and coming in from the north. An alternative car route is to go south-west from Glenkiln by Glen and Craigelwhan (another Martyrs' tomb and monument) to Brooklands and the A712 to Crocketford. The side roads between Crocketford and Shawhead and Lochfoot are charming, criss-crossing old tracks, drove roads and footpaths, and passing some old farmhouses and farm sites. Hillhead (853743), for example, dates back to 1611 at least.

For Lochrutton, whether coming from Dumfries or Castle-Douglas, take the A75 to Crocketford, the side road south to Auchengibbert, then south-east to Milton, and then east by Courthill, Barnbauchle Hill, Lochfoot and Easthill to Drumsleet on the A711. This section of the 'Old Military Road' of 1763-1764 from Carlisle to Portpatrick in Lochrutton parish is good walking or motoring with excellent and varying vistas, especially going from west to east. The crannog in Lochrutton Loch (898729) and the promontory on the eastern shore (900731) seem to have been used as the equivalent of a motte and bailey. Masses of twelfth to fifteenth-century pottery were found here in excavations in 1901-1902. Walk through Lochfoot to see the contrast between the 'old' and the 'new' village.

Hillis Tower (912726) can be viewed from the farm track off the Shealinghill to Lochanhead road. The Maxwells' sixteenth-century tower is on the site of a moated manor complex. Note the attached house of 1721, the high enclosing wall, and the important rare surviving example of a small gatehouse with a little upper chamber on the western side of the courtyard. Lochrutton Church (912735) is a classic simple hall church of 1819 with an impressive monument to the parish ministers, the Rev. George Duncan, father and son, on either side of the east door. The hillside location is unusual and attractive, and the churchyard has some good stones with figure sculpture—well worth walking up to. The Glen mill area (926755) on the Cargen Water north of and below the A75 is an example of a mid-nineteenth-century complex of corn and lint and carding mills with a smithy and an early bridge.

Visitors from the south staying in the Stewartry or even in Newton Stewart would enjoy taking a whole day driving from Dumfries or by New Galloway and Moniaive to explore the country north of Thornhill. Go first to *Morton Castle* (891992), the late fourteenth-century hall house (now DOE), on a superb site north-east of Carronbridge; and then to Durisdeer

Leadhills Railway Station on the Leadhills and Wanlockhead Light Railway c.1910. Specially for railway 'buffs'. Excellent detail of the station building and staff and the two coaches.

Church (NS894037) to examine the exuberant or florid, depending on taste, marble tomb with cherubs, garlands and lifesize effigies by John Van Nost for the second Duke of Queensberry (d. 1711) and his Duchess (d. 1709). Romanists could opt to tackle the Antonine fortlet (NS 903049) guarding the pass north of Durisdeer. Country house and castle enthusiasts should not miss the magnificent home of the first Duke of Queensberry (1679-1691), *Drumlanrig Castle*, on the site of an earlier Douglas stronghold. Children will enjoy the gardens and parkland; and the galleries of paintings by Jamesone, Rembrandt, Holbein, Paul Sandby, Ramsay, Reynolds, Gainsborough, van Dyck, Rowlandson and many others are magnificent. Further north still the old lead and silver mining villages of Wanlockhead and Leadhills have a great deal to offer. Note at the former the Lead Mining Museum, the Miners' Library (1756), a beam engine, a smelt mill, a waterwheel pit, and the Loch Nell mine with a level now open for three hundred yards, and an SYHA youth hostel; at Leadhills the Leadhills Miners' Reading Society Library (1741); and at both villages miners' cottages, old tramways and lade systems. The Leadhills and Wanlockhead Light Railway (1901-1938), a Caledonian and L.M.S. branch line, ran from Elvanfoot to Leadhills. Today the Lowthers Railway Society is planning and working on the construction of a narrow-gauge railway line with three stations on the mile-and-a-quarter stretch between Leadhills and Wanlockhead using the old track bed and with at first diesel and then later steam traction. The project should be a great success, as the close proximity of the line to the main road from England to Scotland should guarantee enthusiastic support from the public.

CHAPTER 10

Troqueer, New Abbey and Kirkbean

The parishes of Troqueer, New Abbey and Kirkbean follow the line of the Nith and the Solway south of Dumfries, so there are landscapes of merse, salt flats, old quays and harbours to explore and enjoy; but they also have a quickly rising hinterland of wooded hills, lochs and romantic ruins which combine to make a most pleasing mixture of the sublime and the picturesque.

The little village of 'Brig-en' at the western end of Devorgilla's Bridge became in 1810 the burgh or barony of Maxwelltown, which was amalgamated with Dumfries in 1929. Landscaping and the progressive extension of the urban sprawl has long since obscured the original scale and strength of Troqueer motte (974748) on the bank of the Nith. The nearby churchyard (974750) includes a good monument to William McDowall (1818-1888), the local historian and newspaper editor.

Take the A710 out of Dumfries towards New Abbey. The first landing point on the west side of the Nith was at Laghall quay (973732) opposite Kingholm. After crossing the Cargen Pow at Islesteps (965728) note the ruinous tower of Cargen House, built in the 1870s by the distinguished mineralogist Patrick Dudgeon, and now looking like a 'genuine' romantic ruin. Take the first road to the right towards Barbush and Carruchan for a pleasant stroll down a footpath to St. Queran's Well (956721) near to the Crooks Pow. 'The idolatrous well at Cargen' was a famous holy and healing well, with a reputation for curing women's and children's diseases. It is not in any sense a spectacular site, but the concept of popular medicine involved here is fascinating and for centuries it was, of course, far safer than resorting to physicians and probably as useful as paying the local 'wise women' who provided herbal medicine and the sort of advice now associated with psychiatrists, marriage guidance councillors and fortune tellers. The Picts Knowe (954721) might be a henge or an Iron Age ritual site or settlement or fort, but the location so close to the holy well might make the first and second suggestions more probable than the others.

Continue north on the same road to the A711 and turn left passing Dalskairth on the east and Goldilea on the west with the viaduct of the 1859 Dumfries to Castle-Douglas railway behind. The more daring might climb up to the railway line from the main road further ahead and, no doubt breaking various British Railways bye-laws, walk along the old track across the viaduct, which provides magnificent views over Goldilea. The wooded hill to the north-west has two Iron Age forts at the north and south ends of the hill ridge at 928740 and 930738, and there is another large hill fort at Castle Hill (928749) north of the Old Military Road and above the A75. From the A711 take the minor road from Drumgans of Golilea back to the A710. There are woodland walk and picnic areas in the Mabie Forest. Mabie House is one of a number of interesting eighteenth and nineteenth-century houses now open as an hotel. Note the interesting placenames, Marthrown of Woodhead, Butterhole and Papista Bridge on the old track over the burn at the south-east end of Lochaber Loch, and the panorama looking north from Whinnyhill on the A710. Walkers and motorists will enjoy taking the minor road before Greymorin west by Mid Auchenfad and Trostan to Glensone, passing a late eighteenth-century deserted farm complex with grain-drying or corn kilns at Little Auchenfad (952686) and the cairnfield on Trostan Hill. From Glensone turn west towards the little nineteenth-century estate village of Beeswing. Loch Arthur has a crannog (903690) near the north shore which was the site of a mediaeval, perhaps thirteenth to seventeenth-century, hall house resting on a platform of timber beams and connected to the mainland by an underwater stone causeway. Lotus House has recently been taken over by the Camphill Village Trust as a Christian 'Village Community' for mentally handicapped adults and co-workers. Lotus Hill (what marvellous placenames in this area) has fragments of epidote, beryl, molybdenite and fluorspar. Return by the same delightful road to Glensone and hence to New Abbey.

You should not, however, miss the other approach to New Abbey taking the side road north of Constantinople at Gillfoot by Kirkconnel Flow Nature Reserve, the farm roadends to Gibbonhill and Maxwellbank, and the Maxwells' sixteenth-century L-plan tower with cape-house at Kirkconnel (979680) linked to the eighteenth-century mansion house. The eighteenth-century pier (986675) north-east of Park farm is now separated from the Nith by recent merseland. From Kirkconnel continue on the same road over the hill for the superb view of New Abbey. The ruins of the Abbots' Tower (972666), possibly built by one of the last abbots of Sweetheart, are on Landis farm.

New Abbey ('New' as opposed to Old Abbey or Dundrennan) is perhaps the most perfect unspoiled village in Galloway, with a real feeling of community, succinctly described in an article by L. J. A. Bell in *Scotland*, October 1950, and with a balance between preserving what is best and adapting to the opportunities of tourism and leisure education. This success, as in Gatehouse-of-Fleet, is the result of the work over the years of one or two exceptional personalities.

Motorists should leave their cars in the park beside *Sweetheart Abbey* (965662). Walk back through the village and make a point of crossing the 1715 bridge over the New Abbey Pow and continuing uphill on the main road through the splendidly tranquil avenue of Scots pines planted between 1775 and 1780 for the classic romantic view over to the rose red of Sweetheart. Return to the village centre and take the lane beside the Criffel Inn to follow the magnificent and unique wall of huge granite boulders along the north-west and north-east sides of the thirty-acre abbey precinct. The wall, as much as the abbey church of St. Mary, tells us a good deal about the energy and ambitions of the Cistercian monks and lay brothers who lived here.

Sweetheart was founded in 1273 in memory of her husband John by Devorgilla Balliol. She was buried in front of the high altar in 1289 with John's embalmed heart, which had been stored in an ivory casket, beside her. Whether this is evidence of extraordinary arrogance, or piety, or 'true love' is a matter of opinion.

The church, built by the Cistercians from Dundrennan who colonised Sweetheart and their successors, is full of contradictions. It is excellent evidence of the wealth accumulated from sheep-ranching and forestry and minerals, but is equally false to the original ideals of the Cistercian order of simplicity and austerity in buildings and decoration. In particular the ornate ninety-five feet high tower over the crossing with its battlemented parapet and grotesque corbels would have been seen as an affront and an abuse by the great St. Bernard of Clairvaux. The church is impressive in scale, but not on the whole in terms of refinement or excellence in details. Note the traceried windows, the fairly complete west front and the east gable of the choir. Little but the foundations remain of the buildings round the cloister. Dundrennan and Glenluce, although far less dramatic, are actually better examples of Cistercian architecture and monastic life.

Walk back through the village, noting the single-storey cottage on the north side with a painted stone Cistercian rosette and three figures in a boat, perhaps rowing pilgrims across the Nith; and the old smithy opposite the Criffel Inn with the trade guild plaque and the inscription 'By hammer hand all arts do stand R M 1775'. Note behind the 1887 Masonic Lodge building the restored two-storey and garret seventeenth-century house with forestairs and a datestone over the south window on the east wall showing it was built by John Stewart of Shambellie and his wife, R. Brown, a descendant of Gilbert Brown, the abbot of Sweetheart.

The mill pond and race lead to the overshot wheel of the nineteenth-century *Corn Mill,* all probably on the site of mediaeval structures operated by the Cistercians. The waterwheel and brick kiln and milling machinery, originally for grinding not only oatmeal but also cereals and beans for animal feed, are now again in working order. The mill and mill house were restored for Mr. C. W. Stewart of Shambellie, who handed them over to the nation in 1978. The mill is now an enjoyable and important educational exercise.

Nor is this all, for *Shambellie House* has been open in the summer since 1982 as a Museum of Costume under the Royal Scottish Museum. Don't be put off by the somewhat esoteric titles of the annual exhibitions, for example in 1983 'The Rise and Fall of the Sleeve: Fashion in Britain 1825-1840', as the evening dresses, costumes, cloaks, hats, shoes, children's clothes and jewellery, all collected by Mr Stewart, are delightful and wholly fascinating. Shambellie House itself is a good example of Scottish Victorian Baronial architecture on a small scale by David Bryce, built between 1856 and 1860. Indeed overall New Abbey is a major centre of national culture.

For another hill view of the village from the south-west climb up to the Waterloo Monument, a circular tower about fifty feet high and at the six hundred feet contour line. South-east of New Abbey the grassy ridge above Lochhill is the site of the long cairn with a stone facade (969651) excavated by Lionel Masters and which had evidence of an earlier timber mortuary structure and a timber facade of sixteen uprights of perhaps about 4000 B.C.

The badly battered motte at Ingleston (981651) was probably built by Richard, the son of Troite of Carlisle, about 1170. Nearby the Bogue Quay (977655) on the New Abbey Pow, still in use in the 1920s for moving timber, was probably used by the abbey for its coastal and export trade or for going back and forth along the Solway to Dundrennan.

Further south on the A710 you pass Loch Kindar, which has two islands. The larger half-acre Kirk Kindar island (970642) with an underwater stone causeway to the north-east shore may well have been a Celtic religious site. The ruins are of the mediaeval parish church of Lochinello, the older name for New Abbey parish. The smaller island to the west may have been a crannog.

Continue on the A710 into Kirkbean parish passing the old sawmill at Drumburn (980621) due for demolition in 1985 and at Brickhouse the site between the road and Carse Bay of a nineteenth-century brick and tile

A fine portrait of a Southerness fisherman, Ben Kerr, in a postcard reproduction of a photograph taken outside one of the single-storey cottages c.1910.

works (983602), which had its own little quay (984603), now long disappeared. Don't miss Kirkbean Church (979592), an utterly charming building of 1776, with a dome-shaped tower added in 1835, and a good churchyard with unusual eighteenth-century tablestone ends with somewhat odd-looking women in contemporary dress and with amazingly tiny waists.

From Kirkbean take the old road over to Carsethorn, a delightful and unspoiled place with the uprights still visible at low tide of the nineteenth-century wooden pier running out from the shore and used for passengers and freight in British waters or across the Atlantic. The beach was used for mooring ground at least as early as the seventeenth or possibly sixteenth century. 'Barracks' at the south end before 'Slate Row' and the

'Steam Boat Inn' are marked on the 1850 O.S. map. People locally still remember the days of the twice-weekly summer and once-weekly winter service by steam-packet to Liverpool and Whitehaven.

Remember the excellent potential of the shoreline from Carsethorn to Powillimount for a walking excursion, or take the side road from Kirkbean or Carsethorn to Arbigland, where the formal woodland and water gardens are sometimes open in the summer. Arbigland is famous for the work of its improver owner, William Craik, a leading figure in the 'Agricultural Revolution' in Scotland in the middle of the eighteenth century, and as the workplace of John Paul's father, who was employed here as an estate gardener. John Paul, later the pirate and rebel or American naval hero Paul Jones, was born, traditionally in 1747, at the cottage south-west of Arbigland referred to on O.S. maps as the 'Paul Jones Cottage' (987571). It is not, however, a museum, nor does it look like an eighteenth-century gardener's cottage.

From Arbigland take the road by Moor to East Preston, where the six-foot-high plain yellow freestone market cross of the extinct burgh founded by the Earl of Nithsdale in 1633 was re-erected in the eighteenth century. Whether Preston was also a mediaeval village is open to question. The existence of the cross itself is not sufficient evidence to be very certain of the earlier history of the area.

Southerness should be visited to see the early (1748) lighthouse erected by the merchants of Dumfries as a warning light for the treacherous Barnhourie Bank. Southerness was laid out as a planned village about 1790 by Richard Oswald and remained for many years a small and picturesque fishing community. Whether you prefer the present village is a matter of personal taste: those who wish to avoid crowds should visit it in the winter months, when the whole coastline is especially atmospheric. From Southerness return by the same road passing the golf course and the fragmentary remains of a sixteenth-century tower house at Wreaths (952565) and hence by the A710 to Mainsriddle.

CHAPTER 11

Colvend and Southwick, Urr, Dalbeattie, Buittle and Kirkgunzeon

Entering Southwick (Suthayk) and Colvend (Culwen) from the A710 above Preston Merse, you are quickly into the Victorian 'Scottish Riviera' with its spectacular rocky coastline and cliff scenery from Lot's Wife to Castlehill Point and Rough Firth and its inlets and little coves associated with smuggling days and tales. Note the fine gardens and woodland areas including wild bamboo at Southwick Burn and old oak, holly and hazel in the Needle's Eye Reserve; and the limestone fossil beds towards Southerness, the uranium vein near Lot's Wife, the remains of old copper-mining ventures, and the clumps of amethyst in private collections taken from the Boreland Burn, and also on Screel and Criffel, with the larger pieces making splendid and very special doorstops.

The older villages, Mainsriddle, Caulkerbush, have not prospered, but the enthusiasm for sea-bathing from the late 1860s to the 1890s saw a positive sprouting of holiday villas between Sandyhills and Douglas Hall and Portling, and at Rockcliffe and Kippford, now joined by more recent retirement bungalows and chalets. Don't forget to explore the hinterland along the little roads up the valleys, where the old deserted farms and settlements, mostly not on the 1:50000 map, have evocative placenames, such as Bunghole, north of Clonyard, Jocklig, north-west of Millbank Hill, and Chapman's Croft, just south-west of Southwick Old Church.

On the A710 note Gilbert de Suthayk's castle mound of about 1180, the Brough or Dunjumpin motte (936570) and, almost opposite, the Home Farm with mill wheel and pond. At Caulkerbush go up the B793 to Mainsmill for a pleasant stroll along the side road by Dunmuck, Ryes and Bogfoot. Southwick Church (927573), built in 1891, is charming. Southwick and Colvend parishes merged in 1612, separated in 1894, and were relinked by the Presbytery of Dumfries in 1950.

Continue along the A710 passing Millbank and Plumjordan and take the side road north up the valley of the Back Burn. The churchyard of Old Southwick (906569) is a beautifully sheltered site with the remains of the thirteenth-century church of Our Lady of Southwick visited by Edward I in 1300. The church remained in use until 1743. Churchyard stones include seventeenth-century tablestones to Johannes Lindsay and Isabella

131

McLellan and to Janet Cutler and Parich Young, and a delightful red sandstone piece with a skeleton carved in high relief and the inscription, of universal relevance, 'Hodie Mihi Cras Tibi'. If in doubt, do *not* ask an elderly relative to translate!

Continue north to the B793 and return passing the Castle Farm with one remaining circular tower of the Z plan Lindsay tower house, Auchenskeoch Castle (917588). The farm has a circular horse mill. Slewcairn (924614) to the north has an important excavated long cairn, eighty feet in a north to south orientation, with a granite pillar facade and forecourt. Here again the monument began as a rectangular mortuary structure.

From Caulkerbush take the A710 along the Heughs of Laggan stretch. Do drive with care as it is not entirely whimsical to suggest that you might encounter the occasional dithery dotty driver, although a personal impression is that for the worst of these you have to wait until Wigtownshire! For a circuit take the B794 to Fairgirth (879566), the site of the mediaeval St. Lawrence's chapel and churchyard, and then the road north-east by Drumstinchall, west along the B793 and south on the B794 by Auchenhay Bridge to return to Sandyhills. Interesting placenames of old settlements include Fore and Back Bainloch to the east of Drumstinchall, and Garryhorn east of Garryhorn lochan (883566). Barnhourie Mill (889553) has charming rock and woodland gardens, especially strong on small rhododendron species, and the old mill with an undershot wheel. The ruined house in Barnhourie Wood (886552) appears to be late seventeenth century.

Along the coast to the east round Craigneuk Point the O.S. 1854 map records a chalybeate Spa Well (903553). An older activity was making salt from sea deposits in rockcut depressions on the Saltpan Rocks at Douglas Hall Point. The Piper's Cave (889545) has vertical and horizontal shafts cut in search of copper. The Brandy Cave (883541) on Portling Bay has a twelve feet long inner chamber (natural?), traditionally a smugglers' hiding place. It is difficult here to distinguish between romantic myths and hard facts, but W. R. McDiarmid's excellent *Handbook of the United Parishes of Colvend and Southwick* (1873 and 1895 editions) gives a useful and entertaining account of the Kirk Session in 1741 rebuking seven local sinners for smuggling on the Sabbath, the offence however being not the smuggling but the Sabbath-breaking. There is a small promontory fort at Port O'Warren (880534).

From Port O'Warren take the footpath walk passing Gillis Craig and Cow's Snout to Castlehill Point on Urr Waterfront. You pass the site of another copper mine, the 'Copper Pit' (868528) at the east end of the Glenstocken Sands, and the former Glenstocken mill stone quarry (862526), beside the Bogle Hole and Gutcher's Isle, where soft granite mill stones were worked from the late seventeenth century or earlier. Mill stones were also taken from a small quarry at Barcloy (858525) above the Lagmuck Sands. The promontory fort at Castlehill Point (854524), perhaps also a mediaeval castle site, has a deep landward trench and the remains of a massive stone wall.

The motte marked on the site of the farm of Moat north of Boreland of Colvend is now too irregular to be at all certain of identification. Colvend Church (863541), built in 1911 to plans by P. McGregor Chalmers, replaced the church of 1771, itself on an older site. The churchyard has some seventeenth and eighteenth-century stones, almost layers of them in fact, including one with the pious pelican pecking her breast to feed her young, which is the symbol of the church. Older placenames include Croftmuirhill and Plumbhole, north-west and north of the church, Turnofive, east of Boreland of Colvend, and Tarlillyan, east of Barean Loch.

From the A710 take either of the side roads to Rockcliffe or Kippford to explore this sheltered area which served as a harbour of refuge in the days of sailing vessels. Moreover in the nineteenth and into the present century the Urr was a busy river, navigable to Palnackie for vessels up to 350 tons and to Dalbeattie for schooners up to 150 tons. Looking at the soft gentle landscape—and Rockcliffe in particular has an almost sub-tropical aura enhanced by the flocks of visiting yachts in the estuary in the summer, by the Anglo-Saxon accents and by the general impression of affluence—it is easy to forget that this coastline was until quite recently a busy centre of fishing and quarrying. The old mussel beds, for example, near Castlehill Point and Hestan were worked by the local fishermen.

From Rockcliffe take the Jubilee (foot) Path to Kippford, or vice versa. Rough Island (843532) is a bird sanctuary accessible at low tide. The *'Mote'* *of Mark* (844540) was excavated by Curle in 1913 and Laing in 1973. Although there is some evidence of settlement back to about 4000 B.C. and also possibly of Iron Age fortification, the main period of occupation was between the late fifth and seventh centuries A.D., first as a stronghold of one of the princes of Rheged and then towards the end of the sixth century by Anglians from Northumbria. The ten feet high and wide stone ramparts with a timber framework may have been vitrified when the 'Mote' was taken by the Anglian invaders. What is really important, however, is the evidence of the existence of a major industrial centre here with workshops in iron and bronze producing Celtic decorated jewellery, brooches, pins, mounts, and using iron ore from Cumbria, jet from Whitby, beads from Ireland and glass from the Rhineland.

Kippford or the Scaur (or Scar) developed as a shipbuilding and fishing village at the beginning of the nineteenth century. The Kipp ford itself was much older. Although the 1854 O.S. map refers to it as Kippford or Scar, there may have been some distinction between the Kipp and the Scar as separate places, and certainly David Gibson refers to them in the 1820s in this way. Henry and John Cummings built ships here, mainly schooners of 100 to 200 tons for Cumbria and the south-west of Scotland, from 1812 to 1867. The last may have been the *Balcary Lass* of 240 tons. Repairs and overhauls continued up to 1911, and published photographs show vessels, such as the *Sweetheart Abbey,* right over and onto the road near the present village shop. Gibson, the Baptist itinerating missionary from Auchencairn, describes a visit to the Scaur on 11 July 1826 as involving 'rather a public night with the ships' carpenters. A mast had to be put into a vessel, and there was a lot of drinking, there being English carpenters there'. The 1851 Census Enumeration Book gives a village population of seventy-seven, mariners, fishers, ship carpenters, a ferry boatman, a grocer and a carrier and their families, Cummings, Marshalls, Fergusons, McKnights, Aitkens, Patricksons, Howells. A second and later industry came with the Caledonian Granite Company quarry (841553). But from the 1870s onward Kippford became gradually more and more a seabathing and leisure resort and a retirement village.

Old placenames between Colvend and Barnbarroch include the surprising Segovia and Hedge Wa's near Auchensheeen West and Drumwhinny near Auchenhill. Continue past Barnbarroch, formerly a village with a single long row of cottages and a well. The Moyle (848576) above Upper Barnbarroch and the former Gallowleck quarry in the forest below is large enough at about one thousand by six hundred feet to have been a refuge for a sub-tribal community and its cattle and horses.

Steadstone (836580) has a remarkable garden with grass slopes and zig-zag paths and terraces, rills and a pond, and natural woodland with rich ground flora including orchids, all most dramatically set within an 1838-1909 granite quarry with the remains of crushing and polishing machinery. The riverside quay (833583) was used by the Steadstone and Old Land quarries. The unassuming 'earthwork' on the river edge at Little Richorn (835596), excavated by Coles in 1891, may be a motte; the central mound has a retaining wall of granite blocks.

Continue on the A710 through Urr parish towards Dalbeattie, and take the bypass road parallel to the river, taking you close to the old quays at the

Dub O'Hass (830603), where the river and the burn meet, and at the largely built-over Dalbeattie Port (830604), both busy in the nineteenth century with schooners taking out vast tonnages of granite to the world outside and with steamship services to Whitehaven and Liverpool. This approach gives you a clear view of the rapidly disappearing Craignair Hill granite quarry (821606). Dalbeattie is very much a granite town, but the first developments in the village, founded about 1780 by Alexander Copland of King's Grange and George Maxwell of Munches, were a paper mill, grain mills, and a lint (flax) mill, and later industries included a waulk (woollen) mill, bobbin making, a sawmill, a brickworks, and about 1920/1921 the Burnside Motor Works where a *very* few two-seater Skeoch Utility Cyclecars with Beardmore motor-cycle engines were made. However, it was the success of the granite quarry at Craignair, opened about 1800 but first worked on a large scale from 1825 to 1832 by the Liverpool Dock Trustees and developed further from the 1850s onward, which explains the growth of Dalbeattie into the largest town in the Stewartry, becoming a police burgh in 1858. In the best years between three and four hundred men were employed in the quarries. But the most amazing sight must have been the half-mile aerial ropeway from the Craignair crushing mill over the valley to the railway station above Dalbeattie.

Dalbeattie granite was used everywhere from the Bank of England and Mersey Docks to the Eddystone Lighthouse and the Grand Harbour of Valletta in Malta. In the town itself the rows of single and two-storey houses and the larger and public buildings are impressive, solid, satisfying architecture. To see a good cross-section turn right at the crossroads of the A710 and A711-B794 and continue along Craignair Street passing the quite picturesque St. Peter's R.C. Church (1814). Park at and walk up Station Road, turn right along Albert Street, right down James Street to the A711 or John Street and back to the foot of Station Road. Turn left into the High Street passing 'The Round House' and Water Street. Cross the mighty waters of the Dalbeattie Burn—not as facetious as this at first may seem, as the recent expensive protective walls and structures show—and continue along the High Street. Turn left into Mill Street passing Alma House and the former Picture House, and up the rather ostentatiously named Alpine Street, passing Alpine Terrace on the left, and on to the B793 Southwick Road at the Primary School. Turn left towards Barrhill, the one-time clachan of Cunningham, for the Barrhill grain mill complex (839614) and follow the trackway beside the lade to Maidenholm Forge (842613), with a spectacular lade system and an overshot wheel, altogether a fine group of mainly nineteenth-century industrial buildings, disused, which would make an excellent folk museum nucleus. Return to the High Street by the B793, and from there take Burn Street to the left and hence over the little footbridge back to Craignair Street.

Dalbeattie has a short but proud history. Its newspaper with the marvellously comprehensive title, *The Stewartry Observer and Wigtownshire News* (1889-1954), otherwise locally 'the Squeak', and the Galloway books, including Frew's excellent *The Parish of Urr* (1909), published by Thomas Fraser in Dalbeattie, are further evidence of the high quality of community life in the old independent burghs.

Take the A711 out of Dalbeattie over the bridge (1797) at Craignair into Buittle parish. On the west bank of the Urr just above the tidal limit is one of the most historic and unobtrusive castles in Galloway. Below the A745 you see the farmhouse of Buittle Place (817617), itself a sixteenth-century tower house on the L plan, restored and heightened in the nineteenth century; and behind is the grassy mound with bushes and trees which is the site of Buittle Castle (819616), perhaps first an oval motte and bailey with water-filled ditch and then from the 1230s a stone castle built by John Balliol, the husband of Devorgilla and father of King John Balliol. Concealed under the rubble and undergrowth may well be the foundations of a complete courtyard castle with curtain walls, curtain towers and a drawbridge entrance with round towers on either side at the north-west of the enclosure. The two-acre outer courtyard includes the farmhouse area. The seal of the charter of Balliol College, Oxford was affixed here in 1282. And there was also a burgh of Buittle, possibly going back to the middle of the thirteenth century or founded in a grant of rights and privileges to Sir James Douglas by Robert I in 1324/1325. The castle may have been dismantled in 1313, but was occupied in the 1350s or later. In the seventeenth century there was a bridge over the river at the north-east end of the castle. Unfortunately there is very little to be seen in the summer from either the A745 or the B794.

For a different and more immediate sort of drama, thrills and happily not spills, continue up the A745 to the crossroads at 807601 and then take the 'Highland' single track with passing places on the right—a 'real' road, with grass in the centre and dykes and hedges at the sides. This has superb views to the west and over to Castle-Douglas before the Dalbeattie Reservoir. At the north-west end of the Reservoir, on the east side of the march dyke, is the site of the Rumbling Well (805615), still in the later seventeenth century a place where the country people left money and clothes on the first Sunday in May and drank the water to cure their illnesses and sicknesses. The Slot Well (814616) was much stranger, as here they left as offerings the bands and shackles used for their oxen and collected the water to take back to wash their beasts and to let them drink from it to cure the disease known as the 'connach'. The old school (801620) is marked on the 1853 O.S. map as the 'Buittle High School'. 'High' it certainly is, with magnificent views to the north and north-west, and an exciting run downhill in front of you. At the foot of the hill turn left by Meikle Knox back to the A745 and return south-east to the Buittle Church crossroads.

Buittle Church (808599) was built in 1819. The former manse, dating from the 1790s, is impressive as a monument to the status and affluence of old-time ministers. The churchyard has the ruined nave and chancel of the pre-Reformation thirteenth or early fourteenth-century church; and some eighteenth-century stones with interesting figure sculpture, a fine pillar monument to David Milligan of Dalskaith, Merchant in London (d.1798), with a ship in full sail, and a good tablestone to Anna Hepburn (d.1706) and William Tod (d.1713), the parish minister.

From Buittle Church continue south by Clone and Courthill to Palnackie (821568), formerly Barlochan Port or The Garden, from the Garden Creek on the next bend to the north. Palnackie was for many years the main port in the Urr estuary and is still an amazing sight when a ship is berthed in the dock. It was exporting Glenstocken millstones in the seventeenth century, but its heyday was in the early nineteenth century when, as the port for Castle-Douglas and Gelston, it exported agricultural produce and imported fertiliser, slates, coal and Baltic timber. Indeed plans were drawn up about 1850 for a canal between Palnackie and Carlingwark at Castle-Douglas to take vessels up to 200 tons up from Palnackie by Big Barwhinny Loch, Douganhill, the Doach Woods and Gelston Lane, with four locks, two at Palnackie and two in the Doach Woods. The coming of the railway probably killed off the project. Palnackie is a most attractive period village, now also known as the GHQ of the 'Flounder Tramping Grand International Festival', actually held at the Glen Isle Sands where competitors use their toes and leisters to hunt for flounders. The Thomson 1828 county map has one placename, 'Purgatory', between Barlochan and Barwhinny, which was omitted from the O.S. 1854 map.

From Palnackie take the A711 west to the road junction at 806560 and the side road south-east to the charming corner sheltering the unique fifteenth-century *Orchardton Tower* (816552) built by John Cairns. The almost doll's house appearance is deceptive, as it has many of the ordinary features of a Scottish tower house of the period, a vaulted basement for storage, an entrance on the first floor originally on the east side of the

A lyrical view of Orchardton Tower showing the kitchens and stables and retainers' quarters to the right of the round tower. Good details of the wall walk and cape-house.

building, and a crenellated battlement, but it is still singularly different in being cylindrical rather than rectangular. It is a delight to look at, but not very practical to live in, very cramped and probably quite exceptionally claustrophobic when floored. Note the sweet little private corner in the round hall, the narrow staircase in the wall thickness, and the wall-walk and cape-house details. Return by staying on the same road and swinging north for Palnackie, and then by Kirkennan and the Munches to Dalbeattie, passing some fine woodland and reclaimed bog land on the bank of the Urr and another old quay at Kirkclaugh east of Kirkennan (832579).

To explore Kirkgunzeon parish the fast direct road from Dalbeattie is the A711 by Edingham and Lower Porterbelly, but the best route is by the B793 up the hill and the side road at Aucheninnes north by Barclosh Hill and Loch Fern, and (passing the road on the left to Quahead and the former Southwick Halt on the railway line) north by Bargrug, Tarkirra and Congeith. On this you pass close by the site of Barclosh Castle (855625) and the Iron Age forts at Tarkirra (867648 and 870644). The hill east of Glaisters and Plascow has many small cairns and old field bank and runrig lines (8965). Old placenames include Clawbelly, south of Isles, and Sheil and

Kirkgunzeon Village, c.1910. Three small boys in the centre and adults behind and to the left having a long look at the photographer. Good details of the bridge, road and houses.

Sheilleys on the Sheil and Glen Burns south-east of Glaisters. Turn left on to the A711 passing the remains of the tower house at Corra (867661) and take the road passing Conniven farm on the west for Kirkgunzeon.

Kirkgunzeon is now almost a lost village which few visitors notice from the main road. But it is both an old settlement, quite possibly a mill village from the second half of the twelfth century when the Cistercians of Holm Cultram were given land grants in this area, and a good example of a once self-contained community with a blacksmith, a tailor, a grocer, a resident minister, and even a railway station. Don't miss it. Note the church (1790) and the former manse (1804) and the site of St. Winning's Well upstream above the grain mill complex at Millhill or Betwixt the Waters (865669), once famous for its oatmeal. Take the road to the left passing the farm road end for Killymingan and Alleyford and the first road to the right for Branetrigg and Drumcoltran.

Drumcoltran Tower (869683) is a very fine sixteenth-century L-plan tower house, latterly used for storage for the adjacent farm. The whole complex could again be a much earlier one. The compact north-west wing was added to the original rectangular tower. Do get the key from the farmhouse and climb up to the wall-walk, from which the view is surprisingly spectacular. Note above the doorway the wise advice for dishonest men everywhere (in Latin so that only the clergy and schoolteachers could read it!)—'Keep hidden what is secret; speak little; be truthful; avoid wine; remember death; be pitiful'. From Drumcoltran return to the Kirkgunzeon road and go north by Byrecroft, Barbey and Green Burn to Milton on the Old Millitary Road.

Milton of Urr (849706) is one of a number of decayed villages on the O.M.R. (1763-1764). The line of much of the road is older, certainly mediaeval and in part possibly Roman. Some sections of the present road are later diversions, for example between Milton and Courthill in 1825 and between Hardgate and Haugh of Urr in 1812. As the coach route until the opening of the line from Springholm to Crocketford after 1800 the Old Military Road was a busy thoroughfare with villages and inns and stopping places along the way. Milton still had a sawmill, a corn mill, a smithy and a school (at Bridgestone Bridge) in 1854, and nine or ten houses when Frew was writing in 1909. Interesting placenames include Blaw Wearie, north of Milton Mains, and Cowdieknowe, south-east of Meikle Culmain. Take the side road north to Milton Loch, which has a crannog (839718), excavated in 1953, a large round second to fourth-century A.D. farmhouse on a circular timber platform with an underwater timber gangway to the shore, a small harbour on the east side of the island, and a line of stakes for a fish trap; and also the quite unusual Green Island promontory fort (838716), variously regarded as Dark Age and Norse or as mediaeval.

Take the road south just before Auchengibbert by Meikle Kirkland, the site of a chapel and churchyard (826697), east of the fort on Barr Hill (815694), and by West Glenarm to the crossroads near Blaiket Mains. Note the very old road from Milton to Glenarm and Barr of Spottes towards the Old Bridge of Urr. On the O.M.R. continue west passing the line of the old village of Blackford and by Hardgate down to Haugh of Urr and the splendid hump-backed bridge over the Urr. The Haugh was once a busy crossroads with several inns, including the Fish Inn and the Dog and Duck. Old placenames include Bonsuck north of Blackford. The whole length of the O.M.R. from Milton to the Haugh is a good walk with fine vistas. The area from Spottes Hall north to Glen of Spottes is a fascinating corner, with the ancient chapel site (805672) where the ninth/tenth-century bronze flask was found and interesting farm and old corn mill buildings. There was another chapel nearer the A75 at 797674. Note also the horseshoe-shaped promontory fort, possibly Iron Age and Dark Age, at Waterside (809659) above the river to the south of the Haugh, and a fort with three concentric ramparts on Camp Hill (807650).

Take the road south-east from the Haugh to Urr Church (816658), a 1914/1915 church by P. McGregor Chalmers on a much older site. The

Haugh of Urr village looking down the Old Military Road to the south-west, c.1910.

parish minister from 1806 to 1813 was the Rev. Alexander Murray, the shepherd's son who became Professor of Oriental Languages at the University of Edinburgh in 1812. The churchyard stones include some good and some sad reading. Robert Kerr (1811-1848), born at Midtown of Spottes and buried here, was one of the best Galloway poets. He tried his hand as a packman in the Colchester area, but came back to work as a ploughman at Redcastle. A collection of his work, *Maggie O' The Moss: and Other Poems*, was published by Fraser of Dalbeattie in 1891. The most memorable is 'My First Fee', but 'Maggie O' The Moss', a description of a local witch attending an international conference of witches at the North Pole is great fun, and 'The Widow's Ae Coo' may still have its followers. It is a good Galloway book to have. Continue back to the B794 by Redcastle, which on the 1854 O.S. map is credited with not one but two standing stones, and a sundial and a bowling green.

Take the B794 towards Dalbeattie. You soon get a clear view of the massive Motte of Urr (815647), ranked generally with the Bass of Inverurie as the finest twelfth-century earthwork castle in Scotland. You also get a splendid view from the other side of the river (over Stepend Ford or the foot bridge at Netheryett) from the road near West Logan. There was also a town here, probably on the east side of the motte. Its burgesses, Adam Clerk and Hugo Sprot, were witnesses to a charter in 1262. The motte, which was excavated in 1951 and 1953, was almost certainly the *caput* of Walter de Berkeley, but whether fortified by him in the 1160s or the 1180s or by someone else back in the 1130s is uncertain. The river flowed at that time on the west side of the motte. The entrance to the bailey was at the

The Motte of Urr from the north-west. The engraving from Francis Grose's *The Antiquities of Scotland* (1797) is also interesting evidence for the state of local roads at the end of the eighteenth century.

north-west end, not the quite recent approach at the other, south-east end. Access to the top of the motte was by a flying bridge, perhaps as illustrated in the Bayeux Tapestry. There was a solid rectangular timber tower or blockhouse in the middle of the motte and a timber palisade with 'foxholes' or pits round the edge for archers to fire down through embrasures, a feature found in mottes in Ulster. The ditch below the motte was up to nine feet deeper than as seen today. Evidence of a great fire six feet below the present top of the motte suggests a total destruction of the buildings at some date (in the 1170s or 1180s or even 1235?), with a subsequent heightening and rebuilding with the 'foxholes' added at this stage. It is difficult to appreciate the immense size and scale of the whole castle without climbing to the top, but it is still part of a working farm, so 'coos' and horses have a prior claim to grazing and access over tourists.

CHAPTER 12

Kirkpatrick-Durham, Corsock, Castle-Douglas, Kelton, Balmaghie, Crossmichael, and Parton

From Haugh of Urr take the Old Military Road south-west up the hill passing the entrance for Corbieton (796658), a charming small house incorporating an older tower and with a large rectangular dovecot nearby. Note at the junction with the A75 the entrance for Ernespie House Hotel (771633), which lies between the Broad Bonnet and Horse Hill. The area to the south is interesting with two standing stones (775632), which may be the remains of a circle of eight or nine monoliths, and Willie's Well marked on the O.S. early maps below in the same field.

Take the A75 north-east passing Mollance (house and lodges demolished) and King's Grange. The hill south of Dunjarg above the main road and Dunjarg Loch has a fort (789655), and there is a St. Michael's Well (778655) east of Fordhouse between Mollance and Gerranton. Springholm is an early nineteenth-century strip development along the line of the new coach road, but also with two mills, the Auchenreoch corn and meal mill and the Newbank woollen mill, formerly working from the Culshan Burn south of the village. The Auchenreoch Loch has two possible crannog sites.

Crocketford or the Ninemile Bar has a quite outstanding early nineteenth-century toll house, but is perhaps better known for its association with the notorious Buchanite sect. Notoriety is, of course, relative, and the prophecies and hocus-pocus theology (a sort of menopausal blight?) of Elspeth (Luckie) Buchan (1738-1791) may not seem any more weird or eccentric now than the once conventional wisdom of other saints and sinners. By the time Mother Buchan, the Friend Mother in the Lord, the Third Person in the Godhead, the woman in Chapter XII of *Revelations,* moved from Irvine to New Cample near Thornhill in 1784 and then to Auchengibbert near Crocketford in 1787 she had a following of some forty to sixty men, women and children. Their beliefs included the communal ownership of goods, abstinence from marriage and what Burns, who knew most of the group personally in Irvine, describes as holding a 'community of women', and the expectation of a second and physical rising to Paradise led by Mrs Buchan, alive or dead. Her band subsequently itinerated post-1791 with her corpse which was variously with them at Auchengibbert, Larghill, Crocketford, and finally at Newhouse on the New Galloway road.

More than half the group emigrated to America. There was no second rising, but for further reading see J. Cameron, *The History of the Buchanite Delusion, 1783-1846* (1904).

From Crocketford take the A712 New Galloway road to the crossroads at Brooklands Bridge and the side road south-west by Minnydow and Loch Patrick to Kirkpatrick-Durham. Minnydow is interesting with an oval fort (797710) north-west of Mains farm, St. Patrick's Well (798711) and a kirkyard site and the Meikle Cairn nearby. The holy well was visited by local folk every March 17th for its healing cures, but the folklore collector Walter Gregor reported (1897) the gruesome tale that a woman drowned her child in it and that afterwards the healing virtue departed from the water. Note the old Lochpatrick corn mill (791710) on the road north of the loch; a good walking road to the north by Culfad, Blackhall, Bardarroch and Wellhill; the old chapel site of Kirklebride (783747) close to the A712 north of Areeming; and the road from Kirkpatrick-Durham to Barmoffity and Pipercroft. The 1854 O.S. map refers to the area between Barmoffity Hill and the Black Loch as the 'Wilderness'.

Kirkpatrick-Durham is one of the most attractive planned villages in Galloway, and it retains the purity of its original simple cross plan of four intersecting streets. The unspoiled single-storey cottages are particularly good and give it the unique atmosphere and feeling of days gone by which make it so worth exploring. The village was founded by the minister, landowner and author, Dr. David Lamont (1753-1837) of Erncrogo and Culshand, who was appointed to the parish in 1774. Lamont was important, chaplain to the Prince of Wales in 1785, Moderator of the General Assembly and (a distinction of a sort) the preacher before George IV in St. Giles in Edinburgh on his Scottish visit in 1822. The village was laid out after 1783 with feus given on generous terms, cotton and woollen manufactories, seven inns and ale-houses, a racecourse, and an annual fair fixed in 1791 as the last Thursday in March. Although the industries largely failed, the village prospered, and there were 500 people living in it in 1844. Lamont built his own house just outside it at Durhamhill. The fair was very much older as it was really Patrick's Mass Fair held at the church over the centuries on March 17th. The church (1748, but with additions and major alterations in 1849 and 1949) may have been on this site from the thirteenth century, and the Durand family castle may have been on the site of the totally removed Marl Mount Moat Hill (795692).

For a long and fascinating drive through the 'real' Galloway of rolling hills and farmland and moors take the road west at the Kirkpatrick-Durham crossroads to the B794. Kilquhanity is an old estate which, since 1940, has housed a co-educational boarding school operating on A. S. Neill of Summerhill principles. Go north passing Walton Park and take the side road west to Knockvennie Bridge and then turn north by Paddock Hall and Glenlair. 'Remote' Glenlair, a ruin since a disastrous fire in 1929, was the home of the great scientist James Clerk Maxwell (1831-1879), the first professor of experimental physics at Cambridge and the founder of much of modern theoretical physics. Continue by Hurkledown Hill, passing the road for Ardmannoch, Mochrum and Little Mochrum, and then by Hillside, Blackhills, Hallcroft and Corsock House and Loch. There was another old corn mill at Millbrae.

Turn left on the A712 by Corsock church (Corsock became a *quoad sacra* parish in 1863) and take the side road north at Corsock village (758764). The 1854 O.S. map uses the old name of 'Howemoor Village'. Continue north by Crogo Mains. The site of Crogo Tower (758774), a possible moated manor complex, is to the north-east near the Water of Urr. There were old corn mills on the river north of Knockdrockwood Ford and at Crogo Mill. The enormous log cabin belongs to the Loch Lorien community—the name is from the 'Lord of the Rings' and has no local reference. Knocklearn Moor (755800) has a number of small cairns, and indeed the whole valley is full of evidence of occupation and settlement over the centuries. Continue by Glaisters Bridge, Monybuie Flow, Nether Monybuie and Waterhead. The 1854 O.S. map includes Monybuie School on the road north of Nether Monybuie.

Loch Urr is bleak, but rather wonderful. Rough Island (762844) on the south-west side is a crannog with an underwater stone causeway to the shore. It also has the remains of three or four enclosures or buildings, including possibly a thirteenth-century hall. The six-acre 'White Island' promontory (759842) at the south-west end of the loch has a ditch and bank across the landward end and may have functioned as a bailey to the island castle. Further north the Watch Knowe (743864) at Craigmuie is a rectilinear fort with the clear remains of two ditches and two ramparts at the rounded south-east corner—not Roman, but perhaps a refuge camp or strength built by local people in the fourth or fifth century A.D. who had seen Roman fortifications. The Physic Well Wood beside the road had indeed at one time a chalybeate well at the south-east corner.

Returning south take first the road north of Loch Urr by Craigenvey Moor and Castramon Hill, and then south-west by Letterick Hill and Craigenputtock (771823), the home between 1828 and 1834 of Thomas Carlyle and his wife Jane Welsh, and then by Glaisters, Nether Glaisters and Upper Barr to Kirklebridge Bridge on the A712; and then down the

B794 by Arkland, where there is a rath or circular homestead (768740), Margley, which has a small fort (770733), Over Marcartney, Kilquhanity and the Doon of Urr fort (774689) to the Old Bridge of Urr (776677). The bridge here is probably eighteenth century, but may incorporate an earlier sixteenth-century structure. Old Bridge of Urr is recorded in 1725 as having the right and privilege of holding a weekly market, so it may have been a place of some importance before the development of Kirkpatrick-Durham. The corn mill complex on the north bank of the Water of Urr with a high breast-shot wheel and a free-standing kiln is an outstanding example of a country grain mill. Unfortunately plans in 1976-1978 to develop the site as a milling museum were unsuccessful. The O.S. 1854 map also includes here Dubbidale carding mill, and there was the site of a waulk mill further north at the Waulk Mill Pool (770685). The rath near Trowdale (758690) is similar to the site of Arkland.

Take the road south from Old Bridge of Urr and continue up and down hill by Chapelerne and Clarebrand, where the fort (770662), so clearly marked on the modern O.S. map, is only barely visible as the slight remains of two concentric terraces. Hence to Castle-Douglas, and after the peace and loneliness of Monybuie and Loch Urr the metropolitan business and bustle is something of a culture shock.

The names for the clachan, first Causewayend and then Carlingwark, and for the town, Castle-Douglas, which became a burgh of barony in 1791, are very appropriate for the stages in the development of the busiest market centre in the Stewartry. The area around it was important over the centuries because of its central geographical location. There is some fascinating evidence of early settlement and civilisation. The famous votive deposit found in Torrs Loch (781617) about 1820 consisted of three separate pieces mistakenly 'repaired' into a composite object and sent to Scott at Abbotsford by Joseph Train, then exciseman in Castle-Douglas. The main piece was a superb Celtic pony cap of about 250 B.C., and the other two were the ends or terminals of drinking horns. Glenlochar to the north, of course, has the important Roman fort complex. And the crannogs with causeways in Carlingwark Loch, Ash Island (763611) and Fir Island (763609) were occupied both in the Iron Age and mediaeval periods. Either Fir Island or the clachan at Buchan (761613), or both, may have been the location of thirteenth and fourteenth-century forges; but the extraordinary local tradition that 'Mons Meg' was made at Buchan for the 1455 siege of Threave Castle has to be abandoned, since it is known now that it was manufactured in 1449 by Jehan Cambier at Mons for the Duke of Burgundy who sent it as a diplomatic gift to James II of Scotland in 1457.

Carlingwark village, as opposed to Causewayend, was founded by Sir Alexander Gordon of Culvennan in the 1760s. Drainage of the loch in 1765 and the removal of vast quantities of marl reduced the water area from 180 to 100 acres. Gordon had a canal, the Carlingwark Lane, cut from the Buchan Bridge (762614) north to the Dee near Threave Island (744625), and this was used to take marl up to the Glenkens on barges. Another canal, the Culvennan Cut round the 'Barony Isle', was dug for him in 1780 from the Dee near (735635) the Fortalice of Greenlaw by locks at Culvennan to the river opposite Boatcroft (734643). Some stretches can still be seen, but they are not suitable for casual exploration.

Sir William Douglas (1745-1809) established Castle-Douglas as his burgh of barony by the charter of December 10, 1791. Douglas was a successful Virginia and West Indies merchant who had 'retired' to his native Galloway in 1785 and purchased Gelston, Hallmyre, Carlingwark and Mid Kelton between 1786 and 1790. His town was planned as both a centre of industry (cotton mill, tanneries, brewery) and of commerce (with his own bank, the Galloway Banking Company of 1806 to 1821). He was also involved in other innovative schemes which did not get beyond the planning stage, including in 1788 a canal from Carlingwark to Orchardton Bay, and with Gordon and the Earl of Selkirk the ambitious Glenkens Canal project of 1796 and 1801 for a waterway from Kirkcudbright through ten locks to bypass the Tongland rapids and on to Dalry (twenty-six miles), and even eventually to Dalmellington. Castle-Douglas became a very successful market town with its own cattle and horse fairs, and by the second quarter of the nineteenth century had replaced Keltonhill as the main centre in Lochelletun or Kelton parish, with banks and inns and, from 1858, its own newspaper, the still thriving *Kirkcudbrightshire Advertiser* or *Galloway News*.

Castle-Douglas is a fine example of a spaciously laid-out, planned town with three parallel streets, Queen Street, King Street and Cotton Street, and five intersecting streets. In such a busy town the best time for a perambulation is either before breakfast or after dinner. Start from the Market Hill opposite the hexagonal market building. A hundred years ago the horse fair was held here, with booths and stalls all the way down King Street from the Crown Hotel to Davis Corner, and farmers and country lads and lasses, hucksters and sleight o' han' men, gangrel bodies and the swell-type mob in seedy suits and others displaying a decayed gentility swarming round them. Go past Jenny's Loaning and down Queen Street, which has some good small painted houses and a few larger buildings. Rosebank and the King's Arms and, round the corner, the 'Palace' Picture

King Street, Castle-Douglas c.1905 in a picture postcard published by Rae of Castle-Douglas and printed in delicate pastel shades in Paris. Very much still the age of the horse economy.

House are all good examples of their type of architecture. Take the B736 road to explore the south-east side of the loch and return to Queen Street by St. Andrew's Church (1868) and the Scottish Episcopal Church (1874). If the main road is quiet, walk along the lochside by Carlingwark House to Buchan. In the occasional severe winter it is sometimes possible to hold a curling bonspiel between the Stewartry and Wigtownshire on the loch. Return by Carlingwark Street, where walkers can get buses for Dalry, Kirkcudbright and Dumfries (Post Office minibuses may be running to Mossdale and Auchencairn from the Post Office, but check locally at the P.O. in King Street). King Street has some impressive buildings. The Douglas Arms with a wall plaque by J. Affleck of Dumfries (1827) showing the mileages relevant in cattle-droving days, hence Huntingdon, is charming, and the Royal Bank of Scotland 'skyscraper' (1864) is massively reassuring—your money must be safe here is certainly the message it conveys!

To explore Kelton parish take the minor road at 771626 by Upper Torrs, Corra and Caigton. Turn right onto the B727 road to Gelston, passing Castlegower, where there is a vitrified hill fort (793589). Gelston Row village had a population of 147 in 1844. Only a few of the older cottages are left now. Note the old corn mill at the north end of the village—last worked in 1950. At the crossroads turn left to the south, passing Gelston Castle estate and

Ingleston motte (774579) on a high rock outcrop above the road. The name of the house (778574) at the end of the Ingleston farm road is listed on both the 1853 and the 1954 O.S. maps as 'Keep Clear'. This is an interesting corner of Galloway with the site of Gelston church and the churchyard behind Kirkland of Gelston farm (778573), hill forts at Ingleston (772577) and Dunguile Hill (773572), a possible rectangular moated homestead or manor, The Ditch (783572), immediately north of Boreland of Kelton farm, and also at Boreland a typical nineteenth-century meal or threshing meal. You are in rich cattle country here (Galloways, South Devons, Charolais and their crosses) and fine rolling landscapes, including the view south towards Hestan island.

Return to Gelston and turn left at the crossroads by Craigley, Airieland and Castlehill. Park at the road junction (747558) and walk up to Corra Hill fort (743554)—fine views north to Rhonehouse and Threave and east to the hills. Take the rolling road north by Lochdougan and Slagnaw and turn right at the junction south of Rhonehouse by Slackburn Bridge and Longsheds to Kelton church (759601). The present church was built in 1805-1806. The mediaeval and earlier church site was at Mid Kelton farm. Joseph Train (1779-1852) is buried in the churchyard. Note the large mausoleum for Sir William Douglas near the manse to the north.

Threave Gardens with the National Trust for Scotland School of Practical Gardening is open to the public through the whole year. The house itself (1870) is private. Leisure gardeners who prefer to look and plan rather than to dig and real enthusiasts alike will greatly enjoy strolling through the grassy glades and seeing the various special gardens—Peat, Rock, Water, Vegetable, Heather, Winter, Rose, Woodland and Walled—plus an Arboretum and a Pinetum. Trees and shrubs have come from all over the world from Gigha and Sikkim to the Magellan Straits.

From Threave Gardens take the north road by Midtown, Hillhead and Slatehole to Rhonehouse or Kelton Hill, a superb period village with the Fair Green for cattle and horse markets at the open west end and houses along the roads to the south-east and north-east. Any walking circuit by Rhonehouse, Gelston and Bridge of Dee is a delight. The old Keltonhill Fair, held on the festival of St. John the Baptist on the first Tuesday after June 17th, was one of the largest in the south-west of Scotland. It may have been held at different places over the centuries, at Furbar hill or Hightae farm or Kelton church or at Kelton hill (the site of Threave House and Gardens), but Rhonehouse was probably the better site. The Fair was moved to Castle-Douglas Market Hill in 1860. Rhonehouse was a busy place itself in the old cattle-droving days with weekly cattle markets during part of the year and perhaps as many as six inns, the Rodney, the White Horse, the Blue Bell, the Cross Keys, the Crown and the Boar's Head. The village population in 1844 was 235.

From Rhonehouse take the road south-west. Auchlane farm (741584) is on the site of a Maclellan moated manor or castle with the remains of water-filled ditches. Kirkcormack motte (716574) on the banks of the Dee and the adjoining church site are part of a fascinating area with evidence of a deserted mediaeval village and field system and an old road, and St. Ringan's Well just north of Mayfield farm. Further south the 'motes' at Gillfoot near the Cow Ford (711561) and Netherthird (711554) might be mediaeval or earlier. The 'cave' on Billies is probably a gallery worked by miners prospecting for copper.

Return to Rhonehouse and take the road by Boatcroft to Bridge of Dee village north of the Grainy Ford (730597). Druim Cheate (722588) on the north bank of the Dee north-east of Argrennan is traditionally the site of a battle or skirmish on June 29, 1308 between Edward Bruce and 'the English Party or Galwegians'. An extraordinary 400 metre-long rock tunnel (now sealed) was found recently thirty feet below the ground on Boatcroft with vertical shafts to the wood above—possibly worked by miners during the early nineteenth-century copper and lead-mining mania period. The slight circular earthwork at Dildawn (733585) might be a rath or a mediaeval homestead site. Cross the delightful Old Bridge of Dee (1737-1740) to the south of Threave Bridge (1824-1825). Bridge of Dee (population 243 in 1844) is yet another in this group of villages near Carlingwark. Walkers should take the Kirkcudbright bus from Castle-Douglas and ask to be let off at the road ends for Bridge of Dee, or at Kelton Mains for Threave Castle.

Threave Castle (739622) is visible from the A75 and from the Netherhall road west of the Dee, but the river island on which it stands can only be reached from Kelton Mains (car park) and the zig-zag path to the ferry. Excavations between 1974 and 1978 indicate the probability of twelfth or thirteenth-century occupation with defensive ditches east of the castle; but the history of Threave belongs especially to the Douglas period between 1369 and 1455. The great five-storey seventy-foot-high tower house built about 1369 by Archibald the Grim is one of the earliest and largest in Scotland. The curtain wall on the south and east is one of the earliest surviving artillery defences in Europe. It was built about 1450, just prior to the great three-month siege by James II in 1455. Note the three corner towers and the wall-slits, keyholes and dumb-bells for crossbows, longbows and hand guns. The island site with the natural barriers of the river and its marshes, the rock-cut ditch, the artillery wall and the great tower made

Threave Castle in an Edwardian card posted in 1905 and published in the 'Galloway Series' by John Low of Castle-Douglas.

Threave a fitting castle for the Douglases, the most dangerous of the over-mighty subjects of the Scottish kings. The island was almost a self-sufficient economy, with grazing land for animals and workshop areas for carpenters, blacksmiths and lead smelters. The rock-cut harbour contained an enormous mass of throwaway objects, including in particular rare wooden bowls and platters with the Black Douglas 'heart' underneath. After 1455 Threave was for a time a royal castle, but from the early sixteenth century was usually held by the Maxwells. The Civil War siege in 1640 and its aftermath resulted in major dismantling, although it was used as a barracks for French prisoners during the Napoleonic Wars.

From Bridge of Dee crossroads take the road by Netherhall and Threave Mains to Glenlochar. Before visiting the Threave Wildfowl Reserve contact the Warden (confirm details with the Visitor Centre at Threave Gardens). At Glenlochar take the road north parallel with the Dee to Balmaghie church (723663). This watery area is at its most dramatic when seen in wind and rain and storm and flood; but even on the softest summer day *The Kirk Above Dee Water* (to use the title of H.M.B. Reid's book published in 1895) is in a wonderful setting. The present church with its sweet little bell-tower was built in 1794, but its site, above an old river ferry crossing, is much older. S. R. Crockett (1859-1914), was was born at Little Duchrae (666690) and spent his childhood in Balmaghie and Castle-Douglas, is buried in the churchyard. He was not as great a writer as his early success suggested, but it is unfair to dismiss his work as 'another crop of kailyard'. Although some of it is very dated arcadian escapism, he could and did turn out some rattling good adventure stories using Galloway history and landscapes. *The Raiders* (1894), *The Men of the Moss Hags* (1895), *The Grey Man* (1896), *The Standard-Bearer* (1898), and *The Dark O' The Moon* (1912) may be his best Galloway novels. The short stories in *Bog Myrtle and Peat* (1895) and his Galloway book, *Raiderland* (1904), are also worth looking at. There are another sixty books for real enthusiasts!

From Balmaghie church try the walk by Gateside and Morrison to the old Kirk Road south of Dornell Loch and the road north along Loch Ken by Livingstone Hill to Mains of Duchrae. Laurieston and the western section of Balmaghie parish are included in Chapter 13.

Cross 'through the water of Dee' by the bridge of Glenlochar beside the barrage with sluice gates operated from Tongland Power Station and into Crossmichael parish. The B795 goes across the north-west corner of the great Roman fort (734645) discovered by aerial photography in 1949 and excavated in 1952. Almost all the fort is in the flat fields to the south. Few traces of it or of the huge marching camps to the east of Culvennan and also in the Abbey Yard area can be seen unless you bring your light aeroplane or helicopter with you. The glacial mound (748645) west of Greenlaw House may be, as suggested in the O.S. 1853 map, a 'Roman Burial Place.' The 'mote' (752640) is more likely to be a burial cairn; it was also used for Kirkcudbright Yeomanry Cavalry reviews and parades in the early nineteenth century when it was known as the 'Huntsman Knoll.' Greenlaw (754644), built by the Gordons of Culvennan in the second quarter of the eighteenth century, is a most handsome house, which in the last five years has both been converted to an hotel and then gutted by fire. The Fortalice of Greenlaw (741635), an oval moated area with a causeway approach from the north-east, may have been the site of a fortified grange or manor house. Alexander Trotter in his *East Galloway Sketches* (1901), by far the best book on the Stewartry, includes a somewhat fanciful sketch of Viscount Kenmure's tower house at the river end of the enclosure.

The A713 north from Townhead of Greenlaw and Danevale Park (1795) to Ken Bridge provides a series of charming landscapes and watery vistas. But to properly explore Crossmichael and Parton parishes you should try at least two long walks or drives up into the hinterland, where the hills and valleys are rich in evidence of burial cairns, shielings, deserted farms and forts and defended setlements. First take the side road north of Drumskelly by Crofts fort (743659), Ringanwhey (where the 1853 O.S. map lists a school), Clarebrand, Ernambrie fort (760666), and Halferne fort (761669) to Balgerran, where there is a fort to the north at 751689 and an old threshing mill in use up to 1934 at the farm. The 1853 map lists a Free School at Walbut(t). There are also forts at Loch Roan (738692) and Glengappock or Glenroan (750704). From Walbutt go south-west by Erncrogo, Mountaintop, Causewayhead, the former Crrossmichael corn mill (739675) and the Mill Burn and Bilbow Bridge to Culgruff House Hotel and Crossmichael village. Crossmichael church, built in 1751, also has its tower. The churchyard includes the Gordon of Airds mausoleum.

Further north on the A713 you pass the roads for Airds and Blairinnie and for Cogarth. Take the side road at Parton Mill House (717689) by Barbershall and Peathill as far as Loch Lurkie. Return to the road junction at 721701 and take the road by Craichie and Nether Laggan to Diamonds Laggan and hence south-west to the road junction at 695708. The earthwork north of Boreland of Parton (693709) may be a motte, or perhaps more probably an Iron Age or Dark Age period fort. The road by Faminach, Craigmore, Nether Dullarg (fort at 688737), Barend and Glenswinton takes you right into the hills—many fine views and even better ones from Shaw Fell and Upper Dullarg Hill behind.

Back near to the A713 there are the remains of early nineteenth-century slate quarries in Tintum Wood (698704). Kirkland motte (696697), which you can view from the churchyard, is the best-looking 'Christmas pudding'-shaped motte in Galloway. Note the classic proximity of church and castle. The present Parton church was built in 1834 beside its predecessor of 1592. The churchyard includes the burial place of James Clerk Maxwell. Parton village is an excellent example of a small early nineteenth-century estate village, rebuilt in 1901 as a 'model village' and again restored, including the wooden clock tower and the octagonal privy or 'bandwagon', six years ago. Continue north on the A713 beside the old railway line to Loch Ken Viaduct and Airds House and by Drumrash to Ringbane and the parish boundary at the Dullarg Burn.

F

CHAPTER 13

Balmaclellan, Dalry, Carsphairn and Kells

The four parishes of Balmaclellan, Dalry, Carsphairn and Kells are together the 'Glenkens', the farms and moors and hills and hidden valleys beside and around the river and loch Ken. In spite of the extent of State and private forestry there is still a great deal to see—prehistoric cairns and hut circles in profusion, rather fewer Iron Age sites than might be expected (although the Balmaclellan bronze mirror in the National Museum in Edinburgh is an exquisite example of Celtic art), early crosses, and an array of deserted late mediaeval to nineteenth-century ferm-touns and settlements and mills. This was probably one of the last areas in Galloway to have Welsh/Gaelic speakers (into the late sixteenth or seventeenth century). And it was amongst the hillfolk and moormen in these parishes, plus Kirkpatrick-Durham, Kirkpatrick-Irongray, Balmaghie and parts of Minnigaff and Penninghame, that the Covenanting tradition seems to have been strongest. Why this was so is a complex matter. Was it primarily the result of the leadership and political aspirations of local lairds, Gordons, Maclellans and Neilsons, who were opposed to taxation and central government control and the sort of civil and ecclesiastical authority associated with Episcopacy? Or was extreme Presbyterianism particularly appealing for some reason to a depressed peasantry? Those who today share an enthusiasm for the beliefs associated with the Covenanters (not necessarily the same thing as their actual beliefs and practices) will probably know that modern 'conventicles' are still held occasionally in Balmaclellan and Kirkpatrick-Irongray and on Kirkconnel Moor, north of Ringford.

Old ways perhaps lingered here somewhat longer than in the low country to the south. The New Statistical Account (1844) entry for Balmaclellan has a tantalising reference to the effect that 'the little spirited species of horse once so famous in Galloway is now scarcely ever met with', which suggests, of course, that some at least of the Galloway nags renowned as war horses and chargers were still then extant. And there is a memorable article by a local man, H. G. MacCreath, in the Scottish Review (1917) on 'The Farmers of the South-West' in which it is claimed that they are the tallest in Scotland and that the men of Balmaclellan parish are 'the tallest and heaviest men in Europe', average height almost six feet and average weight about fourteen stones. The article is a farrago of fact, fantasy and flattery—for example that the Galloway man 'will seldom tell a deliberate lie, but has a distaste for telling the whole truth, if something less than that will serve his turn...in old Ayrshire, the Galloway men were always accused of being too sweet to be wholesome'. The present crop of belles in Balmaclellan and damsels in Dalry will, no doubt, confirm or otherwise these strange myths.

But enough of such fripperies, and back to Balmaclellan at Shirmers Bridge and Ringbane on the A713, where there is an old lint-mill site with bleaching green on the Shirmers Burn (663742) above the road. Take the unsigned and quite marvellous road for walking or motoring at 655748 before Fauld-O-Wheat Burn. There are old farm sites at Ironcraigie and Mankinhowe on the burn below the road at Fauld-O-Wheat. Take the road to the right at Ironmacannie (662757), formerly a school, to the eighteenth and nineteenth-century Ironmacannie Corn Mill (667753), which was in use up to the 1930s and still has its wheel, and the restored mill house, all in a delightful setting and with a waterfall above. Continue by the fine old farm and steading at Barnshalloch to Holmhead at the road junction below Craig, a splendid and even rather exotic example of countryhouse architecture for Galloway. There is the site of another mill in the Mill Glen below Craig. Go north by Corse to the next road junction. You may turn left and return to the A713 by Ewanston Bridge, Blowplain and Barnhillies; otherwise turn right by Galrinnies and Barlay to the A712 at the old hostelry of 'Bread and Beer', now restored as a cottage. The name has been retained so that this must be one of the finest addresses in Galloway.

Turn left on the A712 by Troquhain, Scroggie Hall, Ironlosh and Barscobe. Barscobe Castle (659806) is an L-plan tower house built in 1648, possibly on an older site, by William Maclellan, whose wife was the daughter of Sir Robert Gordon of Lochinvar. Restored in 1972, it is a good example of the later type of laird's house that is becoming rather more like domestic architecture than primarily a fortified residence. The 1854 O.S. map has what looks like a formal garden to the south-east of the house and Barscobe Mill (in ruins) on the Garple Burn north of Millmark Ford. The castle is just visible in the distance from the road.

The War Memorial—and never forget the devastating impact of the Great War on rural Scotland—on the A712 above Balmaclellan is a good place to stop to look over to the motte (653793) which dominated the village below. It is clearly a largely artificial mound and is requiring urgent repairs to prevent further erosion. In the village the church (about 1750, rebuilt 1835) is probably on an earlier site. The churchyard has some

The Robert Paterson or 'Old Mortality' statue in Balmaclellan opposite Corrie's.

eighteenth-century stones with guild and other symbols and a plain monument to five men who died in the Crimean War. The old school beyond the churchyard is now the premises of the Galloway Clog Company.

Do walk through Balmaclellan village and do not miss the two statues of Robert Paterson or 'Old Mortality' (1712-1800) behind the petrol pumps opposite Corrie's. The upright figure is a very fine portrayal of him as a tough peasant. You might consider here whether the repetitive, indeed unvarying, and crudely one-sided formula used by Paterson when cutting the stone slabs you see all over the south-west of Scotland to commemorate episodes in the 'Killing Times' is likely to be reliable evidence of actual events or rather reflects the fanaticism of one group and its followers. There is another statue near The Holme (645796), the nineteenth-century house north of the village, of Old Mortality and his pony, which is a twin to that at Dumfries Museum.

From Balmaclellan go down the hill to the A713 at John Rennie's Ken Bridge (640783), a five-arch granite structure built in 1822. There were two earlier bridges between 1796 and 1813, both swept away by the river. Previously the crossing was by a ferryboat beside the inn, formerly called the Spalding Arms, or by the ford at Cubbox Isle (642773). Elspeth McEwen from Bogha near Cubbox was examined before Dalry Kirk Session in 1696 and then by a Privy Council Commission, and having been found guilty of being a witch was strangled and burnt in a tar barrel in Kirkcudbright on August 24, 1698. Note the standing stone on Dalarran Holm (639791).

Go back up the A712 towards Balmaclellan and turn left onto the A769 passing the lodge for The Holme. Grennan Corn Mill (643802), where there has been a mill since 1506 at least, was rebuilt in 1835 and restored in 1979. There was another (fulling) mill powered by the burn below Holm Mill Bridge (646809), and there is evidence of lead-mining activity beside the Garple Burn above the bridge. Jean's Wa's (649806) is another deserted settlement—whether the name relates to an actual person is one of these placename mysteries usually better left alone. The house on the right just before Trolane Bridge is the former Bogue Free Church manse (now called Garpol Linn). There is another probably mediaeval chapel site on Bogue above the Trolane Burn at 642817 north of the Fiddlers Bog and the Brownies Green. The Tower Moat (637818) seems to be natural. There is another old corn mill site at Gordieston (656816) above the bridge on the A702; and turning west towards Dalry—a wonderful landscape in all seasons—you pass Moss Roddock Loch, a resort for curlers in the winter. Walkers who prefer to stick to the Southern Upland Way can follow it from Dalry north-east to Ardoch (633832), the site of another old corn mill, and hence north to the Lochinvar road.

St John's Town of Dalry is almost too idyllic with its well-kept houses with granite or painted frontages and its manicured gardens and the exquisite vistas. The most important place is the motte (618813) behind the Town Hall (1858) and above the Stepping Stones path down to the river and the footbridge for the Southern Upland Way. It is a big motte. You need to see it from the west bank of the river or be on the summit to appreciate its size. The ditch incidentally is wetter in places than it looks! The ferry below at Boatweil and the Kirk Ford were used for crossing the river until a bridge was built at Allangibbon in 1800. There were other fords at Waterside, Glenlee, Saughtree and Boat Knowe. The church (1770, rebuilt 1831) is adjacent to the earlier (1564) structure. The old manse (1784, rebuilt 1828) round the corner on the main road is a fine example of its type. The churchyard has some good stones. The upright to James Douglas, 1747, with tools and guild cap is the best. The houses in the upper part of the village at Midtown were in an area which had developed before the lower end at Underhill was feued out by the Earl of Galloway in the eighteenth century.

Ernest E. Briggs' *Angling and Art in Scotland* (1908) includes plates of his delicate watercolours of Dalry and the Glenkens. The vast output of members of the Trotter family of New Galloway, Dalry and Dalshangan includes some very worthwhile and some (unintentionally) diverting material. Look for the hilarious *Lowran Castle* (1822), a collection of tall tales including 'The Gold Wells of Cairnsmore', 'The Witch of Hannayston', 'The White Snake of Dalry Moat', and 'The Fairy Horsemen of Holm Glen', and, amongst some truly dreadful novels, *Derwentwater* (1825), all by Dr Robert Trotter (1798-1875); the *Memoirs of the late Robert Trotter* (1736-1815) (1822) by his talented daughter Isabella Trotter (1796-1847); *Galloway Gossip...Wigtownshire* (1877 or 1878 editions) and *Galloway Gossip... the Stewartry* (1901) compiled by Dr Robert de Bruce Trotter (1833-1907); the *East Galloway Sketches* (1901) and the 1856 journal, *To the Greenland Whaling* (1979) by Dr Alexander Trotter (1835-1901); and *The Clachan Fair* (1872) by Dr James Trotter (1842-1899).

From Dalry take the A713 to the side road at Milton Park Hotel up to the B7000 near Blawquhairn. Earlston Castle (612840) in the estate to the west is another L-plan tower house, with a very attractive stairway turret. It was built for William Gordon in 1665. Old placenames nearby include Fumart Liggat, Gallows Glen and Widows Leys. Continue north by Todstone, Barlaes Hill, where there is a nineteenth-century slate quarry (623856), and as far north as the SYHA hostel for the splendid views over to Glenhaul (608878) and Kendoon village. Retrace your steps on the B7000 to take the fine moorland road with passing places at 618857. There are deserted settlements at Cleughhead (621866) and Chapelyard (622864) north of the Ministers Moss. After Mackliston you can link up with the Southern Upland Way on the road to Butterhole Bridge and then walk over Culmark Hill (near a Bronze Age cairn at 634895) to Stroangreggan. There is a cairnfield area on Glenshimmeroch (644880). Continue on the Lochinvar road by Corseglass Bridge (641858), where there used to be a school, and by the Peat Rig north of Corseglass Hill to Lochinvar. Lochinvar Castle (658854) was on an island towards the north end of the loch. 'Young Lochinvar' in Scott's *Marmion* may still be coming 'out of the west', but you are unlikely to see anything now of the island as it is completely covered by the water level of the modern reservoir. Continue south by Duchrae, where a cup and ring marking was found on a rock outcrop at 661837 towards Knockman Loch, and Lochinvar Filter Station and Milnmark to the A702.

Take the A702 north-east by Corriedoo Forest towards Moniaive. The Bronze Age White Cairn (681833) is to the east of the Regland Burn. Continue by Holmhead and the Blackmark Burn towards Lochrinnie and the Minnygryle Burn. The twelfth-century castle mound at Lochrinnie (728871) is unusual with a rectangular motte and a triangular bailey. There is a chapel site to the west. It is very remote from the Glenkens and should probably be seen as one of the group of mottes in the Glencairn-Moniaive area including the fine examples at Ingleston (799899) and Maxwelton (817896). Moniaive, the old terminus of the Cairn Valley Light Railway (1905-1943), is a good stopping-place—a charming village with a Mercat Cross (1638) and interesting hotels. To the east Maxwelton House on the estate bought by the Dumfries merchant, Stephen Lawrie, in 1611 is well known because of its romantic associations with the Annie Lawrie (1682-1764) of the song by William Douglas. The garden, chapel and museum are open at times which you should confirm with a Tourist Information Office.

From Moniaive village test out your car engine and your passengers' nerves by driving straight up the hill near the bridge on the A702 by Hillhead for Tynron village and the spectacular Tynron Doon (820939), which has a history of occupation from Iron Age hill fort to sixteenth-century tower house. You might find something to enjoy in the sprawling volume of essays and pieces by James Shaw of Tynron, which was edited by Robert Wallace with the title *A Country Schoolmaster* (1899). Another walk or drive is along the road up the Dalwhat Water from Moniaive by Craigdarroch, *the* farm centre to see what well-dressed sheep are wearing in winter, that is polypropylene coats which retain body heat, and into the hills at Benbuie and Cairnhead.

From Moniaive take the B729 Carsphairn road by Dungalston, Knockaughley, Auchenstroan and Carroch to the Stroanfreggan Burn south of Cornharrow, where there is a cairnfield (661929), and Manquhill. Note in this valley and further north at Dalquhairn and also between Carsphairn and Lamford the number of green glacial mounds. Stroanfreggan is an interesting area with evidence of occupation over the centuries from the denuded Bronze Age cairn (640914) and cairnfield (647934) to the Iron Age hill fort (637920) on the ridge above the Smeaton Burn and the pagan and Christian Dark Age sanctuary site at the Image Pool (644916) below Stroanfreggan Bridge and the former school. Walkers can take the Southern Upland Way over Manquhill Hill or the road by Craigengillan, Polifferie Bridge and Strahanna to Dalquhairn and Lorg. Note the site of a Bronze Age cairn (657988) between the Spout Burn and the road south of the Washing Pool Bridge over the Water of Ken, a cairnfield at NS645006, the 'Whigs Hole' on Altyre Hill (NS670002), a natural hollow by tradition used as a place of concealment and for holding conventicles, and the galena mine shaft at Clennochburn (NS622006). Placenames near the Clennoch Burn include the Shoulder of Mulbane and the Hags of Poljargen. The track marked on the O.S. 1853 maps south of Coranbae Hill as a 'Roman Road' and then west from Nether Holm of Dalquhairn as a 'footpath' may be the line of a Roman or mediaeval pony trail from Nithsdale towards Ayrshire.

Take the B729 from Smeaton Bridge to the junction with the B7000. Do not miss the High Bridge of Ken (619901), a splendid narrow two-arch bridge rebuilt in 1745-1746. The bend in the Water of Ken below has the odd name of College Brow. The B729 is most pleasant by car or on foot. Walkers can use the (infrequent) Castle-Douglas to Dalmellington bus service on the A713 either at Carsphairn or by using the metal bridge near Carminnow (606908). Going north on the B729 you pass Knockgray, which has a cross from Kirkinner in the garden, brought here about 1887 in an exchange of items of antiquarian interest. Carsphairn village is quite charming. The parish church (c. 1815) is a simple building in white, and the churchyard, with delightful views south and west, includes the burial enclosure of the McAdams of Waterhead. Lagwine (558938) is the site of a McAdam tower house, and there is a Bronze Age cairn site behind at 560939. The deep Green Well of Scotland (557945) on the Water of Deugh was probably a holy well. The 1853 O.S. map marks the site of Bank Mill just above it, and a 'Midgie Ha' and a 'Willies Cave', making an extraordinary group of placenames. The irregular circle with thirteen stones near Holm of Daltallochan (553942) is not too convincing, but probably was what it is generally assumed to be. The garden at the farmhouse (555942) has a simple tenth or eleventh-century wayside cross.

The Woodhead lead mines (532936) on the Garryhorn Burn were worked between 1839 and 1873. As many as 300 people may have been in the valley in the busiest years. There are the remains or sites of at least eleven deep vertical shafts, long horizontal adits, a complex lade and sluice system, a thirty-foot water wheel at the crushing plant, smelting houses with high chimneys, a powder magazine and belfry post, roads for carts and pack horses, rows of miners' cottages and a school, and a Free Church chapel at Lamloch (524962). The workings and spoilheaps are fascinating, but it is obviously important that visitors, as on all estates and farms, should take local advice on access and exercise discretion in approaching these and other mining locations with vertical shafts and other potentially dangerous areas. The haematite mine, or rather trial shaft, at Coran of Portmark (503938) is amazingly inaccessible.

To explore Loch Doon you have to venture into Cumnock and Doon District of Strathclyde Region. Take the A713 north by Lamford and Polnaskie Bridge to the side road at NS493040 and then the long drive down the west shore of the loch. If in Glasgow make a point of visiting the Hunterian Museum in the University to see the two huge dug-out canoes from Loch Doon. They are a vivid reminder of how strange (to us) life must have been here many centuries ago. Loch Doon Castle (484950), a thirteenth-century enclosure castle with an eleven-sided curtain wall, was moved from its island site in 1935 when the level of the loch was raised by up to forty feet as part of the hydro-electric scheme. The quality of the ashlar masonry and the pointed doorway is impressive.

The Loch Doon School of Aerial Gunnery, the centrepiece of a scandal of epic proportions between 1916 and 1918, involved a plan to train pilots of planes based at Bogton Aerodrome near Dalmellington by attacking targets moving on a monorail system on Cullendoch and Craigencolon, the hills on the south-east of the loch. The construction phase alone, including a daft attempt to build an airfield near the Garpol Burn, cost enormous sums of money, and in the end the whole plan had to be abandoned as a catastrophic failure. For the full story see Peter Connon's *An Aeronautical History of Cumbria, Dumfries and Galloway Region* (1984).

Do go on to Dalmellington to climb up the motte (NS482058), possibly the *caput* for a lordship including Carsphairn, and the museum in the weavers' cottages built in 1744. Continue on the A713 to Waterside to see from the road the remains of the Iron Works at Dunaskin, closed in 1921, and the complex railway network serving the coal mines. David L. Smith's *The Dalmellington Iron Company* (1967) is an excellent and very readable book. Just outside Dalmellington take the Gateside Road at NS472062 and turn left by Sillyhole and beyond the old Minnevey Coal Mine, now the centre of the Ayrshire Railway Preservation Group's Museum of Locomotives, and take the pot-holed road straight up Craigmark Hill and then left as far as the cattle grid (NS465084). From up here you have a

The tenth/eleventh-century wayside cross from Dalshangan now in the garden behind Broughton House in Kirkcudbright.

magnificent view of Minnevey and Bogton and the whole decaying industrial landscape. Gluttons for punishment should take the B741 road from Dalmellington to New Cumnock where you go through a modern ravaged landscape of conifer plantations and open-cast coal mining.

To explore the rest of Carsphairn and Kells return by the A713 to Carsphairn and south by Dalshangan to Polmaddie. The wayside cross from Dalshangan is now in the Japanese garden behind Broughton House in Kirkcudbright. The mediaeval and eighteenth-century deserted village and ferm-toun complex at Polmaddie (590878) is well worth studying. Take the forestry road from the A713 and cross the burn by the footbridge or at the Cumling Ford, on the line of the bridle track or pack road running through Polmaddie and then north to Braidenoch Hill, or at the Ballensack Ford just upstream. Look for the walls of the inn at Nether Ward on the pack road to the east of the site, the corn mill with dam and lade, four or five corn kilns (the best-preserved above the burn over on the west side), three or four groups of houses (including a smithy) with vegetable or kale yards, and rig and furrow lines in the field land. The pack road runs north-west to Braidenoch Hill, where there are two tenth or eleventh-century wayside crosses (571908). There is also a good deal of evidence of Bronze Age occupation and activity in the area, with a round cairn and a ring cairn and a cairnfield on the Braidenoch and Bardennoch Hills. Further north Cairn Avel (559924) above the Water of Deugh is a long cairn.

Take the A713 south from Polmaddie by Stroangassel and Knocknalling to Polharrow Bridge, and walk up the road by Crummy Bridge, Stroanfasket and Dukieston to Burnhead Bridge below Forrest Lodge. There is the site of a saw mill (591843) in the gorge beside Crummy Bridge and of a smithy just above the bridge at Burnclose. There is an extensive cairnfield area on Knockreoch (575863). Old settlements include Aitkin's Wa's east of Nether Knockreoch and Altibeastie on Adams Burn in the forest south of Burnhead. The 1853 O.S. map marks Pulharrow School at Woodfoot on the A713 at the Knocknalling Estate entrance, but the later school was at Gateside west of the Crummy Bridge. Note the eight-foot-high figurehead from the Olsen Shipping Line 'Black Watch' in the grounds of Forrest Lodge.

Continue south from Polharrow Bridge to Allangibbon Bridge and then take the A762 by Waterside to Coom Bridge near Glenlee. Take the side road by Glenlee Bridge and Garroch Sawmill (602813) to Knocksheen and Drumbuie. Hill walkers may wish to continue by the old settlement at Allwhillam to Clenrie and the Rhinns of Kells range. From Glenlee take the side road by the Craigshinne Burn (lead-mining adit in the forest at 585793) to join the Old Edinburgh Road and the A712 Newton Stewart road near Clatteringshaws. The Bruce Stone marks a skirmish at Moss Raploch in 1307—the probable site is, like the Old Edinburgh Road, covered by Clatteringshaws Reservoir. Note the huge dam completed in 1935 and the old bridge (1790) below. For details of the hydro-electric scheme at Glenlee and Clatteringshaws see George Hill, *Tunnel and Dam* (1984). Do visit the *Galloway Deer Museum* and perhaps try the Forest Drive (or walk) following the line of the River Dee to the east through Cairn Edward Forest.

Take the A712 towards New Galloway joining the line of the Old Edinburgh Road again at 613775. Note the old waulkmill location (621772)

The Adam and Eve upright (1707) for Robert Corson and his wife Agnes Herese and their nine children. In Kells Churchyard.

above the Knocknairling Burn and the site of an extensive mill dam at 623778 on the west side of the A712 beyond Achie Cottage, and the old churchyard site (621780) west of the site of Damcroft and east of Upper Achie farm. The minor road east of Achie Cottage is the Old Edinburgh Road line into New Galloway and then down Katie's Vennel beside the Kenmure Arms Hotel towards the Ken Bridge or to the Cubbox Ford. The present Kells Church (1822) is at 632783 on the A762 towards Glenlee. New Galloway itself was founded as a royal burgh under the charter of 1630 granted to Sir John Gordon of Lochinvar, so it is in a sense a new town compared to Dalry or Balmaclellan. It is, of course, probable that there was an earlier clachan between the town and Kenmure Castle or at the ford. Several excellent walking circuits are obviously possible using the A762, A712 and the Old Edinburgh Road. Do not miss Kells churchyard, one of the best in Galloway, with three Adam and Eve stones of 1706-1707 and the delightful upright for Captain Gordon's gamekeeper, John Murray.

Kenmure Castle (635764) on a magnificent natural hill with water defences must probably have been the site of a mediaeval castle. The sixteenth to nineteenth-century buildings erected by the Gordons are now in a very dangerous state and should be ignored. You will still spot the ice house near the entrance on the A762, but little remains of the old formal gardens, and the canals and moat are difficult to follow. Little Kenmure (638756) in the marshes south of Kenmure Holms might possibly be an earlier castle site.

Robert Heron (1764-1807) of New Galloway, historian, geographer, working editor of Sir John Sinclair's *Statistical Account of Scotland,* and the first biographer of Burns, may have been a failure by his own standards, but he achieved a great deal from inauspicious beginnings. Do read his travel book, *Observations made in a Journey through the Western Counties of Scotland* (1793).

Take the A762 from New Galloway by Lowran Bridge and Lochside of Ken to Mossdale (the former New Galloway railway station). The Burned Island (657728) in Loch Ken is a possible crannog. The cairn on Cairn Edward Hill (628733) is probably Bronze Age. Hard walking is possible on the old railway line by Loch Skerrow, the Big Water of Fleet Viaduct and the Clints of Dromore to the B796 north of Gatehouse-of-Fleet, or a short pleasant walk on the Airds of Kells road east of Mossdale.

Going south on the A762 you are now in Balmaghie parish again. Holland Isle amongst the Black Water of Dee to the west has the site of a corn mill (660696), perhaps once used by the people from the settlements to the north at Clachrum and Boddon's Folly or from the Duchrae (Hensol) Estate farms. The earthwork above the road at Little Duchrae (663696) may be a ringwork or a later mediaeval moated site. The road at Crae Bridge by Banks of Dee farm to Slogarie Bridge (653688) is a pleasant stroll. The A762 soon runs parallel with Woodhall Loch, or Loch Grennoch. Blates Mill (676668), with a large mill dam above, was the site of a corn mill at least as far back as the seventeenth century. Continue by Urioch, Laurieston Hall or Woodhall, and North Quintespie to Laurieston village, or Clachanpluck to give it the old eighteenth-century name. The Crockett Memorial here was erected in 1932. The O.S. 1852 map includes a corn mill and Bessy's Steps sawmill in the village.

Ornithologists should take the circuit from the A762 at Willowbank by Mains of Duchrae, Livingston, Balmaghie Church, Glenlochar and the B795 back to Laurieston. The C road through Laurieston Forest by

Lochenbreck, the site of a spa and well for stomach disorders and a hotel pre-1914, and Grobdale of Balmaghie is a splendid drive or trek. To the south there are Iron Age and/or Dark Age forts at Craig Hill or Lochengower (691660), Dinnance (674637) and Edgarton (673630), and an island crannog or fort at Bargatton Loch (695618).

CHAPTER 14

Tongland, Rerrick, Kirkcudbright, Twynholm and Borgue

Continuing on the A762 from Laurieston towards Ringford in Tongland parish you are soon into the fertile landscapes which are rich in the evidence of man's past from cup and ring markings and Iron Age forts to castles and abbeys and defended homesteads and manors. There is a minor prehistoric complex west of Loch Mannoch with a cairn and a circle site (662614) with eleven stones now largely under the ground and a large block in the centre, and a standing stone (663609). Kirkconnell Linn (673612) on the Water of Tarff is a fifty-foot waterfall. Kirkconnell farm (675602) is possibly the site of the tower house of the Covenanter William Gordon, and there is another Martyrs Monument erected in 1831 on Kirkconnel Moor (667598) north of the 'Towers of Kirkconnell'. Note 'Pharaoh's Throne' (661589) on Little Culcaigrie Hill—a very odd placename. Barstobric Hill (687606) to the east has the slight remains of an eight-acre hill fort, and the monument to James Beaumont 'Hot Blast' Neilson.

Continue on the A762 by Leggatecheek and New Mills through Dullarg Wood by Rummel Dhu to Ringford, formerly 'the village of the Red Lion'. Dunjop (710604) earthwork might be Iron Age or mediaeval. The rectangular enclosure at Fellend or Queenshill (689590) west of Culquha and to the east of a little burn may be the site of a moated manor or farm with ditch and bank defences. From Ringford take the A75 by Meiklewood and the former Tarff Station on the dismantled Castle-Douglas to Kirkcudbright railway line (1864) and the A762 passing Chapel, Underwood and the old single-arch Low Bridge of Tarff to Tongland. The hill fort on Bar Hill (689544) has the sort of impenetrable mass of thorns and brambles that can be guaranteed to give you a ripping time.

There is another Iron Age fort, Carse 'mote' (695533), above the Dee on the east of the river, and a possible motte at Culdoach (706537) reached over the 1737-1740 bridge at 697536. The disused (1813) parish church is the site of Tongland Abbey (698539), the Premonstratensian house founded in 1218 from Cockersand. Nothing is left of the buildings except a doorway in the small ruined post-Reformation church and a few fragments of sculptured stones including one with a kirtled figure carrying a club at the Meikle Yett Nursery. Abbot John Damian, 'the frenzied friar of Tongland', achieved a sort of immortality as Scotland's first airman (failed) when he attempted to fly from the ramparts of Stirling Castle in 1507.

Tongland Bridge (1805) and the railway bridge on the Kirkcudbright to Castle-Douglas line behind.

The superb 1804-1808 bridge (692533) with a hundred and ten feet arch and three narrow arches on either side is by Telford. Note upriver the piers of the railway bridge. Sloops and schooners of up to forty tons used to come up to Melville Port (690532) and the High Birth Port below the bridge on the south side of the river, and indeed the old bridge of 1868-1926 at Kirkcudbright had a centre section which opened to let shipping go on up to Tongland. The doachs and the salmon fishermen using shoulder, draught and ladle nets are now only a memory to study in old photographs and accounts, and instead the area is dominated now by the *Tongland Hydro-Electric Power Station* completed in 1934-1935 for the Galloway Power Company. The SSEB offer guided tours of the dam, fish ladder and turbine hall. Although a plan in 1790 to turn the clachan of Tongland into a new town failed, nevertheless over the last two hundred years a succession of industries have been located on the river here from corn, farina, paper and saw mills to Gillone's biscuit factory and, in the 1920s, the Galloway Motor Works. The Galloway two-seater, by Arrol-Johnston of Dumfries and Tongland, cost in 1924 the very considerable sum of £250. You can see one in the Glasgow Museum of Transport.

Take the A711 into Kirkcudbright (pronounce 'Cur-coo-bree') to the Moat Brae, probably originally a motte, at the end of the long L-ridge of the High Street above what was once the harbour creek ten feet under the present car park and above tidal marshland where there are now houses and grassland between St. Cuthbert Street, St. Mary Street and the High Street. The mediaeval town was on something in the nature of a promontory or even island site with walls, gates, ditches and banks from the Water Gate, at Moatwell House, and Moat Brae behind the gardens on the east side of Castle Street by the Meikle Yett near the Selkirk Arms and back behind the L of the High Street. The cluster of churches and religious houses and castles in and around Kirkcudbright marks stages in the development of the town from the twelfth to the sixteenth centuries. The first record is probably the account of the visit of Ailred of Rievaulx on 20 March, 1165; the most dramatic the successful defence against a detachment of the English army of invasion in February 1547.

At Moat Brae, Greyfriars Church incorporating part of the Franciscan priory church (1455) was used as a parish church until 1838, as the Castle School, and after restoration by P. McGregor Chalmers in 1922 by the Scottish Episcopal Church. Inside, the Maclellan monument (1597) is a magnificent example of a Renaissance altar tomb with a Gothic figure in full armour, classical architectural details and conventional symbolism. *Maclellans Castle,* built by Sir Thomas Maclellan of Bombie between 1569 and 1582, is a large town house on a complex variation of the L plan, domestic architecture in the castle style with turrets and gunloops to express the status of the occupants. Auchengool House (1-3 Castlebank) may have been the town house of the McCullochs. The group of old buildings and warehouses, including Shore House, the Old Granary, the *Harbour Cottage Gallery,* and Greyfriars House, are outstanding—photograph in the setting sun for superb colour effects.

The High Street and the closes off it are a fascinating mixture of elegant and refined and merely cosy mainly eighteenth and early nineteenth-century houses. The group from Moatwell House to Broughton House and 14, 16 and 18 High Street, and 1, 2, 5, 19, 23-25 High Street, and Atkinson Close, Hart's Close and Greengate Close are charming. E. A. Taylor and Jessie M. King lived and worked at 46 High Street and E. A. Hornel at *Broughton House,* the early eighteenth-century town house of the Murrays of Broughton. Hornel's garden, with Scottish kitchen and Japanese themes and featuring the Dalshangan Cross, is a delight, and the house contains a marvellous collection of books and manuscripts. Hornel (1864-1933) and King (1875-1949) are the best-known 'Kirkcudbright artists'; E. A. Taylor, Wm. Mouncey, Bessie MacNicol, W. S. MacGeorge, John Copland, Wm. H. Clarke, Phyllis Bone, Charles Oppenheimer and Anna Hotchkiss are among the galaxy of those who have worked in the town. Jessie M. King of the faery knights and pale ladies on book jackets and in

A print of Kirkcudbright from a drawing by Alexander Reid (1747-1823), who was more famous as a portrait painter, and published in London in 1792. Note the warehouses, some evidence of shipbuilding at Moat Brae, and the landing place on the mudbank on the left.

illustrations for children's stories and plays and small volumes of all kinds, for example *The Little White Town of Never Weary,* is now a major international figure. Hornel, best known for his gorgeous little girls frolicking in springy blossoms in Japan or Galloway, is very much in favour again with dealers and collectors. Don't, however, underestimate him as his early work is very interesting. 'In the Town Crofts, Kirkcudbright' (1885), 'The Kirkcudbright Stick Gatherers' (1888), 'The Bell Ringer' (1886), 'Pigs' (1887), 'Green girl in white and bronze' (1888) and 'The Brownie of Blednoch' (1889) are great stuff, and the early joint work with G. A. Henry, 'The Star in the East' (1891) and 'The Druids: Bringing in the Mistletoe' (1890), is important. The last three are in the Kelvingrove Art Gallery in Glasgow, as are the marvellous Henry 'A Galloway Landscape' (1889) and Sir James Guthrie's superb 'Old Willie—A Village Worthy' (Kirkcudbright 1886). Don't miss them.

The lane beside Broughton House takes you down to the river and along to Castledykes (6771 5088), the grass-covered mounds of the four corner towers and wide ditch of the massive later thirteenth-century courtyard castle, occupied perhaps between 1288 and 1307, and excavated in 1911-1913. Finds included pottery from the English Midlands and south-west France. Edward I probably stayed here between 19 and 31 July, 1300. Take the path and road by Castlemains and Kirkcudbright Academy, on the present site since 1818, back to the High Street at the Tolbooth. The Tolbooth was built after 1579, with repairs and alterations in 1591, 1625 and 1751. Note the jougs (iron manacles) to which vandals and petty criminals were handcuffed for public chastisement—still a splendid idea—and the market cross (1610) in front. The group of seventeenth-century buildings east of the Tolbooth, the Tolbooth Gallery, Ironstanes and Milroy's Close and 74 High Street and Cannon's Close, and the eighteenth-century 76-84 High Street are exceptionally good.

St. Andrew's and St. Cuthbert's Catholic Church (1886) contains a fine Stations of the Cross by Vivien Redpath. Castle Street and Union Street are part of the later eighteenth and early nineteenth-century 'new town'. Further along the High Street note the two socket stones in the pavement on the site of the Meikle Yett demolished in 1771, and the Selkirk Arms, an hotel since 1777, which has in the garden behind a large fifteenth-century font from Dundrennan Abbey previously used in an outhouse at Bombie, as a stepping stone in the Buckland Burn and as a water-trough at St. Mary's Isle! In St. Mary Street round the corner don't miss the excellent and lively *Stewartry Museum,* with outside the Kirkandrews Cross, the Dunrod font and casts of the High Banks cup and ring markings, and inside a superb collection of photographs, models, Jessie M. King books, shipping records, material on Paul Jones and on Thomas Douglas (1771-1820), the fifth Earl of Selkirk (of Red River Settlement in Manitoba, Canada fame), and much more. The Church of Scotland church by William Burn (1838) has Kirkcudbright's own 'leaning tower', hardly surprising given that the old soaperie and eight tanpits were located nearby and that the whole area was once swampland.

The Augustinian priory of Trail or Trellesholm on St. Mary's Isle was founded before 1220, possibly on the site of an earlier Celtic monastery. The location was probably close to or under the eighteenth-century house looted by Paul Jones on 23 April, 1778 and the 1897 house later destroyed in a fire. Both this site (675492) and possibly also Inch Island (671483) need detailed study and possible excavation. The map references to the Great Cross and the Little Cross refer to long-lost monuments.

Do visit the Old (Corn) Mill Pottery with the lade system running down Shillinghill behind, and take the footpath on to the B727 up to St. Cuthbert's Churchyard, with grand views over the Dee valley. Note the ornate Renaissance Ewart monument at the entrance and the large number of seventeenth, eighteenth and nineteenth-century stones with conventional symbolism and the trade tools of hammermen and shoemakers, the upright for William Marshall (1792) and more Covenanting martyr monuments. On the B727—good walking circuits by Whinnieliggate and Meikle Sypland and the Buckland Glen—you pass the drained Loch Fergus meadowland with, at the north end, Palace Isle (698511), traditionally the site of Fergus of Galloway's 'palitium', and at the south end Stable Isle (698507) with the remains of a long rectangular building. Brockloch (707517) farmhouse may be on a homestead moat site. The old grassy road beside it goes past the lochan to the south-east to Meikle Sypland. At the B727 just beyond the site of Whinnyliggate Loch turn south-east by the former Whinnyliggate School and Camphill (717519), where there is a good example next to the road of a rectangular moated manor or homestead moat; and there is another similar and larger site at 714518. There is a hill fort to the west of Meikle Sypland (709512) and the site of St. Michael's Church (730512) in St. Michael's Glen south-east of Balgreddan. Kirkland (704507), east of the Glenley Burn, is another possible mediaeval farm site. Take the road to the left (north-east) at Buckland Bridge. The important cup and ring marked rock surface at High Banks (709489) is in a field south-east of the farm. There is another rectangular homestead moat at Clownstane (708502), north-east of Clownstane Bridge. The Maclellan castle site at Bombie in the glen above the Gribdae Burn (715505) may be on an earlier ringwork.

Continue into Rerrick parish by Noggie, Auchengool and the road north by Drumboy Bridge (743495) and then east towards the Kirkcarswells, rather than the road by Auchnabony to Dundrennan. There is a cup and ring marked rock surface, difficult to find, on Newlaw Hill (733488). Note the unusual placename, the 'Old Man' (746502), east of Drumbuie Hill and south of the Loch Moss. You pass a small roughly circular earthwork fort on West Kirkcarswell (749495) and an oval hill fort (752497) north-west of East Kirkcarswell. Take the A711 east by Bankhead and Over Hazlefield, and then the side road from Drungans Bridge by Culnaightrie, east of Suie Hill fort (766508) towards Auchinleck. This quiet valley was a busy place by 1770 and especially in the middle of the nineteenth century with up to six shafts being worked for haematite. The iron ore from the Auchinleck mine (771526) was sent for smelting to Birmingham. On the hill ground above there are forts at Hess (766534) and Dungarry (758536). The road by Bluehill and Collin Mill Bridge takes you by the cemetery where a great man, Joseph Heughan (1837-1902), blacksmith, stonemason, bookbinder, cabinet-maker, linguist and poet, is buried. There are examples of his exquisite miniature ploughs and candleholders in the Stewartry Museum. The site of the Ring or Ringcroft of Stocking (791518) is now forgotten, but a malevolent spirit caused chaos and disasters here between February and May, 1695. The parish minister, Alex. Telfer, wrote an account of the affair in his pamphlet 'A New Confession of Sadducism . . .'(1696). More seriously in 1671 Elspeth Thomson from Glenshinnoch, accused by witnesses from Potterland, Screel, Rigg, Drongans, Bankhead, Kirkmirren and Rerrick, was burnt as a witch in Dumfries along with Janet Macmurdoch from Airds on Loch Ken.

Auchencairn, now a leisure and retirement orientated village, developed in the eighteenth and nineteenth centuries more because of the success of local mining and smuggling ventures than because of the mills (cotton, paper and woollen factories were attempted, and corn and sawmills established). The 1851 Census Enumeration Book lists the, mainly English, iron and barytes miners living in the cottages in the village. Hestan Island, accessible with care at low tide, has the site of Edward Balliol's fourteenth-century manor house or hall within an enclosure (838503) and two copper-mining shafts worked by a company which sent the ore to Swansea, again in the nineteenth century. The two enclosures on Seaside and Auchenfad (804508 and 805505) are small forts or Iron Age or mediaeval homesteads. Walking to Balcary Bay and Point you pass Balcary House, used as a base by the Manx smuggling syndicate of Clark, Grain and Quick, and raided by Inspector General Reid of Customs in December 1777. Note the old road south-west by Airds Cottage, formerly Guttery Liggat, to Loch Mackie. Take the Balcary Heughs cliff path by Lots Wife. There are forts at Adams Chair (819483) and on Big Airds Hill (814486), and evidence of barytes mining at Airds (817484).

Walk along the cliffs or take the road from Auchencairn and Moss Side to Rascarrel Bridge (799482), which has fragments of a sculptured stone in the parapet, and to Rascarrel Bay, where there is the site of a coal-mining shaft on the shore (809482). Castle Muir (796470) is a promontory fort between Rascarrel and Barlocco Bays. There was a barytes mine near Airyhill (788474), and the huge Black Cave (788467) and White Cave were traditionally smugglers' hiding places. There is a hill fort near Nether Hazelfield (786482).

On the A711 to Dundrennan take the side road by Heart Moss and Upper Rerrick. There are two cliff forts west of Orroland Heugh at Spouty Dennans (765457). On the road you pass St. Glassen's Well (759469) and then Rerrick Old Churchyard (760467) east of Fagra with the remains of the pre-Reformation chapel and post-Reformation parish church (in use to 1865). There are some good stones including one with a sweet trumpet-blowing angel. Continue by Fagra to Dundrennan village and turn right on the A711 to Barend or Stock Bridge before the road climbs up into Balmangan Glen. Kirkcarswell motte (754487) above the road was perhaps

The 'lost' village of Abbey Burnfoot in a postcard c.1906.

built about the same time as the abbey was founded. The rectangular platform area on the flat land below may have been a bailey and/or the site of the eighteenth-century Murray of Broughton mansion house.

Dundrennan Abbey (749475), founded in 1142, was a daughter house of Rievaulx and was visited in this capacity by Ailred in 1165. In the church the twelfth and thirteenth-century north and south transepts and the choir in the Norman and First Pointed style leave an impression of the quality, simplicity and clarity of early Cistercianism. Note the contrast in the more ornate late thirteenth-century chapter house and the remains of its six pillars and wall seating. The sculptured monuments are quite outstanding, in particular the figure of the murdered thirteenth-century abbot with his pastoral staff and his kilted assassin below with anatomical details; the fifteenth-century cellarer, Patrick Douglas; and the nun or wealthy lay patron (Devorgilla?). Note also the fine former Church of Scotland manse (1790 and later) to the south-west.

Continuing up the hill on the A711 you pass the road for Port Mary (753454). When open—it is at the edge of the Army Range 'Danger Area'—you pass the former Fagra corn mill (748467) and the site of the Nether Mill or Mill o' Kirns (744453). As a landing place Port Mary is very open to the sea, but it may have been used by the Cistercians and may be the place from which Queen Mary sailed to exile in England in 1568. Castleyards (753455) is a promontory fort and the Hanged (or Hangit) Man to the east is an arch of barytes. The coast from here west by Lovers Bower to Abbey Burnfoot and to Mullock Bay, Gipsy Point and Balmae Ha'en is not readily

174

accessible. Abbey Burnfoot (742447), earlier Netherlaw Burnfoot, developed in the second half of the last century as a community of eleven or twelve salmon fishermen's cottages and larger villas with a breakwater or quay and a grocer and coal merchant's shop. The village and Netherlaw House have now disappeared under the Range and survive only in photographs and memories. The 'Danger Area' from Townhead to Dundrennan was taken over by the Army during the War and is now an experimental and testing location for tank weapons and defences, especially armour plating, under the Armament Wing of the Military Vehicle Engineering Establishment (MVEE). Most of the land is let on grazing or farming tenancies, but for obvious reasons of safety and security is not open to visitors. Varying degrees of difficulty would be encountered going to Glenapp (727451), Craigraploch (724440) and Balig (719469) hill forts; the Maclellans' Raeberry Castle (699437) and St. Margaret's Well; the cup and ring markings on Howell (702457), Little Balmae (686447) and Townhead (698471); and Dunrod moated manor and mediaeval village site (699459) with extensive rig and furrow patterns, and the mediaeval church and the churchyard (699460).

Along the A711 there are Iron Age or mediaeval earthworks at Milton (703470) and North Milton (710480 and 706482). The rich and complex cup and ring markings on Galtway Hill are lost under the turf somewhere. The old parish church of Galtway (703485) and graveyard is south-east of Low Banks. The deserted mediaeval village site (707487) is marked on the O.S. 1854 six-inch map beside a small quarry on a plateau above the church and south of High Banks.

On the A711 coming down towards Kirkcudbright take the side road at 691484 south passing a good cup and ring marked rock outcrop with very deep cups at Grange (687471), Drummore Castle hill fort (687457), Torrs, The Battery (684463), the site of a fort removed in 1889, and The Lake to Mutehill (687486) on Manxman's Lake. And hence by Cannee (687501) or by Buckland Glen, haunted by a headless lady, and Orchard Bank Plantation to Buckland Bridge and by High Kirkland fort (692507) to Kirkcudbright.

To explore Twynholm and Borgue parishes start from the Low Bridge of Tarff (684541) above the channel of the Dee where the Mesolithic red deer leister-prong now in the Stewartry Museum was found. Aerial photography has shown up a settlement with triple ditches across the promontory above the Water of Tarff (683541). Cumstoun House (683533), built about 1824 on the west bank of the river, is placed between a fragment of the Kennedy, Maclellan and Dunbar tower house (682532) within the remains of a rectangular barmkin enclosure and a possible earlier mediaeval earthwork site on Castle Hill (684534). Next take the road west of the bridge and through the crossroads to Twynholm Church (1818) at 664542. One of the best things about Twynholm is that within a very small area you have a picture of the history of Galloway over the last thousand years. On the west the Doon Hill (660543) has a fine double-ditch and rampart hill fort, and there is a multivallate Dark Age fort on Campbelton (658539); and opposite the church and above the Kirk Burn there is a sweet little twelfth-century motte (663542) at the bottom of the garden. In the eighteenth century Twynholm was a busy mill village with a corn mill at Ashland and a sawmill and a waulk mill where woollen blankets and tweed were produced into the 1920s. Since the A75 bypass was completed the village has come into its own again as a place to live.

Barwhinnock (654549) to the north of the A75 is a wholly charming Georgian small house or 'bungalow' with a single-storey frontage and unusual windows. It was built in 1844 by Major Irving of the Bengal Cavalry. To the east on the A75 take the side road north by Redfield to Trostrie (656574), a very large motte, possibly with some evidence of later stone structures on top. It quite dominates the nearby farmhouse. The 'mote' at Culcaigrie (657575) is perhaps a smaller mediaeval earthwork. To the south-east the road by Mark and Lochhill takes you past Spout Glen and the Fairies Well beside Trostrie Lane. To the west there are cairns and hut circles and fort or settlement sites on Irelandton Moor.

On the A75 again continue west and take the A755 at Minto Cottage by Auchenhay Bridge towards Kirkcudbright. The magnificent de Moreville motte on Boreland of Borgue (646517) on the top of the hill to the north of the road is one of the most spectacular early castle sites anywhere in the south of Scotland. Aerial photographs suggest that there may be a bailey to the south-east. The little road at the crossroads (659518) down by Newton to Nun Mill is a delightful walk. Otherwise continue on the A755 and then take the B727 along the west bank of the Dee passing the site of a whisky distillery operating between about 1790 and 1820 near the old parish church of Kirkchrist (675514), Gibbs Hill Point, Kirkeoch, and Seaward and the Old Fish House cottage in Fish House Wood (663493) opposite the 'Slate Harbour' site on St. Mary's Isle. Walkers should confirm in Kirkcudbright whether the Borgue Post Bus Service is operating.

The Cistercian nunnery of St. Evoca founded before 1423 may have been close to the site of the old mill and the former Doon School at Nun Mill (659488). Other possible locations are at Kirkeoch farm or on Luskies Burn near the site of Nunton Castle. The Doon (657488), the Iron Age horseshoe-shaped fort in the trees at the top of the wooded precipice above Nun Mill or Doon Bay, has really huge double ditches and ramparts and an annexe at the south-east corner. Access is poor, but it could, if ever it were to be excavated and restored, be a site of major importance. Even at the moment it is one of the most impressive Iron Age promontory forts in Scotland. The wreck in the bay is the *Monrieth* of Wigtown which was grounded in a storm in 1900. Nunton Castle (648491) and the Witches Thorn lay to the east of Luskies Burn between the single-storey farm cottages at Low and High Nunton; the castle site is difficult to identify from the mounds and bumps now left in grassy pastureland.

Continue on the B727 to the side road for Ross Bay and Brighouse Bay. The field at Clauchendolly (643472) has a number of cup and ring markings including ovals and a dumb-bell. Senwick House is now an hotel, and both the building and the gardens are worth visiting. The old parish churchyard (655460) continued in use as a burial place long after the parish of Senwick was amalgamated with Borgue in 1618. It is unusual to find a fragment surviving beside it on the shore side of the pre-Reformation presbytery, which was also probably occupied by two post-Reformation 'readers'. The churchyard contains the mausoleum of the Blairs of Dunrod and the burial place of John Mactaggart, who died in 1830. Mactaggart, the author of the remarkable *Scottish Gallovidian Encyclopedia* (1824) and *Three Years in Canada* (1829), the latter arising from the time he spent as Clerk of Works to the Royal Engineers on the Rideau Canal, was brought up on Lennox Plunton and Torrs. His *Encyclopedia* is a great book, a dictionary of words and phrases and a collection of the children's games and songs and spells and customs and gossip of the area. If you don't know what 'allicomgreenzie, babie cloots, belly-timmer, bochle, clashbag, cutty-glies, dingle douzie, flaiper, gill-pies, gabbie labbie, jumpers, maillies, mowdiemen, peelaneets, troggs, wassocks' and many more words mean, then make a point of borrowing or purchasing, if still available in Kirkcudbright, a copy of the 1981 reprint edition. Anyone with a special interest in language and dialect should also read D. R. A. D. Riach of the University of Newfoundland's papers, based on surveys in 1971 and 1980, on Galloway dialect in the *Scottish Literary Journal* and in *Scottish Language* and his *Glossary of the Galloway Dialect* to be published by the Association for Scottish Literary Studies. Find out, for example, what Gallovidians mean by a 'scutt', a 'huggery', a 'tudderie', a 'slitter' and a 'clart'.

Continue by Balmangan, the site of a Maclellan tower house, to Ross Bay and Meikle Ross with the site of Manor Castle at 654443 to the north and Little Ross island to the south-east. Both Ross Bay and Brighouse Bay were used in the past as anchorages, and there are the remains of a jetty and breakwater at Rockvale (636452) on the eastern side of the latter. After returning to the B727 continue left by Culraven, Pringleton (the former Free Church manse) and Borgue House (in ruins) to Borgue village. Here the dominating building is probably Borgue Academy, founded in 1802 with an endowment from Thomas Rainy, who had left Carleton some fifty years before and made a sufficient fortune as a planter in Dominica. Under William Poole, the rector from 1803 to 1843, it achieved a reputation for sound and practical education and its boarding-house section attracted boys from all over the south-west of Scotland. The secondary department closed in 1947 and the building that is left is now the village primary school. Borgue Church (1814, with additions in 1889) had one outstanding minister between 1792 and 1816 in Samuel Smith, whose *General View of the Agriculture of Galloway* (1810) is one of the most sought-after Galloway books. The churchyard includes a fine stone for David McKissock (1763/1767) and the mausoleum of Lt. Col. Sir William Gordon of Earlston (1830-1906), who had the good fortune to be one of the magnificent men who made up the Six Hundred in the Charge of the Light Brigade at Balaclava in 1854. It is a very pleasant walk along the B727 north of the village by the former manse (1802) to Black Briggs.

G. O. Elder's *Borgue* (1897) is a highly readable short book with good dialect pieces; and the articles by I. A. N. Henderson in the issues of the *Scottish Field* in the 1970s describing boyhood days in Borgue have a delightfully whimsical touch, for example his description of a group of lassies from England coming to demonstrate 'Keep Fit' techniques to the ladies of the Borgue 'Rural'. However, the packman poet, William Nicholson (1783-1849), should also be mentioned, even although the collection of poetry published and sold by him in 1814 and more generally available in the 1897 edition published by Harper of Dalbeattie contains a great deal of flawed material. His best work, in particular *The Brownie of Blednoch*—
On his wauchlie arms three claws did meet
As they trail'd on the grun' by his taeless feet—
and parts of *The Country Lass, Johnny Gill, To Tobacco* and *The Braes of Galloway,* has some lively and memorable lines, perhaps some collected by him from older folk tradition while travelling through Galloway as a chapman. The bronze panel near the Academy by Shannon of Glasgow and based on the painting by John Faed was placed there in 1900.

From Borgue Church take the road west by Swine Drum and Chapelton Row. The coast from Brighouse Bay to Meggerland Point has fine cliff scenery at Borness and Muncraig. The most important fort is the Borness

Batteries promontory fort (621447) with the famous Bone Cave, which yielded Iron Age period bone combs and needles, at the head of the inlet below the cliffs and well above the present high water level. There are also forts at Manxman's Rock, Meikle Saddling Bay near the Dove Cave, Heugh Hill south-west of Muncraig and Barn Heugh. Inland take the road north-west from Chapelton Row to Barmagachan (613494), where there is a fine pudding-shaped motte beside the road and a small Maclellan seventeenth-century laird's house, with a steep and narrow gable-end, later converted into a farmhouse, on the rock platform to the west. Just north-west of Barmagachan take the road south by Rattra and Roberton motte (603485) beside the Pulwhirrin Burn. There are cup and ring markings with up to six rings beside the dyke on the south side of the road west of Tongue Croft (603483).

Kirkandrews churchyard (600481) is a very old site, probably pre-mediaeval and with links with the Celtic Church and Iona. The thirteenth? century cross from Kirkandrews is now outside the Stewartry Museum. The parish itself was amalgamated with Borgue in 1657. Churchyard stones include a typical Covenanting Martyr slab and an inferior and late (1790) Adam and Eve carving. Symson records that the old fair of St. Lawrence was held annually—an occasion for great debauchery—on 9 August in the kirkyard. Sailing ships came into a landing place in the bay (598480) to lie below the church. The village between the church and Balenstock Bridge included in the O.S. 1854 map Kirkandrews Corn Mill, Guttieside, Meggerland, Craighouse and Knockkennock. As seen today the castellated cottages belong to the 'Cow Palace' school of architecture most evident in the group of barns and stables and an eighty-foot water tower (which, in practice, did not work) at Corseyard (591485) built for James Brown of Knockbrex in the 1900s. Mr Brown also excavated and reconstructed in 1905 the D-shaped galleried dun at Castle Haven (594483), listed in one book as one of the '100 Wonders' of Britain. Unfortunately, the 'Borg', which it may be called as there is some evidence of Norse occupation, was so heavily rebuilt that such a rating is extravagant. However, it is an important example of Edwardian restoration of a specialised Iron Age stone fort.

Continue west looking over to Barlocco and Ardwall Islands and Murray's Isles. Knockbrex 'castle'—an amazing sight—was built in 1906 in the cow palace castellated style as the garage courtyard block, inspired by Warwick Castle, for Knockbrex House. The quay (582495) was probably built to take yachts in those splendid spacious days of conspicuous and unnecessary expenditure. Ardwall Island (573495) can be reached across the mud when the tide is out (remember that it does come in again!) from the Carrick road. Still used for grazing sheep, it has the site of a small monastic settlement beginning with an Irish seventh-century timber chapel and shrine, with on top an eighth-century chapel and enclosed cemetery, and a mediaeval hall house. The eleventh-century cross from the chapel site is at Ardwall House.

Walkers may continue to Sandgreen and Gatehouse-of-Fleet or cross Fleet Bay at low tide to Skyreburn or Mossyard Bay (but don't try to race the incoming tide). Otherwise from Knockbrex take the road north-east by Margrie and Lennox Plunton to the A75 at Barharrow. Plunton Castle (605507) is an L-plan McGhie and Lennox sixteenth-century tower house: it sits on a plateau which looks very like a major thirteenth-century courtyard or moated manor site, possibly that of the de Campania family. Edward I may have stayed at Plumptone from 16 April to 2 May, 1297. More exciting still, the Plunton bronze armlet of about 160 A.D. was found nearby.

CHAPTER 15

Girthon, Gatehouse-of-Fleet, Anwoth, Kirkmabreck and Creetown

There are probably more romantic ruins, sweet seascapes and idyllic wooded landscapes and hills with great stone dykes toiling up them between Girthon and Palnure than in any other corner of Galloway. The fascination of the coastal strip is well-known, but the hinterland and the old tracks and roads which take the high ground are also well worth exploring.

Approaching Gatehouse-of-Fleet from the east, do consider taking the high road off the A75 west of Twynholm by Muiryard, Tannymass and Townhead. This has fine vistas and allows you to avoid the new bypass speed track from between Barluka and Conchieton straight through Enrick and Cally Park to the Fleet west of Cardoness Castle. And from Lennox Plunton take the road by Rainton and the site of the Miln of the Laick (599528) at Garniemire south-east of Syllodioch to Girthon. The partly pre-Reformation church on the knoll at Girthon (605533), reconstructed in the seventeenth century and in use up to 1818, has a fine piscina in the south wall. The adjacent farmhouse of Girthon Kirk was the manse until 1795. In the churchyard note at the east end of the church the upright to Robert Glover (1775), a gardener on Cally estate, with spade, rake and hoe. The clachan of Girthon, with single-storey cottages and the former smithy near a little single-arch bridge, makes a charming group. Walk into the Cally estate at Bar Hill to look for the amusing Gothic folly called 'The Temple' (606543), built as a 'ruin' in 1778. There are also lead-mining shafts in the Bar Hill wood (603541).

Palace Yard (614544) is the best example in Galloway of a thirteenth or fourteenth-century moated manor site. A clear oval ditch and bank surround a large central area with at the east end the foundations of the pre-Reformation palace/hall of the Bishops of Galloway. Edward I almost certainly stayed here on 9 August, 1300, when he made an oblation at the church and, exercising the sort of power a Tourist Board should have today, fined the tenant of the mill 13s 4d for 'irregularities'. North of Enrick there is the site of the once-famous copper mines (619549) worked between 1819 and 1857 by a Cornish company which shipped the ore out from the Fleet to Llanelly and Swansea. One shaft was two hundred and seventy feet deep by 1837. A speculative and expensive venture in re-opening the mine between

Gatehouse-of-Fleet from the Galla Hill in a print from a sketch by David Octavius Hill, more famous as a pioneer of photography. There is some romantic licence in the overall balance and effect, but the detail is interesting. Note the dam on the south side of the main road, the Scott cotton mill, and the bridge near Cardoness Castle. About 1840.

1908 and 1912 was not a success. Continue into Gatehouse on the old A75, passing the road—a pleasant evening walk—by Girthon Old Manse (610561), the manse from 1795 to 1946, for Disdow and Drumwall, and the old road and grassy track east-north-east from Drumwall by Irelandton Moor to Corse.

Although for a time the centre of the parish may have been at Girthon and Enrick, there is no doubt about the antiquity of the settlements in the river valley near the fords and bridges over the Fleet. This is clear from the evidence of the Roman fortlet north of Gatehouse (595574), excavated in 1960-61, and the Roman cobbled road leading down to the river discovered in 1984. The twelfth-century motte in Cally Park (606556) is in an excellent position to dominate the valley, and it is not impossible that there may have been a mediaeval 'town' or settlement of 'Flete' close to the river below. However, Gatehouse-of-Fleet itself is very much a planned town, laid out in the 1760s and developed as a centre of industry mainly from the 1780s by James Murray of Broughton (1727-1799), whose burgh of barony it became in 1795. Murray, educated in the Arts Faculty of the University of Glasgow between 1741 and 1745, is the classic example of the benevolent capitalist at work developing his vast estates, which extended over ten parishes in

Galloway, and creating modern improved, enclosed, productive and mutually profitable tenant farms. Appropriately his portrait by Reid is now at Chequers.

Cally House (600549), now the Cally Palace Country House Hotel, was originally, as designed by Robert Mylne and completed in 1763, a compact three-storey symmetrical house, albeit with large public rooms. The massive additions in 1835 have not reduced the charm of its setting between pleasure gardens and an artificial lake. The wooded policies and forest paths where there were once deer parks and orchards and little walks and bridges can be explored at leisure. The earlier Lennox and Murray tower house of Cally or Kelly (598554) is on what may well have been a strong marshland site with water defences close to the old line of the river. Note off the avenue from the Victorian baronial lodges the Fleet Forest Nursery and the Cally Cricket Ground. *The* classic Galloway cricket scorecard was recorded in the *Kirkcudbrightshire Advertiser* for 20 August, 1880:

Kirkcudbright v. Gatehouse, at Gatehouse-of-Fleet.

Kirkcudbright First innings 24.

Gatehouse-of-Fleet First innings 19 for 6.

Unfortunately a discussion arose as to a decision given by one of the umpires, and the game came to a sudden termination.

Today there is a certain irony in seeing the line of the bypass, as the old road line from Enrick to the Fleet through Cally Park to Ann Street was changed by the Cally Park (1812-1818) and the Galla Hill Cut (1819-1823) schemes, and the railway track planned to run through Girthon glebe had to be abandoned because of the opposition of Mr Murray Stewart of Cally (instead the expensive and inconvenient route by Dromore was opened in 1861).

For a most revealing perambulation concentrating on Gatehouse as an industrial centre between the 1780s and the 1850s start at the War Memorial (602565) in front of the drained dam at the corner of the Laurieston road and opposite the bay-windowed toll house (c.1828). The water to power the cotton mills was brought down by Barlay Mill from the west end (619608) of Loch Whinyeon in the hills to the north through a system of embankments and lades completed after 1787 at a cost of £1400; it was then stored in dams on each side of the road at the bottom of the Galla Hill. Walk down to the obtrusive Clock Tower (1871) and the Murray Arms (c.1760), which has an excellent west front facing Ann Street. The garages and quarters opposite the hotel to the north were part of a range of farm buildings. Ann Street, quite idyllic in springtime, was formerly the main road through the town. The 'gait house', now a Coffee House annexe to the Murray Arms, may well be mid-seventeenth century. At the top of Ann Street on the left is Thomas Scott and Company's three-storey cotton mill (c.1790), latterly a sawmill and residential accommodation. Neilson Square (c.1812) and Roseville and its outhouse, formerly a brewery, make a most elegant group. The eighteenth-century Cally Estate Office with blue door and window surrounds was formerly a school and hall.

Cross the High Street and take the narrow lane immediately next to the Bank of Scotland, crossing the little lade which you also see in Digby Street (with the Solway River Purification Board notice for what must be its smallest water course) and Victoria Street, and continue over the grid pattern from Catherine Street to Birtwhistle Street. 'Roarin' Birtwhistle' is a particularly good example of late eighteenth or early nineteenth-century workers' housing. From the lower end of Birtwhistle Street turn left and on to Catherine Street and then right to Victoria Street near the Police Station with the former brass foundry and workshop and hence along to the High Street. Note here the larger houses on feus let out to artisans and craftsmen and the general good taste in the colour-washed houses and painted door and window surrounds, much of this the result of example and persuasion by the superior of Gatehouse. The three-storey Angel Hotel is particularly pleasing. Opposite you have Bruachmoor and the large former brewery building, and below to the west Fleetvale, with garages and stores behind, which was a tannery, possibly as early as 1768, with its tanpits in what is now a car parking area below. The main industrial complex of three cotton mills was between Victoria Street and the river. Here the ruinous three-storey cotton mill (c.1785-1795) close to the river and the lade system, with the wheel pit for the larger mill which was above it, may yet become central features of a major museum of industrial archaeology.

The stone Fleet Bridge of 1729-1730, widened in 1771, 1811 and 1965, replaced a wooden bridge of 1661 washed away in 1721. The first of the charming houses in Bridge Terrace to the west of the bridge, and therefore in Anwoth parish, may have been the soapworks (c.1793). Turn left into Hannay Street for Boatgreen (599560), the site of the old harbour and shipbuilding and repair yard. It was difficult for sailing vessels to get up the old tortuous winding line of the Fleet close to Cally House, and in a most imaginative scheme Alexander Murray had a new canalised course cut by two hundred of his Donegal estate tenants between 17 June and 3 October 1823. The *Venniehill Viewpoint* at the west end of Gatehouse has a fine view of the town and of the old harbour. The new harbour built at Port McAdam (595557) between 1836 and 1838 was in use until the 1930s, latterly mainly by coal boats, but it was re-opened in 1974 for small yachts and pleasure craft. Unfortunately the new bypass bridge places severe restrictions on access.

The old A75 passing Port McAdam takes you to *Cardoness Castle* (591553), the McCulloch fifteenth-century tower house on a rock platform promontory site above the estuary. The bleak eight-feet thick walls with gunports and tiny windows of the fifty-feet plus high tower conceal a huge vaulted basement and a labyrinth of passages, mural stairs and closets. The first and second-floor fireplaces and wall presses are excellent. Do not miss the spectacular view from the wall walk over the bypass and canal and over to Boreland or Green Tower motte and bailey at Ardwall (585550).

To explore the hinterland of Girthon and Anwoth start with the B796 from the Anwoth Hotel, formerly the Ship Inn, to the side road beyond Blackloch for the old clachan and churchyard of Anwoth. The Catholic Church in the housing area in Gatehouse off the B796 has a remarkable Resurrection Crucifixion by Arthur Dooley of Liverpool. Walkers will if at all possible take the ancient footpath through the Boreland Hills following the far side of the stone dyke to the north of Trusty's Hill (588561) and then down through a forest break to Anwoth. The view from Trusty's Hill is superb, and the Iron Age and Dark Age Anglian period vitrified fort on top has a clear rock-cut ditch to the north and multiple defences to the south. The Pictish seventh-century double disc and Z rod, dagger and sea monster carving on a rock surface at the entrance may be interpreted as an expression of status and of tribal identity. The granite obelisk on the hill to the south-west is the Rutherford Monument erected in 1842.

The old churchyard and clachan of Anwoth (583562) has a feeling of extraordinary serenity. There was a church here at least from the 1100s, but if 'Rutherford's Well' in the field north-east of the churchyard was a holy well it is quite possible that this was a pagan holy place with a gentle water nymph deity long before the arrival of Christianity. The old church built in 1626/7 was in use until 1825. Note inside it the simple twelfth-century cross and the elaborate early seventeenth-century Gordon Renaissance monument. The yard has a rich collection of eighteenth-century tombstones with classical symbolism and some good calligraphy. The pleasant parish church to the south was completed betwen 1826 and 1828.

Anwoth is famous as the parish where the Presbyterian scholar Samuel Rutherford (1600-1661) ministered between 1627 and 1639, with a gap in enforced exile between 1636 and 1638. His *Lex Rex* (1644) was an important political treatise, but his *Letters* to Gordons, McCullochs and Lennoxes with both local colour and even a little warmth on occasion are more likely to be read today. The collection edited by A. Bonar in 1891 is the best. 'Rutherford's Witnesses' (573556) near Moss Robin beside an old footpath now almost impossible to follow between Anwoth and Skyreburn are boulders on a grassy stretch where S.R. denounced the people for playing football after a Sunday sermon and 'called on the stones to be witnesses between them and him'!

Back in the clachan the old school opposite the church is now a charming house. Walk back by Woodend and Luckie Harg's Brae to the B796, or enjoy the rough walking on the Old Military Road from behind the old school by the site of St. John's Well (580562), King's Laggan, and the old lead mines on Kirkbride (569567) and Lauchentyre (558572) to the Skyreburn road north of Glen and hence down to Skyreburn Bay for the bus service into Gatehouse.

For the northern hinterland take the Laurieston road, passing the former corn mill at Barlay (602573), the birthplace of the immensely popular and successful artists, the brothers John (1819-1902), James (1821-1911), and Thomas Faed (1826-1900). Thomas Faed's history painting, 'The Last of the Clans' (1865), in the Kelvingrove Art Gallery in Glasgow, is a good example of the sheer technical excellence of his work. For further reading see M. McKerrow's *The Faeds* (1982). The track and partly sunken way north of the Barlay Burn towards Crowcleugh Ford (627588) and Glengap may be mediaeval or even Roman period. The road up the hill towards Laurieston has magnificent views back over to Fleet Bay from above Laghead east of the 'Green Lumps', but if possible tackle this road from the Laurieston end. The other road by Fleuchlarg, Low Creoch and Lagg takes you beside the new reserve in Castramont Wood. The farm road by Culreoch and the track along the Little Water of Fleet takes you by the old slate quarry (584627) and the 1908-1912 copper-mining workings down the hillside at the Doon of Culreoch, and a large corn kiln (582639) south of the deserted farm of Cruffock.

For picnic or wet-weather reading remember John Buchan (1895-1940), whose famous *The Thirty-Nine Steps* (1915) is set in the Galloway countryside. His earlier biography of *Andrew Jamieson Lord Ardwall* (1913) is another book for Galloway collectors. Definitely for a dull day is Dorothy L. Sayers' *Five Red Herrings* (1931)—the Kirkcudbright setting is interesting, but it is not one of her best books. The biography by Janet Hitchman, *Such a Strange Lady* (1975), is very good. Miss Sayers (1893-1957) had two aunts and an uncle in Kirkcudbright and area and had spent many happy hours in the High Street of 'Whisky Jean'.

From Gatehouse the B796 passing the rectangular motte at Pulcree (593583) on the Water of Fleet above Stroquhain's Pool north of Heat Haggies takes you above Rusco Castle, which is better viewed from the road west of Castramont Bridge. Rusco Castle (584604) is a fine later fifteenth or early sixteenth-century rectangular tower house, possibly built for Robert Gordon and Marion Carson or Acarsane in 1494. The cape house is particularly good. The hill to the west has the odd name of Mount Pisga (578601).

Continue by Upper Rusko looking over to Murrayton to the track of the former railway line east of Dromore or Gatehouse 'Station'. The Cairnsmore of Fleet National Nature Reserve includes the high ground between the Clints of Dromore, Little Multaggart, the Knee of Cairnsmore and Craignelder, and this area is both a sheep farm and a sanctuary for upland plants and wild life, red grouse, golder plover, raven, red deer, goats and mountain hares. Follow the railway track on the line opened in 1861 for the impressive Big Water of Fleet Viaduct (558643), the Little Water of Fleet Viaduct (586670) and Loch Skerrow with its Craigaherron (604677) and Blaeberry (603679) Islands. The Auchencloy Monument (603708) from Loch Skerrow or Barneywater is for truly dedicated modern 'Covenanters' only. Take the forest road by Meikle Cullendoch for the Cleugh of Eglon and Loch Grannoch. The cairn above the loch 'In Memory of Maggie' is for a pack-pony (d.1911), which worked from the shooting lodge. Unusual placenames include Loopmabinnie (618674), the Flesh Market (601655), the Nick of the Dead Man's Banes (561686), Maggie Ireland's Wa's (553662), and Germany Isle (582611). South of the B796 there are old lead mines on Meikle Bennan (551615).

On the coast road few illusions about the charm of the stretch from Cardoness to Creetown will survive untarnished the realities of today's heavy and fast-moving traffic, but bear with it as there are wonderful places to discover just off it. Ardwall House (581547), a very fine building dated from 1762, is not visible from the road. Stop at Skyreburn Bay to explore the valley behind. Just beyond Skyreburn Mill House (567553), the site of an eighteenth/nineteenth-century corn mill, take the road over the eighteenth-century single-arch Kirkbride Bridge (566554) to walk by Kirkbride to the Black Burn Brae on the Old Military Road (561572). The sub-circular banked area at Kirkbride (561562) and the Lady's Well below may be a very early fifth/sixth century Christian site. Back on the Skyreburn road continue by Whiteside to Cauldside west of Paradise Bridge (550575). The Cauldside Burn and Cambret Moor area has an important prehistoric complex with a cairnfield, a round cairn and adjacent stone circle with ten stones remaining (529571), and a large boulder on the slope of Cambret Moor north-west of the cairn with a cup and ring marked spiral with seven 'loops' and a radial groove. There is a clear hut circle on Cairnharrow (538569) and a brilliant but difficult to locate rock outcrop at 800 feet with cup and ring markings including a dumb-bell (540568).

The round cairn and stone circle near Cauldside Burn looking north-east with Cambret Moor on the left.

On the Skyreburn road continue by the mid-eighteenth-century farmhouse at Glen to the Corse of Slakes Old Military Road, which is quite probably on the line of a much older route. It was replaced as the main road by the coast road by Auchenlarie to Creetown between 1785 and 1790. It is a fine walk, the snag, of course, being that you have to make siccar that you allow yourself time to catch the bus at Creetown back to Skyreburn.

On the A75 continue by Cardoness (formerly Bardarroch). Colonel Wm. Maxwell's parchment burgh of 'Cardiness' (1702) at the 'clachan of Anwith and Marquocher' with a port on the west side of the Fleet failed to develop. The private chapel on the shore (568534), built in 1768, is used for an annual service. When the tide is out walk along the shore from Skyreburn to Mossyard Bay and the Garvellan Rocks. What look like standing stones at Newton (550525) are three pillars which were part of the chamber of a cairn, of which the entire superstructure has been removed. The coast here looks as if it might have Mesolithic sites. There is another flat rock outcrop on Mossyard (545514) with a series of cup and ring markings. Further west do not miss the spectacular early castle above the cliffs immediately south-west of Auchenlarie Holiday Farm. Kirkclaugh motte (534521) has a deep ditch on three sides and a kidney-shaped bailey with an outer ditch and a causeway approach. The eleventh/twelfth-century cross from the outer bank was taken to Kirkclaugh House (532524) in 1898.

Stop beside the old Kirkdale Bridge (517531) designed by Robert Adam c.1785-1790 to explore this fascinating area. Kirkdale House (514533), completed before 1787 for Sir Samuel Hannay to a plan by Robert Adam as a four-storey house with two three-storey wings, has the best, and unaltered, exterior frontage in Galloway. The tenth/eleventh-century wayside crosses from the bridle track above High Auchenlarie and formerly at Cardoness House are now at Kirkdale, as is a unique collection of boulders and portable stones with cup and ring markings from the Laggan, Bardristane and Cairnholy area. The older tower-house site is between the present house and the splendid octagonal stables (512536) up the hill. Further up still is the site of the former parish church of Kirkdale (512541), united to Kirkmabreck in 1636, and the churchyard with Sir Samuel Hannay's mausoleum. Below the A75 shrouded by bushes west of the new bridge is a circular domed icehouse in stone and brick, removed in 1969 from its original site on the bank of the burn now under the road. The 'mote' or 'The World's End' below (516528) is a natural rock pinnacle landscaped in the eighteenth century with walks leading to a 'hermitage' on the top! Serious 'ghost hunters' may want to return at dusk to investigate reports of headless horsemen and a woman in white with half her head cut off seen in Kirkdale Glen. Just above the shore is 'Dirk Hatterick's or Meg Merrilees' Cave' (518526)—the literary references are from Scott's *Guy Mannering*—which may have been used as a hiding place for smuggled goods. Inside there are dozens of stone boxes along the wall for bottles—*very* elaborate indeed. It is not easy to find and you require a rope to clamber up again after sliding down from a small access aperture to the cave fourteen feet below. It may well be dangerous internally and liable to rock falls.

From Kirkdale Bridge walk up the road to *Cairnholy I* (517539), the classic example of a long chambered cairn with a ritual forecourt area in front of a facade of tall monoliths, and *Cairnholy II* (518541), which has a fine capstone. There is a small car-parking space at the former (I have taken minibuses up, but it is not really advisable). The old road over Barholm Bridge (517532), just below Kirkdale Sawmill, takes you up by Barholm Castle (520529), a charming McCulloch sixteenth-century L-plan tower house with unusual windows and a weird doorway with a snakelike animal with human head masks attached above. Barholm farmhouse, built in 1797 and recently restored, has a magnificent view. The walk by Bardristane to High Auchenlarie, where there is a possible stone circle and cup and ring markings nearby (539534), offers fine vistas over Fleet Bay and the coastline to the south. The other road to Claughreid takes you on to an old track by California (513560) and Cambret to the Old Military Road east of

A later nineteenth-century romantic tourist-orientated concept of the Galloway Coast near Dirk Hatterick's Cave with smugglers prominent in the foreground. The print is from a painting by C. Stanfield.

Englishman's Burn. You pass a circle with nine stones and a central boulder north-west of Claughreid (517560). The hills to the east have excellent examples of the great drystane dykes, including march dykes between farms and estates, built in the eighteenth or nineteenth century. Both the dykes and the other local style, the 'Galloway hedge' or 'sunk fence', that is a dyke plus a thorn hedge, are very effective and permanent obstacles. The Stewartry Drystane Dyking Competitions held near Gatehouse and open to professionals and amateurs are well worth visiting to see the old traditions and skills still in use today.

On the A75 *Carsluith Castle* (494541), the Browns' late fifteenth-century rectangular tower house with a north wing added in 1568, has many attractive features. Note the functional and decorative gunports, the pepperpot turrets, the little turret stair to the attic level, and the wall walk with stone cannon and spouts to run off water. The proximity of the farm buildings greatly enhances the impact of the monument. Take the old A75 through Carsluith village, once a busy place with a corn mill (490548) built in 1817 on a site where there had been a mill since 1527, and the Bagbie granite quarries (488549) opened in 1861 and closed in 1954. The old quay (485546) is on the west side of the new A75. Note from here to Creetown the salmon nets and the fine view over the sands and the Cree to the hilltop town of Wigtown.

For the old churchyard of Kirkmabreck (493565) at 450 feet in a wild moorland setting take the road up the hill at 480560 by Kirkmabreck farm. This is an excellent walk climbing up and looking back over the Cree estuary. A new church was built for the parish at Ferrytown of Cree in 1645, but the churchyard remained in use through the eighteenth and nineteenth centuries. The granite obelisk is a monument to the philosopher, Thomas Brown (1778-1820), who was born at Glebe House (478565), the former manse. To the south-east the cairn on Bagbie (498564) has a setting of four stones beside it and a large standing stone two hundred yards to the south. To the west is the Fell Hill granite quarry opened in 1850, and closer to the A75 the now huge Kirkmabreck Quarry opened in 1831 by the Liverpool Dock Company, who sold out to the Scottish Granite Company in 1908. The old quay was at Carskeel Point (473568) north of the site of a lighthouse (473566). The crushing mill on the pier was built by the Scottish Granite Company.

Creetown is and looks like a granite town, but it also has a long history as the mediaeval village of 'Crithe' beside the dangerous fords and ferries over the Cree for travellers and, more especially, pilgrims en route to Whithorn. An early fourteenth-century, or earlier, hospice to provide accommodation for pilgrims and perhaps also for the sick and infirm and owned by the Cistercians of Dundrennan was located near Spittal (4760) or maybe the former Knockdown Ferry House (465604). The cultivation terraces at Blairs Hill (466612) beside the Pulwhat Bridge Mill may be connected to the hospital, although they could equally date to the Anglian Northumbrian period. The early chapel and seventeenth-century church site (476586) near The Hill in Creetown might be related to another ferry point near Barholm Mains or a fording route across the Wigtown Sands further south.

In the late eighteenth century 'The Ferry' or Ferrytown of Cree became a burgh of barony (1791) in the interest of John McCulloch of Barholm with a tannery, and a corn mill, a cotton mill and a woollen mill on the Balloch Burn (sites and some remaining structures at 474585, 477586 and 484588). Vessels of up to fifty tons came regularly into the harbour (473586). Today the bypass from near Cassencarie over the salt marsh to Pulwhat Bridge laid on a blanket of plastic and layers of rock may take away any feeling of proximity to the sea, but it will be of enormous benefit to Creetown.

For a Creetown perambulation start at the Clock Tower (1897) in Adamson Square. Up the hill on the (old) A75 the three-arch Moneypool Bridge (475590) built in 1769 is a superb example of quality classical bridge-building. Opposite the Clock Tower the Gatehouse road, becoming the B796, passes the old school, now the Creetown Gem Rock Museum and Art Gallery, which has a truly international collection. Highlights include a fine 'amethyst geode' and a high-powered ultra-violet mineral display. Come back down the hill to take the High Road, parallel to St. John Street, below The Hill, a compact late eighteenth-century house with nineteenth-century additions in granite, and then Crispin Street where you pass the restored two-storey house dated 1736. The road to the left up a steep slope takes you to the present parish church (1834) and the unusual former 'Girls School of Industry' opposite. Return by Crispin Street to St. John Street and turn left down Harbour Street—good solid eighteenth and early nineteenth-century houses—for the old harbour and waterfront. Mill Street and the partly cobbled lane at the top of Harbour Street are worth exploring.

Take the Old Military Road by Drumrake and Burns to the bridge over the Englishman's Burn. Glenquicken Circle (509582), which has twenty-eight boulders and one large monolith in the centre, is important, but is quite difficult to locate and visit. The area roundabout has other cairn and cist sites. There is a lead-mining trial shaft near the Balloch Burn (488588).

Off the Moneypool Burn road there is a leadmine shaft on Culcronchie (501608) and the road by Mark to the extensive Pibble Hill leadmines (523608 and 528604) with spoil heaps and the remains of a three-storey engine house. Kirkmabreck also has a number of chalybeate springs and wells, including Mount Horeb Well (507608), Red Wells (528616 and 479586), Falbae Well (498608), the Spa Well (480595), Burnfoot Well (455625) and Gernay Physic Well (475636). No doubt some could still be sampled, but it would be much more beneficial today to visit the 'Laird's Inn' at Cassencarie, where you can also study the sixteenth/seventeenth-century tower house incorporated in the nineteenth-century mansion.

CHAPTER 16

Minnigaff, Newton Stewart, Penninghame and the Moors

Old Galloway hands travelling west from Gatehouse will perhaps still be surprised to remember that they have already crossed into Wigtown District well before Creetown, let alone Palnure or Minnigaff or Creebridge. On the fast A75 it is easy to miss the once busy corner at Palnure and the site of the old harbour (454631) on the Palnure Burn at the end of the loops just before the bridge. Vessels of up to sixty tons used to come up here to take away timber, grain and lead from the mines. On the east side of the Palnure Burn shafts are recorded in Wicklow Wood (475635), in Bargaly Glen (466682), and at the Cairnsmore mine (463634), which flourished in the 1840s and 1850s. The cairns on Cairnsmore of Fleet at the north (502670) and south (509654) summits may or may not be Bronze Age in origin. The granite memorial taken up to the top by a United States Air Force helicopter in 1980 is for the twenty-five British, American and German airmen who died in crashes on the hill.

The walk from Muirfad by Strathmaddie and Bardrochwood up the east side of the Palnure burn to Craignine Bridge (460662) at the beginning of Bargaly Glen and then back down the west side by Little Park Wood to Stronord and Daltamie is a delight in all seasons. Bardrochwood motte (459653) at the normal tidal limit on the burn is now an anonymous hillock; Machars Hill motte (470652) is still clearly a mediaeval castle mound, perhaps for a hunting lodge base for the forest to the north or even, very speculatively, as a fortified point for men-at-arms on a Cistercian sheep-farming grange.

The Forestry Commission Nursery at Daltamie, dating back to 1931, and the Kirroughtree Forest Trails are genuinely interesting. Do not miss the idyllic-looking Bruntis Lochs, which are in fact artificial nineteenth-century reservoirs for the lead mines. The former coach road from the old school at Stronord west up the hill passes the sites of the East Blackcraig (446646) and the Craigton or West Blackcraig (433652) mines—and at least eighteen old shafts—and then goes down the steep hill to the A75. Mining began about 1764 and reached a peak in the 1770s to 1790s, but the mines were also busy in the 1870s and 1880s and were revived for a few years in 1917. The depth of the shafts ranged from 25 to an amazing 132 fathoms by 1873. In 1881 there were sixty-three men and women

The thatched houses and the road on the Mines Hill, Blackcraig. Recorded by J. P. Milnes, 'photo artist', Stranraer, c.1901.

working at Blackcraig as miners and lead washers and in other occupations including a carter, an engineman, an engine driver, the agent and the office cleaner, Agnes Paterson. As to visible remains, you will still see some spoil heaps and old shafts topped with concrete slabs. Casual exploration of horizontal levels and vertical shaft sites carries obvious hazards. There are still also remains below the A75 at 435647 including a lade system, spoil heaps and raised causeways, and possibly a water wheel pit and a shaft. Placenames in the area include 'Solomon's Temple' (438646) on Challoch Croft.

To explore some of the hinterland of Minnigaff parish take the A712 New Galloway road. The grass-covered remains of the tower house and ancillary buildings of the McKies of Larg (433662) are in the field north of the farm. The famous Gout Well of Larg was located somewhere in Doon Wood (428664), which is above the former mill dam/curling pond in Kirroughtree estate on the west side of the road. The winding A712 from here to just south (458686) of Dallash is still largely the turnpike section opened about 1802. It offers good walking through a mixed farming landscape with wild flowers and life and colour along the roadside. The side road at 442677 up the hill by the Risk road end and down towards the Auchinleck road looking over to Cumloden Deer Park is even better and makes a marvellous afternoon circuit through 'old Galloway' down by Glenhoise and Cumloden to Minnigaff and Kirroughtree.

Just south-east of the Risk farm road end you cross the line of the 'Old Edinburgh Road', more properly 'The Queen's Way' than the A712, as most of it is the route from Edinburgh to Whithorn taken by pilgrims—by James IV in 1497 and 1501, and by Mary Queen of Scots in 1563 on her itinerary from Glenluce to Whithorn to Clary to Kenmure Castle and then south to Kirkcudbright. The line of the road, now difficult or almost impossible to follow, is marked on the O.S. 1:50,000 sheets 83 and 77 from Minnigaff and then south of Risk, north of Craigdistant, and by the Loch of the Lowes to Talnotry and the Grey Mare's Tail, up the Saddle Loup ('Nothing in the Alps was worse' was Sir John Clerk of Penicuik's comment in 1735) and by the valley north of Craigdews Hill and Brochloch Hill and by Lilie's Loch to Clatteringshaws, where, of course, it is covered by the water. The old road, superseded by the 1790s and in the 1800s by the present A712 route, was close to the nickel and arsenic mines near Talnotry (482717 and 483721), the Grey Mare's Tail (491725) and the Black Loch (494727), and a possible copper venture beside the Pulran Burn (522749). The Grey Mare's Tail is a common name for waterfalls and hanging valleys, no doubt imitating the famous 'Tail' on the Moffat Water on the Selkirk road. The name is also used at a spot north-east of Clawbelly Hill (878614) in Colvend and Southwick parish.

On the A712 itself from before Dallash to near New Galloway you are into the industrial landscape of intensive forestry. The presentation of this development has been brilliantly handled by the Forestry Commission as a public relations exercise with many innovative ideas, including not only marking trails but also reserving areas as zoological parks. More screening may be required when the full devastation which will ultimately be left by felling is revealed. Note from the south the rough roads to the Loch of the Lowes and the Corwar and Dallash holdings; the highly organised Talnotry Forestry Trails; the monument erected in 1835 on the Big Doon to Alexander Murray (1775-1813), the shepherd's son from 'Tennotrie and Kitterick' who became Professor of Oriental Languages at the University of Edinburgh; the *Wild Goat Park* (492720); *Murray's Birthplace* at Kittrick (503717); the narrow bridge at Craigdews across the Tonderghie Burn; the rough road to the Black Loch; the *Red Deer Range* (522732) on Brochloch Hill; the road before Clatteringshaws for access to Lilie's Loch, and along the waterside at Clatteringshaws by Craignell to Craigencallie; and the *Deer Museum* near Moss Raploch and *Bruce's Stone*. Interesting placenames include Poultrybuie (494731), The Sleekit Knowes Loch (493712), Pyot Craigs (507717) and The Types (507728).

At the south end of the A712 beyond Larg the B7079 takes you on to the villages of Creebridge and Minnigaff and the town of Newton Stewart. The flat land, the Camp Park of Kirroughtree, and the slopes of Lessons Park above the B7079 were an important prehistoric area with a number of cairns and standing stones recorded. Note today the sites of the Low

Lessons (424654) and High Lessons (422653) cairns just over the dyke and the round eight-feet-high Bell Cairn, which sits on a wide platform (416656). The ground between the B7079 and the A75 is traditionally the site of a battle in 1308 in the Wars of Independence. Kirroughtree House (422660), now an hotel, was built by Patrick Heron in 1719. Later eighteenth-century additions and alterations make it a most original house. The octagonal dovecot (418662) with 648 nests may also date to 1719. The 'Punch Bowl' (418646) north of Machermore Castle is a natural feature.

The clachan of Minnigaff below the motte and the church on the east bank of the Cree just after the confluence with the Penkiln burn was a busy market centre for the men of the moors and hills, certainly by the sixteenth century and probably long before then. McKie of Larg obtained a charter for a burgh of barony in 1619, and another parchment burgh was attempted by the Herons at Larg in 1698; but it was, instead, the 'Ford-House of Cree', becoming the burgh of Newton Stewart in 1677 to William Stewart of Castle Stewart, which in the long term became the main centre in the area. The temporary change of name from 1778 to 1794 as Newton Douglas, in place of Newton Stewart, was at the behest of Sir William Douglas of Gelston Castle whose venture at establishing another industrial town with a cotton mill and a carpet factory failed.

Creebridge or Bridgend of Cree with its toll house at the bridge and its row of houses remained (perhaps still even now) a separate village entity, certainly throughout the nineteenth century. Creebridge House, now an hotel, dates to about 1780, and the last house at the north end of the row of houses on the west side coming from the bridge has a stone with the date '1769'. Walk from here towards 'Old Minnigaff' passing the handsome Flower Bank Guest House and the very impressive four-storey granite former Minnigaff corn mill (411661), possibly built in 1823. It was in use as a corn and meal mill until about 1900 and later became for a time a carpet factory for Blackwood Morton of Kilmarnock. The old school is now an SYHA hostel. 'Old Minnigaff' from the school to the Penkiln Bridge and the new Indoor Bowling Centre on the sawmill site on Cumloden Road, and including Penkiln Terrace, is still a charming corner. Continue up Cumloden Road to the eighteenth-century former waulk mill (414669), now a house, where blankets and plaids were produced into the 1920s, and cross 'Queen Mary's Bridge', now a footbridge rebuilt after substantial flood damage, to return to Monigaff parish church on the west side of the Penkiln Burn.

The present Monigaff church (for Minnigaff parish) was built in 1836 to plans by William Burn of Edinburgh. Unremarkable externally, it has a

'Mr Minnigaff or the oldest Gallovidian' as depicted on the eleventh-century cross-slab to the right in the tomb recess in the old church.

fine interior to study as an almost perfect example of a Presbyterian country parish church. The stained glass windows to Lt. Col. Patrick Stewart of the Royal Bengal Engineers and James McKie of Bargaly are particularly good. The ruined sixteenth-century church on the site of an older mediaeval building has two important, probably eleventh-century, cross-slabs in a recess in the north wall. The whinstone pillar on the right is sculptured on three faces with the figure of a man (probably 'the oldest Gallovidian' you will see, or 'Mr Minnigaff' for he is a friendly looking little chap), with a series of three panels with spiral and interlace designs, and on the back a fish and bird monster which is almost impossible to see even with a mirror. It was found in use as a lintel in a house demolished in 1880. The

The Creebridge United Free Church, evicted from their church, marching through Newton Stewart to their hall on 2 July, 1905. After a bitter dispute they were allowed to return to the church on 2 June, 1907.

churchyard has some brilliant carved stones, in particular the upright to Thomas McCreddie and his spouse Margaret Gordon (1767) with smith's tools, vice, pincers, hammer, file, nails, which is on the west side of the yard nearly west of the old church door, and the upright with three ravens and an arrow to Patrick McClurg in Glenshalloch (1746). The steps at the south end of the churchyard take you down into the ditch below the motte (410664) at the end of the promontory between the Cree and the Penkiln Burn. The motte may well be the 'strength on the Water of Cree' described by Blind Harry and taken by Wallace in 1297.

Cross the Suspension Bridge and continue up to the A714 for your perambulation in Newton Stewart parallel with the river towards the town centre. Douglas House was built in 1832 as a school, Douglas Academy, with funds from the Windsor Castle estate in St Mary Parish, Jan.aica, which had belonged to Samuel Douglas (d.1799). After the Ewart Institute opened in 1864 Douglas Academy became, from 1873 until amalgamation in 1922, a school for girls with the Ewart as a school for boys. The modern building adjacent to the south is the new Adult Training Centre. Going south into King Street, formerly Cotton Row, you pass the Cree Mills complex dating back to 1899 and built on the site of the cotton mill, later a sawmill. The Cree Mills have been very busy in 1984 and 1985 with orders for hundreds of thousands of mohair and wool scarves for Russia. The site of the Heugh grist or corn mill was immediately to the south of the Cree

Mills. Next there is 'Solomon's Brewery', now converted into houses. The manager's house is now a Customs and Excise office. Arthur Street was formerly the Gorbals. It is interesting how 'royal' and 'respectable' the street names suddenly became in nineteenth-century Newton Stewart. The Cree Bridge by John Rennie (1813) was built a hundred yards downstream from the site of the old bridge (1745-1806) at the foot of the 'Saltbox Brae'. Note the extraordinary monument to the 9th Earl of Galloway (1875), contrasting with the sober and solid Clydesdale Bank building and the eighteenth-century former Town Hall with a cupola-topped clock tower in Victoria Street opposite the Galloway Arms. For leisure reading it is appropriate to suggest here Mary Curran's *The Country Ones* (1975), which is set in Creebridge and Newton Stewart and area in the post-war era. The dust wrapper in green-brown showing the Loop of Cairnsnaw on the Cree south of Newton Stewart looking over to Cairnsmore is excellent.

For the upper town take the lane beside the Galloway Arms and go up the hill path at the far end. At the top turn right for *Newton Stewart and District Museum* opened in 1978 in the former St. John's church in York Road. The collection of Levee and Court dresses and Charleston era togs, lace and Paisley shawls, old farm and dairying and laundry implements is quite outstanding. At the top of the hill from the Galloway Arms turn left for Penninghame St. John's Church (1841) by William Burn and for the old churchyard further south with interesting Douglas and Ewart monuments. The parish church was first located here in 1777, when this site replaced the clachan of Penninghame kirk (411612) as the ecclesiastical centre of the parish. From York Road go up Corsbie Road, passing the new Douglas Ewart High School, to the top of the hill for splendid vistas over to Cumloden Deer Park and the Minnigaff hills. Turn into Blairmount Park (403654) and take the pathway at the other end down to Princes Street. Turning right on the road takes you to the site of the former Newton Stewart Railway Station (406649), which saw its last passenger train from Whithorn in 1950 (freight in 1964) and from Stranraer in 1965. Turn down Princes Street to Dashwood Square, formerly 'The Angle', with the McMillan Hall (1881) and the bus stop for Whithorn, Girvan, Stranraer and Dumfries. Continue down Albert Street passing the pink and distinctly frivolous Bank of Scotland building with its pillars, balcony and urns into Victoria Street, where there is still (and almost unique in a small town in Britain in the 1980s) a good cinema open all the year round *and* showing recent releases.

Newton Stewart and Minnigaff are fortunate in having open moorland, hill farmland and unspoiled woodland to the north rich in plant, bird and

A busy scene at Newton Stewart Railway Station with the Stranraer train on the left and the platforms for Wigtown and Whithorn and for Castle-Douglas and Dumfries on the right.

animal life and studded with archaeological and historical sites. It is very important that this wonderful country should not be lost and, in particular, that the advance of 'Forestry' in all its forms should be prevented here. Fortunately, the Wood of Cree is now a reserve and most of Cumloden Deer Park and Garlies Wood is still intact. Cumloden Deer Park was created by clearing the previously existing farms by General Sir William Stewart (1774-1827), who retired there in 1814 and built Cumloden Cottage. Stewart, 'The most beloved and chivalrous General in the British Army', as *The Oracle* (1832) described him, was a brave fighting general, a man of 'untamed and boiling courage', who took his troops into battle from the front and fought in seventeen campaigns, most notably in Spain and Portugal commanding the Second Division under the Duke of Wellington. He was also a close friend of Admiral Lord Nelson. The Park he created is a sort of paradise with prehistoric hut circles and cairns, and deserted eighteenth-century ferm-touns and corn kilns, including Clauchrie (412681), Glenmalloch (428690), Closing (419693) and Knockbracks (424697). Garlies Castle (422691)—the barony was held by the Stewarts, later the Earls of Galloway, from 1263—consists of the remains of a tower house at the north-west corner of a courtyard range of buildings, and another outer courtyard or paddock for horses and cattle. The fireplace in the tower has a spirited, but damaged, hunting scene.

The hill farm and moorland to the north have some important prehistoric sites. Boreland cairn (405690) is a long chambered cairn with a crescentic forecourt setting with at least four stones in place. Drumwhirn (393688) is a long chambered cairn. The Nappers (408713) on Drannandow is a denuded long cairn with five chambers, one at the east end and the other four laterally placed. Other stone structures include sheep rees, shielings or bothies, round cairns with cists, and cairnfields or field clearance heaps. The Thieves (404716) are two large standing stones set within an oval banked enclosure. The 1852 O.S. map marks the line—problematical—of the 'Deil's Dyke' running east to west just north of The Thieves.

The Wood of Cree road, running north from Monigaff church, is a wonderful road for walking. You pass by fields still farmed, river pools on the Cree, wild flowers by the roadside, the Coldstream, Washing, Cordorcan and Lagboes of Ballocharush Burns tumbling down to the river, the 524-acre RSPB reserve including probably the largest oak wood left in the south-west of Scotland, and then the sleepy sheet of sluggish river water known as the 'Loch of Cree'. There were lead mines at the Wood of Cree (386694), lead and zinc at the Coldstream Burn (386697) and a silver mine (377728) near the Silver Rig Loch. Return by the same road to Minnigaff or continue to Clachaneasy Bridge (355751) near the old High Black Rack Ford for the A714 to Newton Stewart.

To explore Glentrool, Bargrennan and the moors in the north of Penninghame and Kirkcowan parishes and into Colmonell parish to Barrhill requires weeks or months rather than days. From Newton Stewart take the A714 from the town centre or the bypass road from the A75 by South and North Barnkirk on the west, passing Barnkirk Hill (394664) which aerial photographs show as an oval hill fort with double-ramparts. On the A714 at Challoch you pass the Scottish Episcopal Church of All Saints (384674), built by Mr Stopford-Blair of Penninghame House and consecrated in 1872. Castle Stewart (379690) is the shell of the sixteenth-century tower house of Culquhreauch or Culcruchie with later seventeenth-century alterations by Col. William Stewart. Note the rounded corners of the rectangular tower and the refined fireplace on the second floor. Since 1954 Penninghame House has been an Open Prison, hence the Scottish Home and Health Department title at the entrance. Cut Island (384701) in the Cree, which may be what its name suggests, has artificial banks and ditches, probably early nineteenth-century decorative landscaping to accommodate a boat house and walks.

Pause on the A714 just beyond the site of St Ninian's Chapel, the Old

Kirk of Cruives of Cree (377707), built by John Kennedy of Blairquhan in 1508, to enjoy the wooded scenery and the placidity of the slow-moving Cree to the east. There is a possible deserted village site nearby at 377708. The metropolis of Clachaneasy (355749) has grand new road signs placed in 1983 at either end of the village, which consists of one house. The much-photographed Old Bridge of Minnoch (373759), a high arched four feet wide possibly seventeenth-century packhorse bridge, is now some three miles from the nearest road. For Glentrool continue by the Middle Bridge of Cree to Bargrennan by the church (1838) and take the road along the Black Burn for Glentrool village and Loch Trool. The important White Cairn passage-grave-type chambered cairn (352783) is now very difficult to locate. It would be pleasant on your return journey to take the road south from Stroan Bridge (371785) by High Minniwick to Clachaneasy Bridge or continue by Borgan and the Wood of Cree road.

The forestry village at Glentrool, now a mix of privately owned houses occupied all the year round and Forestry Commission property, has a school, a shop, and the Western SMT buses calling off the Girvan to Newton Stewart service. Here you are into Forestry Commission country with facilities for organised walks and viewpoints. There are Forest Trails from Stroan Bridge south of Glencaird and the Loch Trool Trail as a circuit from Kenmure Moss skirting Glentrool Lodge and Buchan, round the east end of the loch east of the site of Ferrachbae (425801) and Ringielawn before Glenhead, along the south side passing the traditional site (422798) of the battle in 1307, commemorated by the Bruce Stone on the north side of the loch, to Caldons. The oak woods at Buchan, Glenhead and Caldons are sites of special scientific interest. The Martyrs Monument at Caldons is a replica of the original stone by 'Old Mortality' now in Newton Stewart Museum. It is interesting as an example of an unreliable and highly partisan account written long after the events—a series of ambushes and affrays with a final body count of probably six conventiclers and five soldiers—which it purports to describe. Paterson's propaganda does no justice to the conventiclers who were neither fools nor milksop saints and who deserve to be respected as possibly heroic figures and certainly hard, strong men who were ready and able to defend themselves and to meet force with force.

Walkers may link on to the Southern Upland Way either going east towards Loch Dee or west along the south shore of the loch and by the Water of Trool and over the Water of Minnoch north of Holm to Bargrennan. Armchair mountaineers and hikers will enjoy J. McBain's *The Merrick and the Neighbouring Hills* (1929), which is also available in a 1980 reprint but without the excellent photographs and the O.S. map in the earlier edition. A. McCormick's *Galloway: The Spell of its Hills and Glens* (1932) is a book that grows on one. The folklore section is enormously worthwhile, for example chapters on 'The Shiel Folk', 'Aul' Gipsy Flora' and 'Aul' Farrant Folk'. McCormick, the Town Clerk of Newton Stewart, was totally immersed in the history of Loch Trool and its hinterland. One interesting story is his account of finding the Bronze Age hoard from Eschonchan Fell (p. 64), which he suggests actually came from the mouth of a cave on the face of Nig-nag-newan at the north end of the Rig of Stroan during a Great War spy scare search for German aeroplanes and petrol.

Family parties will enjoy taking the minor road from Glentrool village north parallel with the Water of Minnoch to *Palgowan Open Farm* (373832). The northern route suggested from here might well appeal to hill rally enthusiasts. Ordinary motorists should be quite certain that their spare tyre is in order and that they have the necessary tools for modest repairs with them. Take the road by Kirriemore and Kirriereoch east of Loch Moan. The King's Cairn (377854) in the forest is a large round chambered cairn. Continue by Tarfessock, Shalloch on Minnoch, Waterhead and up the Pilnyark Burn with fine views back to the south, and on into Carrick Forest. Another Forest Walk is possible from the bridge (395956) over the River Stinchar which is just starting on its way to the sea at Ballantrae. Continue north through the forest by Genoch to Straiton. There are the remains of an unusual village settlement or shielings with turf huts and lazy-beds on Knockskae (NS 370014 and 369011). At Straiton take the B741 over the Girvan Water passing Blairquhan (NS 365054), an impressive 1820-1824 'Tudor'-style house by William Burn (1789-1870) for David Hunter Blair of Blairquhan and Dunskey in Wigtownshire. At Cloyntie take the road south by Balsaggart, Drumyork Hill, the Deil's Elbow (NS 342015), the Pilot, the Black Hill of Garleffin, Pinverains and North Balloch to the Nick of the Balloch road between Glengap Hill and Pinbreck Hill by Brandy Well to rejoin the Straiton-Glentrool road south of Waterhead. The Druid's Grave (338944), an oval chambered cairn with massive capstone and orthostats a feature, is in a sheep fold in the forest on the slope of Bencallen.

For the Wigtownshire moors take the side road south of Bargrennan at 353754 by Glenvernoch, Ochiltree and Beoch to the B7027 south of Knowe. This partly coincides with the Southern Upland Way which mixes moorland stretches with sections of the road and should be used over Ochiltree Hill (327741) for the fine views over Lochs Ochiltree and Fyntalloch and the forest to the south. The two larger islands on Loch Ochiltree may be crannog and castle sites. The Deil's Dyke marked on the

O.S. 1848 map crossing Ochiltree Hill and also south of the site of Meikle Castle farm (314756) and Castle Hill north of Kirkcalla *may* have been part of a long-distance earthwork running through Penninghame and Minnigaff parishes; but the field evidence is not convincing, and 'may' in this instance means that the subject has to be approached with considerable scepticism.

Knowe or The Snap was once a modest clachan with a school, a post office, a public house (the Snap Inn) and a corn mill (313714) on the Beoch Burn. The 1851 census lists twelve households including blacksmiths, a handloom weaver, a stonedyker, Scott Templeton from Inch parish, and the miller, John Stroyan from Minnigaff. The school (311724) at that date was near Knowe farm. The sites of the Beoch (315727) and Carrick (311760) grain mills are a reminder that this was once a healthy mixed farming landscape.

It is useful from here to follow the Southern Upland Way route by Waterside, Tannylaggie, Polbae, Darloskine Bridge and Derry for Linn's Tomb, the Wells of the Rees and the *Laggangairn Standing Stones*. Linn's Tomb (243725) on Craigmoddie Fell is another Covenanting monument, but worth the trachle of getting there for the sweeping moorland vistas around you. Follow the Way through the forest for the Wells of the Rees (229723), north of Kilgallioch, on the Pilgrim route from Ayrshire to Kirkcowan or Glenluce for Whithorn. The 'wells' are three drystone domed structures three and a half feet high, each with a niche/recess for a statue of the Virgin or a saint, sitting over bubbling freshwater. There was also a chapel site in an enclosure to the west of the Wells. Outside the forest—and it must be the most remote and difficult-to-find 'Scottish Monument' in the south of Scotland—you come to the *Laggangairn Standing Stones* (222716), two prehistoric monoliths each with an incised cross with four little crosses at the angles and used as wayside crosses or even as one of a series of Stations of the Cross. The Wells and the Standing Stones are good examples of pagan holy places re-used for Christian purposes. The suggestion that the last word in the placename, the Fell of Eldrig of Liberland (250748), indicates the presence of a 'leper' settlement in the area is interesting, but very speculative. 'Leprosy' in a mediaeval context meant all sorts of skin diseases, and 'lepers' *were* banished to remote locations. If the idea is feasible, then the site of White Eldrig farm (246752) to the north should be investigated. For walkers the Way goes south from Laggangairn on the old packhorse route over the moors west of the Sinks of Plumjordan and the Loops of Brackeniecally on the Tarff Water and across the Mulniegarroch or Purgatory Burn to Balmurrie north-east of New Luce.

Back at Knowe and going north on the B7027, Loch Maberry has seven islands, one (285751) the site of a mediaeval castle or hall and with causeways to the shore and the next island. The island in Loch Dornal (294762) may also be the site of a castle. Continue by the Lavery Burn and the Duisk River to Barrhill and then back on the A714 for Bargrennan with fine views over to the Galloway hills. Cairnderry (316799) is a passage-grave-type round chambered cairn with three chambers and some cup marking on the boulders. Sheuchan's Cairn (338838) on Highlandman's Rig is a round cairn with one chamber, but is in a planted area. It would be wicked to suggest that readers of the *Five Red Herrings* should be required to cycle at speed from Bargrennan to Barrhill to test the validity of Miss Sayers' plot, but such is human nature that no doubt someone sometime will want to do so. The run on the relative flat to Newton Stewart would be much more sensible.

Back in the soft balmy air of Newton Stewart it may be alarming to discover that there are still expeditions to the south and west of Penninghame parish to undertake. Start from Challoch on the B7027 as far as Glassoch for the Penninghame Forest Walks, the Garvachie Lochs, and the roads for Meikle Eldrig, Loch Eldrig and Little Eldrig. Returning on the same road, take the turning south at 375676 by Skaith towards Low Knockbrex Toll (395642). Skaith motte (382662), now obscured by trees and bushes, is a rectangular castle mound with a well-preserved ditch and bank, originally water-filled. The area on the top is just large enough for a small blockhouse or hunting lodge. The O.S. 1847 map shows the deserted village of Old Feys (372652), north of the Old Military Road which here runs north of the A75 from Black Park to Moor Head and north of Barskeoch towards Shennanton. On the sweet peaceful Skaith-Knockbrex road cross the old railway line to Stranraer and then manoeuvre your way over the A75 and continue south by the side road east of Merton Hall (382640) and Drumterlie by Culbratten Hill and Barracr to Barvennan Moss.

Take the road east by Barvennan and Barwhirran and turn south at the Foul Hole junction (412618), near the old railway line to Whithorn, for Penninghame Old Churchyard (411612) and the site of the Clachan of Penninghame (413612). Until the first church was built in Newton Stewart in 1777 this was the ecclesiastical centre of the parish. The clachan on the Foul Junction to Park farm road declined subsequently until by 1851 only a depressed little community of seven households of paupers, spinners, a sewer and a seamstress and a merchant was left. The churchyard has a marvellous collection of memorial stones. The upright for James Heron in

Carnestock (1758) and his spouse Marion Shan, appropriately with cherubs in profusion, since they left seventy children and grandchildren alive and thirty dead, is quite outstanding. A photograph is included in I. Donnachie and I. Macleod, *Old Galloway* (1974). Note in the south wall of the farmhouse a seventeenth-century stone with the arms of the Earls of Galloway and a pelican feeding her young. This whole area was also an important mediaeval religious centre with the possible site of the thirteenth and fourteenth-century palace of the Bishops of Whithorn at 'Penninghame Hall' (409605) on the Bishop Burn east of the site of the Mill of Penninghame (404606). The Bell Knowe (408612) was the knoll where St Ninian's Bell, presumably a handbell, was rung. James IV on pilgrimage to Whithorn in 1507 gave nine shillings to the man who rang the bell. In the fifteenth and sixteenth centuries the Bishop's palace may have been at Clary or Clachary (424603), later the residence of the Earls of Galloway, where Mary Queen of Scots supped and stayed with the Master of Garlies on August 11, 1563.

From the Clachan site continue south to the A714 at Causeway End and turn north by Baltersan to the Carty road (422627) south of Upper Barr. St.Ninian's Well (424628), perhaps for pilgrims landing at St. Ninian's Creek just below, is behind the houses at the road end. The low road to Wigtown by Carty Port, Carnestock and Grange of Cree is a delightful walk or drive through rich pastureland on the Moss of Cree and beside the weaving tapestry of the Cree looking over to Cairnsmore and then to Creetown and the quarries soaring up into the hills behind. The river was a busy highway for commercial traffic over the centuries. Carty Port (431625) behind the Brick and Tile works is an early nineteenth-century 'New Quay' built by the Earl of Galloway to replace the Old Carty Port upriver (427627) at St. Ninian's Creek. Vessels of at least forty tons brought in coal and took away agricultural produce and livestock up to the Great War period, c.1915. There was another jetty at Kelly Port (448613), and the O.S. 1850 map marks a 'Ferry Bell' (461603) with a jetty just south of the area later taken back from the river by the breakwater. Knockdoon Ferry at Spittal is opposite the 'Ferry Bell' on the east bank of the Cree.

CHAPTER 17

Wigtown, Kirkcowan, Kirkinner and Sorbie

Kirkcowan is a huge parish with vast moorland stretches north of the A75. Wigtown, Kirkinner and Sorbie are mostly fine farmland with fat contented cows enjoying the rich grazing and the carefully planned improved landscapes above the saltings and sands from the Cree estuary onto Wigtown Bay and behind the cliffs and headlands from Sliddery Point to Palmallet. Kirkinner and Sorbie are mid-seventeenth century amalgamations respectively of the mediaeval parishes of Kirkinner and Longcastle and of Sorbie, Kirkmadrine and Cruggleton; and Sorbie itself then consisted of Great Sorby and Little Sorby, which were joined c.1235-1253. The small size of Wigtown (possibly originally part of Penninghame) and mediaeval Kirkinner, Great Sorby, Little Sorby, Kirkmadrine and Cruggleton may mean that they correspond to Norse or early mediaeval Anglo-Norman land holdings.

Approaching Wigtown from the north always, time permitting, take the Moss of Cree road by Carty and Barsalloch, not an old route as the road north from Wigtown went only as far as the Bishop Burn until after 1807, but truly a road for all seasons where you feel close to the river and the sky and appreciate something of the lyrical and elemental quality of the watery landscape/seascape at low or high tide looking over to Creetown and across the 'Wigtown Sands'. Nearing Wigtown there may once have been another ferry to Creetown, well south of the Knockdoon crossing at Spittal, from a long jetty marked on the O.S. 1850 map north (459588) of Barsalloch. Drovers and their cattle were also taken over a 'ford' across the Wigtown Sands. The other road, the A714, is particularly good on the stretch going north down the hill towards Baltersan looking towards the Galloway hills. Although there are older roads by the Clachan of Penninghame site and from Carsegowan and Cairnhouse south by Glenturk Moor Croft to cross the B733 at Kirvennie Hill (421552), there is the site of another St. Ninian's Well (423576) south of St. Ninian's Bridge near Glenturk for mediaeval travellers and pilgrims. It is not merely a playful suggestion that the A714 and the A746 to Whithorn might be officially designated 'The Pilgrims' Way'.

On the Moss of Cree road continue by Borrowmoss and East Kirkland by the line of the old Newton Stewart to Whithorn railway (the Wigtown section opened in 1875) to the *Martyrs Stake* Car Park at the foot of the hill up to Wigtown. A sweet walk along the old railway embankment takes you to steps and a concrete track across the saltings to a stark simple stone post placed here in 1936 to mark the approximate location (437556) of the drowning at a wooden stake of the 'Wigtown Martyrs' in 1685. The view over to Kirkmabreck is superb and it hardly is necessary to point out that the fact that it was possible to drown anyone here shows just how much the balance of land and sea has changed in this area.

The 'martyrs' were not from Wigtown. Margaret McLachlan, the widow (aged 63) of John Milligan, was from Drumjargon (409505) near Whauphill in Kirkinner parish, and Margaret Wilson (aged 18) was from Glenvernoch (345753) in Penninghame parish. Details of the occupants of the farm of Glenvernoch and the ferm-toun of Drumjargon are included in the 1684 *Parish Lists of Wigtownshire and Minnigaff* (1916) edited by W. Scot for the Scottish Record Society. Their 'martyrdom' is best seen in the context of a whole series of cases of men and women also charged by the Episcopalian authorities with religious and political offences, that is of taking part in conventicles and in acts of rebellion. Of the others accused, William Johnston, George Walker and John Milroy from Penninghame were hanged. William Kerr from Boreland, Kirkcowan, who was imprisoned with McLachlan, escaped. John Dunn of Stewarton, who was banished, died at sea and his daughter, Janet Dunn, after examination through torture, her fingers burnt with matches and wedged into wimble bores, was sent as a prisoner to Glasgow. In the same way Episcopalian and Presbyterian authorities alike in their evangelical enthusiasm tortured, tried and burnt women and men at the stake as witches. In Scotland the number of those burnt whose names are known was 599, about a third of those executed, with the worst years the 1620s, the 1640s, the 1650s and the 1660s. This is important because seen in this light the case of the women drowned at Wigtown is not strange or even exceptionally wicked, but rather the unsurprising consequence of seventeenth-century Christian fanaticism and intolerance, just as dreadful and just as pointless as all the others. The example of Margaret Wilson seems especially devastating because she was so young, so brave and so foolish. The technically superb Millais painting of her as the 'Martyr of the Solway' (1871) in the Walker Art Gallery in Liverpool expresses all too well the nineteenth-century romantic view of the whole ghastly affair.

Wigtown was a lively mediaeval town as the centre of a sheriffdom (by 1263) and a burgh (1260s or pre-1292) with a courtyard castle and a Dominican priory (1267 or pre-1287). The main settlement was probably on the ridge and plateau above the Bladnoch which you still see clearly behind Bank House, although an earlier site near the castle is quite possible. The landing places and quays on the Bladnoch were certainly in different locations over the centuries. The eighteenth-century harbour at the foot of the hill (436556) near the Martyrs Stake Car Park is shown in William Daniell's print, sketched in 1815, in his *Picturesque Voyage Round the Coast of Great Britain* (1814-1825). The new quay south-east of the town, probably closer to the mediaeval harbour, was developed in 1817-1818 when the river was diverted into a new channel.

There are useful descriptions of Wigtown and more of the Machars in *Wigtown and Whithorn: Historical and Descriptive Sketches* (1877), *Lowland Lore; or the Wigtownshire of Long Ago* (1880) and the *Poems* (1885) prepared and published by the local bookseller and druggist, Gordon Fraser (1836-1890). Wm. McIlwraith's *The Visitors' Guide to Wigtownshire* (1875) is the best county survey, and Trotter's *Galloway Gossip Sixty Years Ago* (1877 or 1878 editions) is a wonderfully wise and comic collection of Wigtownshire stories and 'sensations'.

For a Wigtown perambulation climb up the hill road from the Martyrs Stake Car Park passing Croft-an-Righ, where there is a four-feet-high stone near the gate with two incised crosses (perhaps eleventh or twelfth century). The large parish church (1850) sits below the site and remains of the pre-Reformation church rebuilt in 1730. The tenth-century Anglian cross-slabs (p. 210) lay against the wall of the old church until a few years ago. The churchyard has more Covenanting interest memorials. Note from the War Memorial the splendid view over the saltings and south across to Kirkinner parish. The massive Bank House on the left with a walled garden was formerly the British Linen Company's Bank. The site of the Dominican priory and graveyard may be in the field behind Bank House or further east to the south of Croft-an-Righ. Continue up Bank Street and turn left in the Square at the amazing 'County Buildings' or 'Town Hall' (1863), on the site of the eighteenth-century town house and incorporating part of the old tolbooth. There is now a small *Museum* here. The summer exhibition in 1985 was appropriately on the theme 'Nae Bishop, Nae King'. The old bells include a Dutch example by Henrick ter Horst of Deventer inscribed 'O GOD LET WIGTOUNE FLOURISH BY THY WORD IN CHRIST WHO IS OUR ONLIE HEAD AND ANNO 1633'.

It is difficult now to imagine what the Square, actually a long rectangle consisting of North Main Street and South Main Street from the High Street on the west to Bank Street at the east or lower end, looked like before the West Port at the mouth of the High Vennel and the East Port opposite

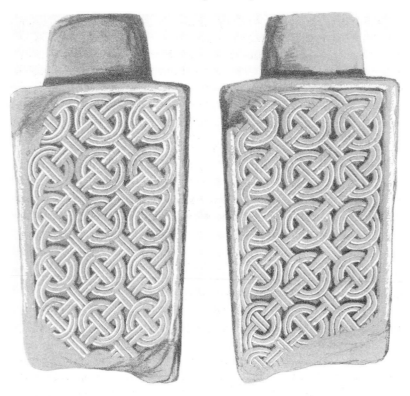

The Anglian cross-slabs at Wigtown. From John Stuart's *Sculptured Stones of Scotland* (1856).

Bank House were demolished to provide access for carriages with wheels in 1761. There may still then have been some lairds' town houses left, for example William Ahannay's tower house (1549) on the north side of the Hie Gaitt. The north side was also greatly altered with the opening up of the new main road from the north in the 1830s. In Wigtown today look rather for the late eighteenth and nineteenth-century merchants' and sea captains' houses, and the painted (blue, brown, pink, grey) fronts varying from the merely elegant to those which might be described as having the petrified toothpaste touch.

From the Square take Harbour Road at the south-east corner, that is opposite the Low Vennel on the other north-east side, passing Applegarth and, on the right, the delightful Southfield Lane behind South Main Street and the former Wigtown Prison (1848) with its fine display of chimneys.

The site of Wigtown Castle (438550) is in the field on the left. The outer gate and drawbridge of this courtyard castle were located on the south-west circumference in an excavation by Captain McKerlie in 1830. The castle was delivered to Edward I in 1291 and subsequently held as a royal castle for King John Balliol by various governors including Henry de Percy in 1296 and John de Hodleston in 1297. Only one earlier castle site is recorded and this only in a legal document in 1503 where there is a reference to the manor house and 'mote of Monkhill' belonging to Simon Makcristan. Monkhill is north-west of the town near the B7005. This and many other useful details are recorded in the *Wigtownshire Charters* (1960) edited by R.C. Reid for the Scottish History Society. At the foot of Harbour Road turn left along the rough road passing the site of Wigtown's railway station to Wigtown and Bladnoch Harbour (438546), opened in 1818 and taking vessels of up to 300 tons. There was also some shipbuilding here, for example the sloop *Britannia* of 50 tons in 1818 for Peter Anderson. Anyone who only remembers it from the 1960s will be amazed at the recent restoration and reconstruction work completed with the assistance of the Manpower Service Commission Special Temporary Employment programme.

Continue west by Seaview, Maidland Place and Dunure (formerly Barbadoes Villa) to the A714 and turn right for the Square by Beechwood, Acre Place, Orchardton, Kilquhirn Road, Southfield Lane and the Grapes Inn. Walk along Southfield Lane for the fine view to the south-east. At the Square turn right for the old and new Market Crosses (1738 and 1816) and go up the High Vennel by the former and classical picture house, a treat for cinema archaeology buffs, and follow the signposts for the Windyhill Monument (1858) at 430554 with superb vistas over the sea and the land in all directions.

It is good to see Wigtown reviving again in the 1980s, although it is unlikely ever to approach again its eighteenth and nineteenth-century pre-eminence before the railway era as the county town. It was perhaps symptomatic of its relative decline that it was in Newton Stewart that *The Galloway Gazette and Stranraer News* was founded in 1870 as a local newspaper to support the Conservative interest in opposition to the *Wigtown Free Press and Stranraer Advertiser* (1843) published in Stranraer and regarded as the Liberal paper. Unlike Kirkcudbright, where John Nicholson published the *Stewartry Times* (1860) for a short time, no local newspaper was even attempted in Wigtown. There was an earlier and short-lived monthly, *The Oracle,* published by T. Tait in Wigtown from 1831 to 1833, but it was a very slim journal compared to *The Galloway Register* published in Stranraer from 1836 to 1837 or later or the *Castle-Douglas*

North and South Main Street from the High Street, Wigtown, c.1900. Note the photographs on display at the shop doorway.

Miscellany (1823-1826) and the *Castle-Douglas Weekly Visitor* (1829-1832). In a different era *The Gallovidian* was published in Dalbeattie from 1899 to 1919 and *The Gallovidian Annual* in Dumfries from 1920 to 1941 and in 1949.

For Bladnoch and Baldoon take the A714 south from Wigtown passing what looks like a small toll-house at the Maidland road end (430547) and a standing stone in the dyke (424542) on the south side of the road in Bladnoch village. Bladnoch Distillery (420542), which produces malt for blending, was established in 1817. Cross the bridge and turn left by the Creamery and the site of the railway bridge on the Baldoon Mains road for Baldoon Castle (425537), associated with Scott's *The Bride of Lammermoor* (1819). Only a fragment of the Dunbars' sixteenth-century tower house remains, but the late seventeenth-century Renaissance-style gateway piers are exceptionally good. The Aerodrome (433533) was a Second World War field also used by a navigators' training school. Barracks and camps nearby housed up to 2000 men.

For the rest of Wigtown parish and then 'out of the world and into Kirkcowan' return by the B7005 passing Fordbank, now an hotel and Bird Garden, at the end of Potato Mill Road near the site (425547) of an extensive nineteenth-century starch manufactory. At the crossroads take the B733 west toward Spittal and Kirkcowan. The Bladnoch below powered nineteenth-century or earlier corn mills at Newmilns (402552) and Torhouse (396553) and a waulk mill (398553). There is also the site of a farina mill beside the road at 403554. The placenames near here are odd:

Megs Hill, Harrys Hill, Elspeths Hill and James Hill, and then Horse Hill and Yett Hill south of the site of Mains of Torhouse farm (386550). The prehistoric complex at *Torhouse Stone Circle* (383565) is one of the best in Galloway. The circle, cleared in 1929 but unexcavated, has nineteen rounded granite boulders, graded in height to the east-south-east, round a low stony mound, and there are three boulders in a line on a raised stony central platform. The mound may conceal cremation burial pits or cists or even be a denuded cairn converted into a major ritual monument. The three standing stones on the north side of the road may be an alignment or even part of a stone row. Note also the stone with a deep hollow cavity in the dyke on the south side of the road which 'the knowing never pass without depositing therein some pebble or gift to pass in peace'. There are also three cairn sites (383566) and a 'fort' or settlement site (379567) nearby.

Leave the B733 at Spittal and take not the B7052 but instead the unclassified road west to the north of Clugston Loch and by Gass and Inchmalloch to High Mindork (307586). This is a delightful road ablaze with the colour of wild flowers and roses and old hedges which hopefully will never be ruined by 'tax-concession' trees and 'financial' forests. The two standing stones (352581) as outliers to the White Cairn, the Doon Hill fort (347585) with double ramparts and the site of Mindork Castle (322587) are less important than the magic of the road itself and the deserted cottages and farms, which include Low Mindork (314590). The chapel site (303590) on the south bank of the Tarf Water opposite Kenmore is probably Dark Age or early mediaeval. Just before High Mindork take the road north over the Tarf Water by Barnearie to the B733 beyond the old railway line. Turn left by the woods concealing Craighlaw Loch, a famous curling venue, and Craighlaw (306611). The tower built by William Gordon c.1500 was restored in the nineteenth century and incorporated in the larger mansion house. Glendarroch (308617) is a timber shooting lodge brought across from Norway.

At Halfway House on the A75 turn east by Kildarroch and take the road north at the crossroads (316623) by West Culvennan and Dirnow. The 'mote' (296655) opposite Ballochadee Faulds and south of The Rhong may be a natural feature. Turn west on the Glassoch-Glenluce road for the Black Loch, Loch Heron, where a crannog site (271647) is recorded, Loch Ronald and the Tarf Water east of Torwood House Hotel. On the moors to the north the most important sites are the Wood Cairn (252687) on Eldrig Fell south of the High Eldrig road and the White Cairn (263676) near Airies Wood. The possibly eleventh-century cross slab recorded as the lintel in the back door of the deserted farmhouse at Low Eldrig (251679) suggests another lost chapel site nearby on the Tarf Water on a route from Laggangairn and the Wells of the Rees to the north to the chapel near High Mindork to the south. An old mill lade is marked on the 1850 O.S. map at 252627 west of Airyligg on the Tarf.

From the crossroads (287663) at Dirnow old schoolhouse take the road east by Drumnabrennan and Kilquhockadale, and then the road south by Carseriggan and Barfad to join the Old Military Road at 334637 towards Shennanton. There are deserted eighteenth-century ferm-toun sites at Crunlae (317634) and old Ardachie (322640) north of the present farm. Note the disused eighteenth-century two-arched bridge (343632) over the Bladnoch and then negotiate your way onto the A75 going west and then take the B735 towards Kirkcowan. Note the line of cairns at 335631 and 338624 with another site at 338628. There is another fine corn mill (340618) south of Barhoise farm and the Linn associated with the 'Brownie of Blednoch'.

Kirkcowan is a classic example of a strip village running from below the church (1834) with outside stairs at the top of the street to the old churchyard with a fragment of the old church (1658) at the bottom. It may have been the location of the parchment burgh of Knockcreavie created in 1642 for Gordon of Craighlaw. The old railway station on the Stranraer line was west (322610) of the school. There is some good period architecture including the Craighlaw Arms and the distinguished former manse, Kirkland House, south of the village. The old chimney and weaving sheds in the distance belong to the late nineteenth-century Armstrong's woollen mills (330602) on the south bank of the Bladnoch. Milroy's waulk mill, eighteenth century and rebuilt in 1821, and also disused, is downstream on the north bank. From Kirkcowan take the B733 over Johnston's Bridge by The Holm and Boreland Fell Quarry and the badly eroded Boreland or Clugston motte (355584) to Spittal and then the B7052 into Kirkinner parish.

The Broom Hill and Chapel Meadow area north of Crows is interesting with, close to the B7052, the denuded round White Cairn and a fine holed stone (365558), now separated by a dyke. The chapel, well and kirkyard site (370557), an enclosure with a low bank or wall in marshy ground in Chapel Meadow, and the rectangular 'moat' (368557), which has disappeared under cultivation, may be a mediaeval group of church, homestead and possible deserted village, but Dark Age and Iron Age dating for the chapel and fortified enclosure respectively is another possible interpretation. Continue south by the former (Dalreagle) school and the old smithy, c. 1840, at Malzie Bridge (371541). At the road junction take the B7005 west to

Culmalzie, where this road continues west by Airriequhillart and Corsemalzie House Hotel towards the A747, and then the B7052 again (the Sorbie road) passing a holy well site (374528) below Chapel Hill and Doonhill fort (380515). Continue by Sheep Park and Slochabbert to Whauphill, a crossroads village beside the old Whithorn railway line which came up from Kirkinner before swinging away down to Sorbie, all real 'Wigtown Ploughman' country.

Using Whauphill as a central point, take first the A714 by March and Culbae passing the standing stone (382481) before the former Longcastle school (381479) and the site of the mediaeval parish church of Longcastle at Kirkland (376474). The side road by Camford to Drummoddie takes you below Annat Hill fort (384465), another rectangular and largely ploughed enclosure which might be mediaeval or Dark Age or Iron Age. The Long Castle (394468), south-east of Boreland of Longcastle, seems to have been a tower house with other buildings on an artificial island site located at the western extremity of the now drained Dowalton Loch. Another chapel site (393473) is recorded on Chapel Hill to the north.

Again from Whauphill the B7052 by the old railway line passes Barwhanny (410494), where there is a fine circular twenty-five feet high windmill tower. For more details and for a description of many other mills, breweries, tanneries, quarries, roads and canals see Ian Donnachie's *The Industrial Archaeology of Galloway* (1971). Take the side road just before Mill of Airies (417481) towards Macher Stewart by Stonehouse, which is north-east of the Dowalton Loch area drained in 1863, when at least ten crannogs were located and some excavated. Further south there is another Doonhill fort (414470) and the site (417468) of St. Michael's, the parish church of Little Sorby beside the road south-west of Culnoag.

Lastly from Whauphill and for the rest of Kirkinner parish, take the A714 north passing Barnbarroch (398515), a Georgian mansion house built c.1780 and with Victorian additions gutted by a fire in 1941 described in the Third Statistical Account of Scotland volume for *The Stewartry of Kirkcudbright and the County of Wigtown* (1965). The estate was held from the late fourteenth century by the de Vaux or Vanses, who had an international 'family' get-together there in 1984. At the crossroads after Barglass take the side road east by Maltkiln Bridge to the A746 south of Milldriggan (421521), a fine large early nineteenth-century mill on a mediaeval site. The cresset stone from Newton Hill farm is in the National Museum of Antiquities in Edinburgh.

In the early nineteenth-century strip village of Kirkinner the parish church (1828) contains the repaired and restored Anglian wheel-headed cross formerly in the churchyard. The church is almost certainly on an early Christian site as the churchyard area does look like an amphitheatre, and this would have been useful for an early preaching and mission station staffed from Whithorn. Andrew Symson (c.1638-1712), the Episcopalian rector from 1663 to 1686, is one of Galloway's most distinguished authors. His *Large Description of Galloway* (1684) is particularly useful as a record of contemporary farming methods and technological levels from the tilling of oatland to obtaining oil for lamps from stranded whales, dyes from cork-lit and lichens, and sacks and ropes from hemp-rigs. Samuel Robinson (1786-1875), who was born in Kirkinner parish, left in his *Reminiscences of Wigtonshire* (1872 and 1984) an excellent picture of the land and the condition of the people, tenant farmers, labourers, Irish immigrants, schoolteachers, smugglers, politicians, in the 1790s and 1800s. A third local author, John Lauderdale, actually an Ulsterman and variously quarryman at Milldriggan, squatter at Claycroft, shopkeeper and schoolteacher, left a slim volume of *Poems chiefly in the Scottish Dialect* (1796 and 1984) with some happy and coarse comments on local life and leisure pursuits.

Take the A746 up the hill from Kirkinner and continue on it to Sorbie rather than taking the B7004 by North Balfern, where the Ring Hill (437509) is a vitrified fort with double concentric defences, and Stewarton and Orchardton to Garlieston. Drive with special care through Kilsture Forest, where the Forestry Commission provides another signposted Walk, and past the modern Creamery where the Newton Stewart to Whithorn railway came in from Claunch to Sorbie Station before going east towards the Old Place of Sorbie and the Garlieston branch line. The row of cottages in Sorbie village on the south side of the B7052 may have been built for the employees of the famous damask manufactory founded in 1789 and which still had 91 hands in 1838. It won a prize of £40 in 1834 for having the best woven cloth in Scotland. The old church almost opposite (438468), built for the united parishes of Kirkmadrine, Sorbie and Cruggleton, was repaired in 1713, rebuilt in 1750 and enlarged in 1826, but was closed by the Earl of Galloway after he provided a new church at Millisle in 1876. Note in the churchyard the stone (1768) for George Bean, White Smith in Garlieston, with hammermen's guild symbols and a broken (1718?) stone leaning against the west gable of the church with two lively trumpet-blowing angels.

Continue on the B7052 by the Old Place of Sorbie (451470), the Hannays' late sixteenth-century L-plan tower house just beyond the rectangular motte (451469) on what had been a strong site surrounded by swamps and marshes. The very active Clan Hannay Society has done basic consolidation work on the tower and cleared the area; and excavations by

Eric Talbot of the University of Glasgow have established that the motte, with originally at least a flying bridge to the top, was occupied by a succession of buildings into the sixteenth century. More remarkable still was the location of a cobbled roadway running out east-north-east from the courtyard. The tower itself is exceptionally spacious and altogether rather grand. Note the human head as a corbel termination to the stairway turret over the entrance. The most unusual Hannay, whether of Sorbie or Kirkdale, was the diplomat and court poet Patrick Hannay, the author of 'A Happy Husband or Directions to a Maid to chose her Mate' (1619) and 'A Wife's Behaviour before Marriage' (1619) and other polished elegies, songs and sonnets:

> The quaking aspen, light and thin,
> To the air free passage gives—
> Resembling still
> The trembling ill
> Of tongues of womankind;
> Which never rest,
> But still are prest
> To wave with every wind.

But the Hannays generally were more likely to be involved with feuds and quarrels with their neighbours, the Murrays of Broughton, than in poesy, and perhaps their ghosts will be happy to see the reviving fortunes of their Old Place in comparison to the virtual disappearance of even the site of the Old Place of Broughton (456452), an oval enclosure north-east of Broughton Mains and in the same field as the site of the Brick and Tile Works opened in 1841. An heraldic stone (1628) from this Old Place is built into Broughton Mains farmhouse.

Continue on the B7052 from the Old Place of Sorbie to experience the contrast in architectural styles in the eighteenth-century great house and planned village at Garlieston. The old Garlieston railway, which opened in 1876 and took passengers up to 1903 and freight until 1964, branched off from the Whithorn line just before Millisle or Sorbie Parish Church (468463) and then ran north of the road until crossing it just before the B7004 junction and going south of the village to the harbour. The stained glass in the church, including a window by Christopher Whall (1849-1924), is unusually good. The site of the mediaeval Great Sorby church (St. Fillans) is just to the north at 470466. Millisle farm is the home of some twenty superb prize-winning Clydesdales. The site of the nineteenth-century Millisle Tile Works is at 468473 close to the B7004. Galloway House (478452), built by John Douglas between 1739 and 1745 for the sixth Earl of Galloway and that family's principal residence until

ADVERTISEMENTS.

Galloway Steam Navigation Co.

GALLOWAY AND LIVERPOOL.

THE FINE STEAM VESSEL

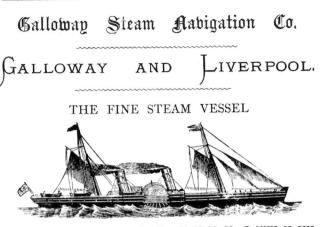

COUNTESS OF GALLOWAY,

JAMES COID, *Commander.*

Sails regularly (weather permitting, and unless prevented by any unforeseen circumstance) between the Ports of GALLOWAY and LIVERPOOL, with Passengers, Cattle, and Goods.

Passenger Fares : — CABIN, 10s, (including Steward's Fee) ; STEERAGE, 5s.

N.B —Passengers must provide themselves with Tickets from the Agents before going on Board. Return Tickets, available for One Month, may be had from the Agents, subject to the printed conditions thereon—

CABIN, 16s. :- STEERAGE, 8s.

Secretary to the Co.—-E. S. BLACK, BRITISH LINEN CO. BANK, WIGTOWN.

AGENTS :—

WIGTOWN, - - - -	JOHN A. M'KINNELL.
GARLIESTOWN, - - - -	ROBERT HIGHET.
ISLE OF WHITHORN, - - - -	JAMES DUFF.
KIRKCUDBRIGHT, - - - -	SAMUEL CAVAN.
LIVERPOOL, MINERS & Co., 9 Chapel Walks, S. Castle St.	

FOR PARTICULARS SEE HANDBILLS.

Gordon Fraser's *Wigtown and Whithorn* (1877) has a back section with sixty pages of advertisements for everything from steam threshing machines and cheese presses to 'London Nourishing Stout highly recommended by the medical profession' and, as here, steam packet company publicity material.

A postcard view of the Crescent, Garlieston (here the older spelling as Garliestown) c.1908, with the Bowling Green to the left.

1908, is a dignified, plain, solid house. The grounds, with originally seven porters' lodges and a massive boundary wall, were and indeed still are exceedingly impressive with great trees, parterres, walkways and drives, and even balconies cut out above the cliffs south of Sliddery Point. From 1947 to 1977 Galloway House was used as a residential school for children from Glasgow's Primary Schools. Some of the Glasgow keelies were reputed to have been overcome by the fresh air!

Garlieston was laid out about 1760 by Lord Garlies, later the seventh Earl of Galloway. The crescent round the bay with parallel streets behind makes an unusual and attractive composition. The pier and harbour (481462) were built about 1816, with further improvements in 1854. The Dumbie breakwater was added in 1843. Shipbuilding developed from about 1800, mostly sloops such as the *James Bryce* of 71 tons in 1816, the *Swiftsure* of 28 tons in 1817 and the *Keith Stewart* of 59 tons in 1818. Some larger vessels were built, including the *Lady Mary Stewart* of 100 tons in 1862. Rope and sail cloth was manufactured at a nineteenth-century rope walk at the north-west curve of the bay (480470) north of the site of the corn mill at Mill Bridge. The harbour is still used by vessels bringing in fertiliser. And the 1985 summer cruise by the *Waverley* from Garlieston to the Isle of Man gave passengers an unexpected opportunity to experience the sort of storms the nineteenth-century steamer, *The Countess of Galloway,* might have encountered on her runs from Garlieston or Kirkcudbright to Liverpool.

North of Garlieston Bay the site of the castle at Eggerness (494477) in the wooded area above the cliffs beyond Port Whapple is only suggested by the ditch at the north end. The remains of the mediaeval parish church of Kirkmadrine and a small burial yard (475482) are on Penkiln farm, directly south of Innerwell Port (478493) and Fishery.

South of Garlieston take the B7063 into the mediaeval parish of Cruggleton. Rigg or Cruggleton Bay was used in 1944 for testing the 'Mulberry Harbours' in preparation for the Normandy landings. Cruggleton church (477428) was rebuilt in 1892 with funds provided by the Marquis of Bute. It was a fairly extensive restoration as all the walls had collapsed by 1884. The simple nave and chancel are probably twelfth or early thirteenth century. Cruggleton Castle (485428), on a large and spectacular promontory site visible in the distance from further south on the B7963, has a very complex history. The kitchen vault which is still standing and is such a prominent landmark belongs to a late fifteenth or sixteenth-century tower house; excavations at the end of the 1970s have established that underneath lie the remains of the late thirteenth-century courtyard castle with a great eight foot thick curtain wall occupied in 1292 by John Comyn, who obtained a licence from Edward I to dig for lead in ruins in the Calf of Man to cover the eight towers at Cruggleton; and underneath this is a motte and bailey with wooden buildings including a twelfth or thirteenth-century tower and an earlier, perhaps eleventh-century, single-storey hall. The cliffs are dangerous and erosion is a problem.

CHAPTER 18

Whithorn, Glasserton and Mochrum

The geographical location, the long coastline and the rich farming country behind made Whithorn, Glasserton and Mochrum parishes attractive and accessible from the earliest times to settlers from England, Ireland and the Isle of Man. Ploughing and field clearance over the centuries have left only sparse evidence of great cairns or stone circles, the funerary and ritual monuments of the Neolithic and Bronze Ages. But only mid-Argyll in Scotland is better in terms of the number of rock outcrops with cup and ring markings and of their artistic quality from the spiral at Gallows Outon (448420) and the marvellous carvings at Broughton Mains (450452), first reported in 1974, to the better-known sites near Monreith. These are described in detail in R. W. B. Morris, *The Prehistoric Rock Art of Galloway and the Isle of Man* (1979). The vulnerability of the area to raiders and invaders in the Iron Age and Dark Age world is suggested by the number of fortifications along the coast, for example south of Cruggleton at Dinnans (479405), Dinnans—The Old Fort (478402), Cairn Head (486382) and Stein Head (485371). Iron Age or Anglian and Norse period or early mediaeval occupation are all possible. The Old Fort with formidable banks or ramparts and a protected rock inlet approach up which boats could be dragged is very interesting as a possible Norse fortification.

Using the same seaways, early Christian saints and missionaries and their mediaeval successors and propagandists made Whithorn a major and a cosmopolitan centre for the propagation of the faith and for pilgrimage—a sort of combination, for kings and common folk alike, of penance and early tourism—to St. Ninian's shrine. And, trafficking in brandy and tea rather than in souls, smugglers found the coast from the Isle to Auchenmalg a haven in the eighteenth century for their nefarious activities. Just as romantic in its way was the coming of the Wigtownshire Railway, which finally reached Whithorn from Sorbie via Broughton Skeog and Chapel Outon in 1877. Full details of the line and its history are available in D. L. Smith, *The Little Railways of South-West Scotland* (1969). Until 1939 it was possible to go in a through coach from Whithorn to Edinburgh and return in the same day, an amazing contrast in convenience and comfort to public transport facilities by bus in the 1980s. The last passenger train left Whithorn in 1950. Freight continued up to 1964.

The classic view from the south down George Street on a card posted in Whithorn on 10 February, 1906.

Entering Whithorn from the north, the A746 from Sorbie by Castlewigg and the B7004 from Millisle by Gallows and the Stirnie Birnie Bridge (447412) meet just south of the site of the Wigtownshire Railway station (445408). The best approach, however, is from the B7063 by Cruggleton taking the side road at 472406 by Drummaston and Claywhippart Bridge (454404) into Whithorn from the east and looking south to High Skeog where the Court Hill (454397) seems more like a small Iron Age fort. Note on the left in Castle Hill road the buildings of Whithorn School and in the playing fields opposite the site of the castle or episcopal palace and fortalice of Balnespik (448403). Castle Hill takes you out at the Grapes Hotel towards the north end of George Street, the long main street originally with 'ports' at either end which sweeps down the hill from the south.

Rather than going immediately to explore the Priory area off the pend, Bruce Street, behind the gatehouse and archway with the Royal Arms of Scotland built by Bishop Vaus (1482-1508), visitors should first enjoy a Whithorn perambulation. In particular do not miss walking up the hill to the south end of George Street and looking back from the site of the 'port' at the 'narrows' before the High Street. The wide street and the later eighteenth and nineteenth-century houses with their painted door and window surrounds make a finely balanced composition. The old town hall with square tower, steeple and weather vane was built in 1814 to replace the tolbooth which, according to Mr Nicholson writing in 1839 in the New Statistical Account of Scotland, was in the middle of the street. King's Road, almost opposite and with good views back to George Street, was perhaps on the mediaeval pilgrims' route from the Isle by Prestrie and north of Mains Loch. The Ket (burn) running from west of the Priory and eventually south-east to Portyerrock actually still ran *across* George Street at the end of the eighteenth century.

Although the burn served a tannery (446402), and a windmill (446398) which stood at the top of the hill at the end of Isle Street generated the power for grinding corn, Whithorn was not an industrial town but rather a service centre for a large rural area. The 1851 Census gives a fascinating breakdown of the town population, the carriers, blacksmiths, cattle dealers, bankers, booksellers, Presbyterian clergymen in four varieties, lodging house keepers, drapers, saddlers, teachers and small farmers, and the china merchant, cabinetmaker, mangler, ragman, flowerer, staymaker, musician Andrew Denniston, thatcher John Murphy, 'Qack Doctor' Hugh Irving, retired Jamaica planter James Lawson, and the group of English travelling players, the comedians and actresses George F. and Jane Adams, James and Eliza Bostock and Joseph and Martha Williams. Another lively picture of later nineteenth-century Whithorn is contained in J. F. Cannon, *Droll Recollections of Whithorn and Vicinity* (1904) and in the poems by David McWhirter of the Isle, *A Ploughman's Musings* (1883), including his 'Cloopie an' the Poachers' and 'Candlemas Day at School'. Walk round the churchyard and by The Ket from the George Street entrance for the church (1822) and the stones with some fine calligraphy for Whithorn burgesses and mariners and farmers, and the best, the most honest and the most believable Covenanting Martyrs stone for Janet Brown and her husband Hugh Dunse, who 'endured persecution' in the reign of Charles II 'but kept steady in the faith and a good conscience'.

The *Museum* in the old school (1731) in Bruce Street has a marvellous collection of sculptured stones, including the mid-fifth century memorial for Latinus and his daughter, set up by his grandson Barrovadus; the seventh-century St. Peter's Stone, possibly from an oratory and cemetery site (443392) south of Whithorn; the probably tenth and eleventh-century cross shafts and disc-headed crosses in the Anglian style commemorating individuals and brought together from landholdings, farms and chapels in Whithorn, Longcastle, Mochrum and Glasserton and including the Monrieth Cross originally from the Court Hill of Moure (382433); and the seventh to eleventh-century slabs and stones with incised crosses from St. Ninian's Cave.

Although there is no evidence of any Roman fort or camp at Whithorn, and a naval base at the Isle seems as or more likely, there is no doubt that Whithorn was a (possibly urban) settlement with a partly Romanised and partly Christian British population by the fourth century. Recent excavation finds of fourth-century pottery from Alexandria and late Roman glass provide further confirmation. Whether this should be called 'Leucophibia' is altogether more speculative. St. Ninian, it now seems, came as a bishop, c.396/397, and not necessarily the first, to an already established Christian community. This does not in any way underestimate his importance or his success and reputation for sanctity in developing the community at Whithorn, in erecting a stone church c.400-430, possibly the building under the east end of the Priory church although this could also be later fifth or sixth century, and in making Whithorn a powerful evangelical base for outgoing missionary endeavour. It is even possible that his shrine was attracting pilgrims as early as the sixth or seventh century. Far less is known about the Celtic/Anglian monastery—recent excavations in the glebe field may have located part of the vallum or enclosing wall and boundary ditch—and whether and in what state it survived the period of Norse domination when Hvitsborg may have been a Norse town and wintering station. Certainly a workshop for making sculptured stones was active into the tenth and eleventh centuries.

The restoration of the bishopric by Bishop Gilla-Aldan after 1128 and the development of the *Cathedral Priory* with the arrival of the Premonstratensian canons from Soulseat c.1175 or earlier and under Bishop Christian (1154-1186) mark a new period of growth and prosperity. Only the twelfth-century south-west doorway in the church, with fine Romanesque decorative detail, suggests the quality of the new buildings. The rich collection of grave goods of thirteenth and fourteenth-century bishops from the east end of the church is unfortunately in Edinburgh. The magnificent crozier (c.1200) in gilt metal and enamel decoration with the figures of four bishops and sixteen prophets holding scrolls, plus beasts and monsters and birds and fishes, is outstanding. Mediaeval Whithorn is, however, associated in particular with the immense popularity of pilgrimages to St. Ninian's shrine at the east end of the Priory church, a journey undertaken by the kings of Scotland from Robert I in 1329 to James IV (frequently) and James V. Whithorn itself became an ecclesiastical burgh by 1325 or earlier. There is no doubt that this was a very profitable activity for the town, which was by far the most cosmopolitan in the south of Scotland, nor is there any doubt about the devastating effects of the banning of pilgrimage by the Scottish Parliament and General Assembly in 1581. Modern pilgrimages were begun by the Catholic Church before the War and resumed after 1945.

To explore the southern part of Whithorn parish take the Castle Hill road by Low Skeog and Stairfield, passing a standing stone in the dyke (467398), and the B7063 by Portyerrock (476389), formerly the site of a grain mill and a salmon fishing station, to the Isle of Whithorn. The village on the 'mainland' is clustered round the former Bysbie corn mill on the Drummullin Burn and the L-plan tower house (476365) or 'castle' built in 1674 by Patrick Houston of Drummaston. At the end of the eighteenth century the 'castle' became the local headquarters of the Revenue Prevention Service under Sir John Reid, and it seems to have been more or less continuously occupied since then, for example in 1851 by the village butcher John Findlay and into the 1940s as a boarding house. From the bridge walk along the artificial 'mole' constructed c.1790 and carrying the row of houses opposite the church, which was built in 1844 as a Free Church on a site below the high water mark provided by Whithorn Town Council, and between the Stinking Port and the harbour to the 'Isle' proper. Continue by the Steam Packet Hotel and the old warehouses along the quayside to the pier (c.1790 with later additions and major repairs) and then to *St. Ninian's Chapel,* built in the thirteenth century for pilgrims arriving at the harbour or landing just to the south at the Chapel Ports East and West on the Isle. The Iron Age and Dark Age promontory fort (480360) with three ditches cut across at the landward side is at the south end of the Isle.

The Isle of Whithorn was a busy nineteenth-century port with a tradition of shipbuilding from at least as far back as the *Cutcloy* c.1799 and the sloops, the *Sir William Maxwell* and the *Jane and Mary,* of 45 and 57 tons respectively in 1804 and 1817. The 1851 Census shows that the Isle was a village of mariners, seamen, ship carpenters and carters, and with a tailor, a grocer, the joiner and shipbuilder William McWilliam employing eight men, the miller William McCredie, the schoolmaster and parish Inspector of Poor Isaac McConnel, and the innkeepers Thomas Broadfoot, Jane McWilliam and Charlotte Logan from the Isle of Man.

Take Tonderghie Row by Drummoral, which has a fort (461362), and Cutreoch, which has a Gallows Hill and the site of a castle at 467357, and Cutcloy for Burrow Head, where the caravan site complex is on the site of a large Second World War military camp. There are promontory forts west of the Devil's Footsteps (459341), at Burrow Head (457341) and at Castle Feather (448342). The 1850 O.S. map records the site of 'Bysbie Old Mill' beside the little stream at 452342. The shafts of the copper and lead Mary Mine (440347) south of Tonderghie were opened in the 1790s with further attempts in the 1840s and perhaps exploratory work during the Great War. Further west the site of another castle or fortification is recorded at Carghidown (436350).

For *St. Ninian's Cave* (422359) take the A750 from Isle of Whithorn and the A747 Port William road to the signposted access road for the charming walk through Physgill Glen and Gilhow Plantation. The cave, which contained the cross slabs discovered between 1883 and 1886 and now in the Priory Museum, was used as a retreat by St. Ninian and his successors in the sixth and seventh centuries and quite probably into the mediaeval period. It is still possible to see the incised crosses on the walls of the cave. The modern Catholic pilgrimages are centred on the Cave rather than on the Priory. Port Castle (426358) at the east end of the bay may be in origin an Iron Age fort, but there seems to have been later occupation and building activity whether mediaeval or eighteenth-century (smuggling related?). The present compact Physgill House (428367) is an interesting example of a country residence expanding and contracting over three centuries to meet changing needs. Other houses with Victorian excesses to cope with have been less fortunate.

Continue west on the A747 for Glasserton Church (421380), an admirable building of 1732 with additions in 1836, approached through the carefully planned parkland of Glasserton estate. The belfry (1580) is from Kirkmaiden church near Monrieth. Note the mural monument in the north wall of the burial aisle at the east end of the church for Lady Garlies (159-), with two rows of human heads, five male and six female. Part of the head of a cross found in the 1890s is inside the church. Other Anglian cross-shafts from Knock and Craiglemine are in Edinburgh. The very atmospheric churchyard has some striking stones with conventional symbolism, including the upright for John Conning in Applebie (1761).

Glasserton House was the principal residence of the Earls of Galloway until it was burned down in 1734. The later mansion (site at 418376) in Cairnsmore granite was built for Admiral Keith Stewart (1739-1795) c.1780 or after 1767. It was the power house of a planned estate with splendid 'pleasure grounds' and functional buildings including the farm offices (417378), a rectangular dovecot (416379) and a dairy (417377). The 1851 Census gives an idea of the scale of the operation in the middle of the nineteenth century, as it lists eleven servants at the House, a footman, a housekeeper, a nurse and a nurserymaid, a kitchenmaid, a cook, two housemaids, a laundress, a dairymaid and a messenger, and at the Mains the head groom Alexander Morton from Kelso with six men, the gardener Alexander McMorran from Minnigaff with two apprentices and sixteen labourers, Elizabeth Steel from Carsphairn in charge of the poultry, and the tenant farmer John Dinwoodie from Moffat with fourteen labourers and five others.

Glasserton House from the south in an engraving from a drawing by J. P. Neale published in London in February, 1829.

The 'mote' (413371) on a ridge to the south partly within Broad Lane Wood may be Iron Age or Dark Age rather than mediaeval. There are cup and ring markings on an outcrop (407375) between Broad Lane Wood and the Fell of Carleton. Further west Laggan Camp (398372) is an Iron Age fort. The 'Mill Stone Howe' (397376) recorded on the Fell of Carleton on the 1850 O.S. map may be a millstone quarrying site, and there is an old slate quarry at 401379 south of Slate Heugh. Unusual placenames include the Howe Hill of Haggagamalag east of Tonderghie and, on Glasserton Mains, the 'Sleeping Man' and 'Man-Wrap' as field names.

From Glasserton take the A746 to Whithorn by Long Hill and the Rispain road end. *Rispain Fort* (429399), which has been in State care since 1890, has a massive rectangular ditch with rounded corners and inner and outer banks. Excavations (1978 to 1981) have established that it is neither a Roman camp nor a mediaeval moated manor but instead a first/second-century A.D. fortified homestead with three round timber house sites. It is at least possible that the Novantae farmer-builders were imitating Roman military architecture encountered elsewhere in Galloway. A report is contained in the *Transactions of the Dumfriesshire and Galloway Natural History and Antiquarian Society*, LVIII, 1983, a series which is required reading for and should be subscribed to by all Galloway enthusiasts.

For the north of Whithorn parish and moving west into Glasserton and Mochrum take the A746 by Chapel Outon, where there is a chapel site at 448421. In the trees west of the road is the now derelict Castlewigg (426432) built c.1800 by Captain John Hawthorn and incorporating a tower house (Castle Wigg), at the south-west corner, perhaps by Archibald Stewart of Barclye (Tonderghie) who acquired the estate from Sir John Vaus in 1584. The Anglian-style cross, now in the Priory Museum, found in a field between Castlewigg and Bridge House (Brighouse) c.1890, may indicate that the Wigg was the focal point of a much older landholding.

On the A746 take the side road for Ravenstone at 433456 by Barledziew and Grennan. Ravenstone Castle or Castle Stewart (409441) is another and larger derelict house last occupied c.1930. The late sixteenth-century L-plan Maclellan tower house and the late seventeenth-century Stewart house are overwhelmed by the later eighteenth-century double-bow extension and another block added by Lord Borthwick in 1874. The nineteenth-century pump house and horse-powered water pump are unusual. The castle site west of Drumgin (402444) is perhaps an earlier tower house or moated manor site with marsh and water defences. There is also a crannog at the east side of the White Loch of Ravenstone (401440). Mr Clanaghan, writing in the New Statistical Account (1838), notes that the loch contains 'leeches of a superior sort'. Leeches were still prescribed by doctors well into the nineteenth century, hence the opportunity for the 'gill-gatherers' as described by Mactaggart (1824) to collect leeches in the marshes, presumably for sale. They were 'commonly old women' who waded 'about with their coats kilted high. The vampires lay hold of them by the legs, when the gill-gatherers take them off, and bottle them up'.

Continue south-west to the B7021 junction at the former Ravenstone school (396426) and turn west above the Dowies or Monrieth Burn. The Old Place of Dowies or Ballingrene (381430) is a sadly derelict sixteenth-century L-plan tower house occupied by the Maxwells until 1683 and converted into a farmhouse and steading in the early nineteenth century. Interesting details include the stair turret, a gun port and a gargoyle head. The much older Court or Castle Hill of Moure (382433), where the Monrieth Cross stood, is on the north side of the burn. There is another castle site (401408), a not very convincing motte and bailey, on the Dowies Burn west of Appleby.

There are cup and ring marked outcrops on Big Balcraig (at 374440 and 376445), including cups with seven rings, one a very large carving of twenty-five inches diameter. The *Drumtroddan Cup and Ring Marked Rocks* (363447), reached by the farm road off the A714 and then south of the farmhouse, have an excellent display of cups with rings and radial and connecting grooves. The *Drumtroddan Standing Stones* (364443), 400 yards to the south, are an impressive alignment (to what is a matter for free speculation). The two stones still standing are over ten feet high; the third stone has fallen to the ground.

Monrieth estate policies south of the B7021 between the A714 and the 'Clachan of Myrton' (368439) on the north and Blairbuie on the south have an important group of sites, including the crannogs at the south end of the White Loch (358432) and on the former Black Loch area (361428). The Lady Well (363431) south of Monrieth Mains is probably a holy well site. Myrton Castle (360432) is a motte with a McCulloch tower house c.1500 built inside it, perhaps replacing a timber blockhouse or tower, and with a seventeenth-century wing added on the north side of the mound. James IV stayed here on pilgrimage to Whithorn and granted a charter for the burgh of barony of Myrtoun in 1504. (This is quite distinct from the burgh of barony of Myreton at Merton Hall in Penninghame parish granted to John Kennedy of Blairquhan in 1477.) Monrieth was purchased by Sir William Maxwell in 1683. The present Monrieth House was built in 1799. C. H. Dick's *Highways and Byways in Galloway and Carrick* (1916) has a particularly good description of the house and the White Loch. The owner, Sir Herbert Maxwell (1845-1937), was a remarkable man, naturalist, botanist, essayist, historian and antiquarian, an accomplished artist producing in his '70s and '80s exquisite flower paintings, and chairman of the Royal Commission on the Ancient and Historical Monuments and Constructions of Scotland. This last distinction explains why the Reports for the *County of Wigtown* (1912) and the *County of the Stewartry of Kirkcudbright* (1914) were preceded only by Berwickshire, Caithness, and Sutherland, and also why so many monuments were taken into State care in Whithorn and Glasserton parishes. The White Loch was reputed to have extraordinary detergent *and* curative properties. Symson (1684) records that the water 'will wash linnen as well without soap, as many others will do with it . . . it is an excellent place for whitening and bleeching of linnen, Holland and muzlin webbs . . . several persons, both young and old, have been cured of continued diseases by washing therein . . . I cannot approve of their washing three times therein, which they say, they must do; neither the frequenting thereof the first Sunday . . . of February, May, August and November . . .'

For Monrieth Bay take the A714 by Cupid Hill west of the White Loch and the side road by Airlour and South Barsalloch to join the A747 in Monrieth village. Continue east on the A747 by Clarksburn Bridge and take the golf course road to the car parking area on Back Bay. Monrieth

Bay, Front Bay and Back Bay may have been smugglers' landing places, and the coastline to the east has a series of caves to below Cairndoon and another Grey Mare's Tail (374390). There is a small promontory fort (369393) south-east of Back Bay. Walk back by Front Bay and up to the sweetly sequestered Kirkmaiden church (365399), probably an early site, as a tenth/eleventh-century cross-slab was found here, and as romantic a ruin as will be found anywhere. The churchyard was the burial ground of the McCullochs and the Maxwells of Monrieth. Note the monument placed here in 1960 for Commander Thurot of the French navy. His body was swept ashore after the sea battle in Luce Bay in 1760 between three French and three British ships. The Chincough or St Medan's Well was at the north end of Front Bay at 364400. Walk up the road to see Penny Wheatley's otter sculpture for Gavin Maxwell (1914-1969) above Kirkmaiden churchyard and with magnificent views over to the Mull of Galloway, the Scares and the Isle of Man. The Knock spiral cup and ring marking is on the same rock outcrop (364402).

North of the A747 there is the site of a tower house on a rocky knoll west of Barmeal (378412) and an Iron Age oval hill fort with the remains of a chevaux de frise at the south end of the Fell of Barhullion (374418). Take the side road by South Barsalloch for Blairbuie farm and the *Wren's Egg Standing Stones* (361420), two standing stones with an erratic boulder (the 'egg'), a 'stone arrangement' and not, as Masters' excavation has established, part of a circle. There are also two standing stones on Milton Hill (362416) west of Blairbuie Loch.

Monrieth, or Milltown of Monrieth as it is shown on the map printed with the New Statistical Account (1841), is now a leisure-orientated and retirement village. The Monrieth Burn, however, formerly provided power for a tile works with a kiln (358413) north of the village, a waulk mill and the 'old' (probably grain) mill below the road. The 1851 Census includes an innkeeper, a tailor, a grocer, a joiner, a weaver, a cooper, a shoemaker, and Alexander McClure, unusually both weaver and schoolmaster.

Continue west on the A747 by Monrieth Bridge and above the bay from the Black Rocks to Port Whapple (348410) and Barsalloch Point. The old cliffs along the road at Barsalloch (343422) and Low Clone (333453) are the site of Mesolithic camps and scooped hollow shelters. *Barsalloch Fort* (347412), on a promontory above the road and approached by scrambling up the rough slope of the old cliff, has a very clear horseshoe-shaped ditch and banks on each side.

Port William, founded by Sir William Maxwell about 1775, was laid out along the raised beach level and eventually up the old cliffs behind where

The busy corn mill and the Bank House in Port William on a postcard printed in Saxony c.1910.

they were cut through by the Killantrae Burn. There would almost certainly have been an older fishing settlement (Killantrae?) on the same site and a landing place on the shore, and the smuggling trade was flourishing and immensely profitable along this coastline in the second and third quarters of the eighteenth century. The scale of the operations by the Manx 'firm' of Morrison, Gault and Company, the Clone brethren, and other local smugglers is suggested in the letter from James McWilliam, formerly excise officer in Wigtown, describing events in 1777, and sent to Joseph Train in 1840: 'I remember... counting 210 horses, laden with Tea, Spirits, and Tobacco, accompanied by about half that number of Lingtowmen, passing within a mile of the town of Wigtown, in open defiance of the supervisor, two excise officers, and about thirty soldiers, stationed at Wigtown, to assist the revenue officers in the suppression of smuggling ... I accompanied my father, who was then excise officer in Wigtown, and the supervisor, with about twenty-five soldiers, to Port William, where two Luggers were lying ready to discharge their cargoes of contraband goods. One of these Luggers mounted twenty-two guns, the other fourteen, and each had a crew of about fifty men ... I remember my father going several times with a party of soldiers to the farm of Drumtroddan ... having received information of there being a cellar for the reception of smuggled goods ... the entrance was ... discovered ... immediately under the fire of the kiln ... Mr Reid, Inspector General of the customs ... in December, 1777 ... discovered so many of these under-cellars both at the Clone and at the Mull of Galloway, that in the course of a

231

few days his party seized about 80 chests of Tea, and 140 ankers of Gin and Brandy, with nearly as many bales of Tobacco . . .' A military barracks and customs post was established at Port William in 1788 to bring an end to this trade.

From the Monrieth Arms Hotel, formerly the Noble Seiner Inn, note the very large early nineteenth-century three-storey corn mill and warehouse complex on the burn. Walk round on the A747 south to Saltpans Point (337432), noting the cut behind the Monrieth Arms diverting the Killantrae Burn from its original course out through the harbour. The first small pier and harbour was built in the late 1790s, and another longer pier before 1848, but a good deal of the present harbour works and warehouses are probably post-1875. There was some shipbuilding at the Port, including the brig *Robert and Ann* of 81 tons in 1817 and the *Dirk Hatteraick,* a sloop of 47 tons, in 1818 and owned by Sir William Maxwell.

To explore the hinterland of Mochrum parish take the A714 north from Port William by Landberrick to Airyhassen (372466) and then the minor road west across country by Blairshinnoch and Glentriplock Bridge to the crossroads village of (Kirkton of) Mochrum. Walk from the churchyard north up the Barrachan road and climb up *Druchtag or Boghouse Motte* (349467), a fine large truncated cone type motte with a summit area considerable enough for a blockhouse and ancillary buildings. The steep and slippery grass banking gives visitors an excellent idea of just how difficult it would have been to attack a twelfth-century castle mound. The parish church (1794 with galleries added in 1835) is a very pleasant plain building with outside stairs. The eighteenth-century manse, with additions in 1822 and 1901, is now the Greenmantle Hotel. The churchyard has some excellent stones, in particular the upright for John Leyburn in Drumshoge (1737), with hour glass and skeleton and Father Time and a central figure holding a Bible with a text reference to Psal. CXIX, ii. Another castle site (Druchtag Castle) is recorded at 343462.

The road north passing Druchtag motte takes you by Skate to Barrachan (362495), where a small village developed in the second half of the nineteenth century. The famous old Scotch plough, which may have been taken to Chilcarroch farm (350498) about 1793 and was subsequently used at Culbae and at High Elrig until about 1880-1890, is now in the museum in Stranraer.

The classic local novel of the 1930s, now extremely rare and obtaining extraordinary sums at auctions even for a well-thumbed copy, is John McNeillie's *The Wigtown Ploughman: part of his life* (1939). It was regarded

The upright for John Leyburn in Drumshoge (1737) in Mochrum churchyard.

then as a wee bit coarse, but deserves recognition as an interesting attempt to write a Lewis Grassic Gibbon type elegiac novel in a Wigtownshire setting. McNeillie's *Morryharn Farm* (1940) and *Glasgow Keelie* (1940) are at least as scarce. Writing as Ian Niall, McNeillie has achieved widespread recognition for his beautifully composed essays and commentaries on rural matters in *Country Life* and in books including *A Galloway Childhood* (1967), *The Galloway Shepherd* (1970) and *Country Matters* (1984). Gavin Maxwell's *The House of Elrig. An autobiography of childhood* (1965) is a very different sort of book. I enjoyed the descriptions of Mochrum Loch and 'herons after dusk' and the surprising facts that emerge, for example not only that earlier generations of Maxwells kept a foxhound pack at Monrieth but also that the racing stables they maintained there produced a St Leger winner. The sketches of Myrton, Monrieth and Ballingrene (Dowies) are charming.

The circuit from Mochrum village by Elrig, Elrig Loch and Auchengaillie makes a fine walk or drive. The whole area west from Elrig to Auchenmalg Bay in Old Luce parish is now lightly populated compared to centuries past, at least judging by the evidence of the number of prehistoric cairns, Iron Age and later forts, 'earthworks', 'enclosures' and crannogs, Dark Age and mediaeval crosses built into farms and farm-steadings, and deserted farms and settlements and villages. In the area near Elrig itself, for example, there are forts or earthworks on Elrig (324481), Ringheel (338491), Milton Fell (311479) and Airyolland (308477), and crannog sites in Elrig Loch (321489 and 325492) and at two adjacent locations on the drained Rough Loch (318492). A deserted village and chapel site is recorded on Airylick (309498), and there are deserted ferm-touns with corn kilns west (312494) and north (315505) of Airylick and to the south at Clays of Airrieolland (311488). The famous House of Elrig (311495) north-west of Airylick was built after 1909. And Elrig village itself was once a thriving centre of industrial activity. The Elrig, or Mill of Mochrum, complex (323473) of late eighteenth-century and nineteenth-century bone and meal, farina and oatmeal mills was the largest in the Machers.

The Carlin Stone (326497), a fine standing stone over five feet high, is east of the road running north from Loch Head to High Glenling. Take the other road from Loch Head north-east by Derrie and west of the Flows of Elrig, Drumnescat and Airriequhillart to the B7005 and then turn west by Glenling Moss to the Drumwalt road west of the former school (306510) at Culshabbin. The 'mote' (326526) north-east of Crailloch looks more like an Iron Age or Dark Age rock-cut fort, but with continued mediaeval occupation including the sixteenth-century tower house held by Patrick Dunbar in 1539. A chapel, a 'castle well', a corn kiln and a possible early mill site are adjacent. The Doon of May (295515) is a vitrified hill fort. A cross-head is built into the wall of the byre at May farm (301515).

Walk or drive along the Drumwalt road by Mochrum Loch, the Black Loch and Loch Hempton, and the Fell Loch to Loch Wayoch west of Craigeach. There are crannogs on Loch Wayoch (302561) and Fell Loch (310550), and the remains of buildings on the Long Island (300526) in Mochrum Loch. The buildings on Castle Island (293541), where a programme of excavation and restoration was carried out by the Marquis of Bute in 1911, include a possibly fifteenth-century hall house and a chapel. At a much earlier period Castle Island, or indeed Long Island, may have served quite different purposes as retreats or hermitages. The Dunbars may have moved from their hall house on Castle Island to build their new tower east of Mochrum Loch about 1500. The Old Place of Mochrum (308541), magnificently restored by the Marquis of Bute in 1876 and 1911, is an example of the application of the rather sophisticated concept of building two towers. The first, the rectangular west tower of c.1500 with a corbelled parapet, is straightforwardly defensive in character, but the second late sixteenth-century east tower block with fine crowstepped gables was added primarily for comfort and additional accommodation.

The 'Old Mill of Mochrum' stood on a rocky site near the Old Place. In Galloway it used to be said of anyone who yearned for the unobtainable that—'He's like the auld Mill of Mochrum, which aye wanted a back-door'. And to busybodies wanting to know where you were going you could, more or less politely, reply—'I'm going to the Old Mill of Mochrum'.

From Culshabbin take the B7005 west to the A747 to explore the coastline from Philip and Mary or Bar Point (324455) to the Craignarget Burn (260511). Note the site of the Bar Mill (319462) south of Elrig, a carding mill on a very old water-powered location going back to the sixteenth century at least, and the series of forts and defensible homesteads at Chang, Chippermore and Corwall, and the 'ports' at Chang (298474), Chippermore (287480), Alticry (271496) and Garheugh (269499) with a common feature of access paths cleared through boulders on the foreshore. There is another Grey Mare's Tail at 265504.

Corwall Port (277489) is suitable only for landing on the beach, but the adjacent location of *Chapel Finian* (278489) suggests that it may have been a place of some importance. The small, perhaps tenth-century, chapel within a rectangular enclosure and the holy well to the south-east may be related to pilgrims crossing Luce Bay for Whithorn. But it is also possible that it was instead an oratory and landing place en route to an early and lost monastery in the Elrig area. St. Finian of Movilla (Mag-Bile) in County Down, an important monastery until it was plundered by the Vikings in 824, died according to the Annals of Ulster in 579. The dedication could, of course, be later, but it is possible that his chapel here was a Celtic sixth or seventh-century foundation from Ireland. The suggestion, however speculative, is interesting and is useful to bear in mind remembering the proximity and relevance of Ireland for the Loch Ryan and Luce Bay area. Another building and kiln (280489) are marked on the 1850 O.S. map on the south side of the road zig-zagging up to Corwall and then either north towards the Doon of May or east to Airylick and Elrig.

CHAPTER 19

Old Luce, New Luce and Carrick

The Luces (Old and New Luce became separate parishes in 1646) take in a huge area from the sea between Craignarget Burn east of Auchenmalg Bay to the Luce Sands and Torrs Warren west of the Piltanton Burn, and then north to the Ayrshire border between, on the east, the Tarf Water and, to the west, Glenwhan Moor and the Main Water of Luce from north of Galdenoch. The most remarkable feature is neither the vast hoard of flints, stone axes, coins and pottery from the sandhills nor the Iron Age, Dark Age and mediaeval sites along the coastline and up the river valley, but rather the extraordinary profusion of prehistoric hut circles and cairns on hill and moor ground. Hut circles are recorded on Culroy, Knock Fell, Craigenveoch Fell, Dirnean Fell, Carscreugh Fell, Camrie Fell, Glenwhan Moor, Bught Fell, Gleniron Fell and Kilfeddar; and cairns on Craignarget Hill, Challochmunn, Culquhasen, Culroy, Glenwhan Moor, Carscreugh Fell, Airyhemming, Garvilland, Barnshangan, Balmurrie Fell, Kilfeddar, Craigbirnoch and Miltonise.

On the A747 on Luce Bay you pass Craignarget farm (256513), where the important ?tenth-century cross-slab now in the National Museum in Edinburgh was found. It is covered with Christian symbolic crosses, circles and a swastika, and also with cup, cup and ring and dumb-bell designs. Continue north by Gillespie, Auchenmalg and Paradise, and the Cock (of Luce) Inn on Auchenmalg Bay, a smuggling landing stretch until a barracks for an officer and up to fifty men was built at Sinniness (230519) as a base to patrol Luce Bay in conjunction with the complement from the barracks at Port William. The 1850 O.S. map marks a starch mill on the burn north of Broompark.

At Auchenmalg Bridge take the side road by Long Forth for Milton and Stairhaven. The coastline is interesting with a promontory fort at Garliachen on Laigh Sinniness (215522) and the 'Broken Castle' broch (209533) south of Stairhaven. The broch entrance passage and intra-mural staircase were cleared in an 'unauthorised' excavation in 1977. The thoroughly ruinous pier at Stairhaven or Crow's Nest (208536)—most impressive from the hill to the south—was built by the Earl of Stair in the late 1840s, with improvements in 1894. Local postcard evidence shows that it was in use into the 1910s or possibly later. Castle Sinniness (214531) consists of the remains of a fifteenth/sixteenth-century Kennedy tower house, but the site may well be much older. Other cross-slabs from Sinniness and Barlockhart are also in Edinburgh, and there is an interesting concentration of Dark Age or mediaeval Christian sites nearby including a chapel at Chapel Fey, Balcarry (199560), Kirkchrist Chapel at Jerusalem Park (212550), the Clauchan or Lady Well (214549) and the Chapel Well, east of Kilfillan (211545) and north of the former Kirkchrist corn mill (214544) on the Milton Burn.

For the eastern corner of Old Luce parish south of the A75 take the A747 north from Auchenmalg Bridge by Culquhasen and Challochmunn. There are crannogs in Whitefield Loch—Dorman's Island (237550), Loch Robin (246558) and Barhapple Loch (259591), and a hill fort on Knock Fell (255558), which at 550 feet has sweeping views over vast stretches of forest and moorland. The site of St John's Chapel and Well (262557) is between Knock of Luce and the Peat Loch and north of the track running across by Green Eldrigs to Annabaglish near Mindork Bridge.

North of the A75, the old railway line and the Old Military Road, note the site of a deserted village or settlement at Braid Hill (259600), south-east of Dergoals Moss. Off the A75 east of Glenluce at 214581 take the side road north for a fine moorland walk from the old railway bridge or the cattle grid towards Carscreugh Castle (223598). Note the green grass-covered cairn on the east side of the road and 'The Round Plantation' west of the castle. Carscreugh was a 'modern' castle and a much more complex building than the remains, the south-west tower with a round wheel-stair, suggest. The central block with flanking towers at the north-west and south-west was built or rebuilt after 1665 or about 1680 by James Dalrymple (1619-1695), Professor of Philosophy at the University of Glasgow, author of the *Institutions of the Law of Scotland,* Lord Advocate, and in 1690 1st Viscount Stair. The estates of Carscreugh and Balniel came to him through his wife, Margaret Ross of Balniel. Carscreugh was also the country residence of John Dalrymple (1648-1707), the distinguished politician, who became 1st Earl of Stair in 1703.

The eastern part of Old Luce parish up to the Tarf Water may be explored from the road running north from the A75 in Glenluce village by the site of the railway station (198576) on the Stranraer-Dumfries line, and then by Officer's Croft, Whitecairn, Drumphail and Glenchamber to Torwood House (244640), built as a fishing and shooting lodge in 1875 and now an hotel. The Bennan of Garvilland hill fort (215628), north-east of Bught Fell, is impressive. For a shorter evening walk take the road from Glenluce as far as the junction (206595) between Campbell's Croft and

Whitecairn, and then west by Honey Pig and Gleniron Several to the New Luce road at Glenluce Abbey and south by Back of the Wall to the Bridge of Park for Glenluce.

Entering Glenluce on the A75 from the east, continue down the hill by the Auld King's Arms and turn right opposite The Judge's Keep up Church Street to the churchyard (197574). Although when the essential bypass is eventually completed the village will once again be a peaceful and indeed delightful place, at the moment the heavy lorries going to and from the Irish ferries create a desperate traffic problem. Although a settlement at or near the present village was made, as Ballinclach, an ecclesiastical burgh in 1490-1497 and then, as Glenluce, a burgh of barony by c.1681-1700, the line of houses on the hill may have been laid out only about the middle of the eighteenth century. The village grew rapidly from the 1770s to have a population of 821 out of a total of 2,180 for Old Luce parish in 1831. The Lint Mill Bridge on the A747 suggests that there had been a flax mill on the Lady Burn, and a dye mill is recorded on the 1850 O.S. map at the east end (206575) of the village, but Glenluce was not an industrial village; its function was to be a service centre with inns and shops for the Luce valley area and for the travellers on the Portpatrick to Carlisle road. The last remains of Balkail (199574), a laird's house near the Lady Burn, were demolished in 1961.

The parish church (1814, but with recent alterations including the removal of the outside stairs) is on the site of its 1637 predecessor. The site itself may be much older, as a ?tenth-century cross-slab, again in Edinburgh, was found in the churchyard. Details of the famous case of the Devil of Luce, a spirit which invaded the home of Gilbert Campbell, a weaver, between 1655 and 1658, are contained in *Satan's Invisible World Discovered* (1685) by George Sinclair, the Professor of Mathematics at the University of Glasgow. The phenomenon was attributed to the machinations of Alexander Agnew, a beggar who had been hanged at Dumfries for blasphemy and who had threatened hurt to Campbell's family because he had been turned away by him without alms. From the church walk up the hill, in the footsteps of George Borrow who stayed in Glenluce on 18 and 19 July, 1866 on his Galloway walking tour, and over the disused railway line and then left along a very narrow road with a superb view of the site of the 'mote hill' (193573), the railway viaduct and across to the Castle of Park.

Continue down the hill to the Bridge of Park (191573) and to the very difficult access road off the A75 for the *Castle of Park* (188571). The magnificently restored four-storey and attic tower house built by Thomas

Hay of Park in 1590 is a classic example of a late L-plan laird's house. The superb plateau site looking over the Luce valley was originally laid out with walks and walled gardens. The eighteenth-century two-storey wings, latterly occupied as farmhouse accommodation with the tower house by the 1910s used for storage, had been demolished many years before the recent restoration programme. Note the massive chimneystacks, the steep roofline and the crowstepped gables, and the entrance details including the inscribed panel above the door.

The A75 below is no place for sightseeing, and the Glenluce-Dunragit section is one of the more dangerous stretches and certainly potentially lethal for pedestrians. So for the western end of Old Luce parish either drive or take the bus from Glenluce to Dunragit, passing the modern Creamery on the site of the Ballochjargon Starch Mill marked on the O.S. 1850 map. There are two Iron Age/Dark Age fort sites, the Round Dounan (148579) with double ramparts and the 'earthwork' at 150586 north and south respectively of Dunragit House. Take the A748 south, passing the badly eroded mass of Droughdool motte (148568), to Piltanton Bridge and then west by Genoch House and Mid Torrs to the A715 and the West Freugh 'Danger Areas' to Clayshant Bridge east of Mye Plantation (107530), where the Mesolithic or Neolithic pit traps were excavated. This whole area, and in particular the Wood of Park, the Swamp Plantation beside Piltanton Bridge and the Lochnagappal site (125543), the swamp of the horses, has attached to it folk tales of headless horsemen and headless women carrying off and trapping careless travellers in moss-holes. The 'Danger Area' signs to-day, however, refer to the presence at West Freugh Airfield of an RAF testing range and experimental area. This has an interesting history going back to the establishment of the First World War RNAS Base to patrol the Solway Firth and the Irish Sea—it even had its own newspaper, *The Freugh Gazette*. The Danger Areas between the A715 and Luce Sands are subject to the rival claims of the RAF, of commercial sand quarrying, of the Rhins Motor Cycle Club for scrambling on the sand dunes, of the Nature Conservancy looking after sites of special scientific interest, especially in the Torrs Warren complex, and of archaeologists and antiquarians looking for flints, Neolithic axes, and mediaeval coins, pottery, glass and settlement sites. A thirteenth to fifteenth-century hunting or fowling lodge site at 149554 yielded a fine hoard of Scottish coins from James II to James IV; and the Horse Hill (143556) may be another important site. There is also a Forestry Commission plantation south of the Piltanton Burn with a road down to Ringdoo Point.

The Piltanton Burn may have been navigable for small vessels at high tide up to below the Droughdool motte, and there was a busy eighteenth-century landing place, perhaps at Cuttybatty Ford (168565) below Whitecrook or near Droughdool Bridge. The Piltanton Burn and the Water of Luce join in the bay south of St Helena Island (192558), which was listed—I suspect by a diligent civil servant who did not like nil county returns—in both the 1881 and 1891 Censuses with Barra and St Kilda among 'The Inhabited Islands of Scotland' (number of houses 1, population 4). Both the 1850 O.S. map and General Roy's map c.1750 show it as merse-land which became temporarily isolated during high spring tides. It may have been christened 'St Helena Island' by Admiral Dalrymple Hay on his return from a visit to *the* St Helena. The less likely part of the tale is that he planted willows on it grown from cuttings of the tree at the Emperor Napoleon I's grave!

For the north of Old Luce and New Luce take the road north from the Bridge of Park passing the site of the Bridge corn mill (190573) and Back of the Wall. The old road from the abbey to Glenluce church was probably on the higher ground to the east off the Craigenholly road and by the sites of Auchenmanister, Morrison's Croft (190580) and Kiln Croft, opposite the end of the Fine View farm road. Before the abbey note the site of St Katherine's Well (185587) at the edge of the road.

The Cistercian *Abbey of Glenluce* (184586), founded in 1190 by Roland of Galloway and colonised from Dundrennan, is an excellent example of the layout of a mediaeval religious house: at the north end the church, of which only the late thirteenth-century south transept survives to any height; the east range including the library and parlour, and a fine late fifteenth-century vaulted chapter house with stone seats and a central pillar, Gothic windows, and opposite the carved doorway the remains outside of the cloister walk arcading; on the south the refectory, a brew-house and a kitchen; and on the west the laybrothers' range and a tiny gatehouse. The water supply system with earthenware pipes and junction boxes is particularly impressive and important. Do not miss the excellent museum with examples of thirteenth-century pottery and floor tiles from excavations at the abbey.

Between the abbey and New Luce village note west of the Water of Luce the sites of tower houses, the Old Halls of Craig (172598) on Airyhemming and Larg Castle (166643) on Mains of Larg; and to the east the important Mid Gleniron long chambered cairns with facades (187610 and 188609) and a complex history of growth and change from small oval cairns revealed in J. X. P. Corcoran's classic excavations between 1963 and 1966, and the Kilhern Moss acid bog. The Southern Upland Way may be followed west by Craig Fell, Glenwhan Moor, Chlenry and Balnab to the Black Loch at Lochinch, but the route east along the road from Cruise to Kilhern and then north by the Loups of Barnshangan waterfall to Balmurrie is much more interesting. It takes you close to the Caves of Kilhern (198644), a long cairn with four or five chambers and a passage, Cairn na Gath (212674) long chambered cairn, and deserted settlements with corn kilns and lazybed cultivation patterns at Fauldinchie (191648) and Tierehan.

New Luce, at the junction of the Cross Water and Main Water of Luce, is a charming village. It may never again have, as in 1839, a population of 180 and three shops and three inns, but it has happily experienced a revival in the last decade. The restoration of the cottages in the village street is interesting and lively. The Moor Kirk (1821) is plain and pleasing, and the churchyard has some good eighteenth-century stones, including John McMillan of Lagangarn (1761), 'a youth of great expectation', and the McHarg stone (c.1755).

Crossing the Main Water Bridge and turning south-west by the former railway station, closed in 1965, and Auchmantle into Inch parish, you are in an area with a plentiful supply of hut circles and small cairns. The Auld Wife's Grave (135649) at 750 feet on Cairnscarrow is a Bargrennan type chambered cairn. The Standing Stones of Glentirra (145625) is an arrangement of four stones in a rectangle, reminiscent of Bagbie near Carsluith. On the other side of the road is the site of the highly mysterious 'Stepping Stones of Glentirra' (144617), first located during peat cutting in the 1830s, which may be an alignment or a series of boundary markers or a trackway across difficult swampy terrain. There is nothing to be seen above the ground, but a party, including E. A. Hornel, which conducted a detailed examination of the area in 1923, claimed to have found ninety-six stones laid on rock or gravel under up to two feet of peat. During subsequent discussion Mr McKie of Kilhern claimed in a letter to the *Free Press* that there was another line of thirty stones on Balneil farm.

The road north from the Main Water Bridge takes you to Penwhirn Reservoir, and for walkers the possibility of a cross-country trek west to the Claddy House Burn and down to the A77 south of Cairnryan for the bus to Stranraer. The moors south of the Pot of Currafin near Pularyan Bridge and the Loup of Kilfeather have more deserted settlements, including Fauldslave (153664), and some odd placenames—The Eyes, Almanack Hill and Slamonia.

North of New Luce it is surprising to find the Knockibae lead mines (189665), which were worked by the Earl of Stair before 1782 and again in the late 1780s. In the very far north and west of the railway line Cairn Kenny

'British sight-seers attempting to distinguish the ruins of a Druidical temple from the works of Nature' (top) and more B.Ss. (below) beside the 'remains of an ancient British village'. From *The British Working Man* (c.1880)!

(174752) at 700 feet is another Bargrennan type round cairn. Placenames east of Miltonise and Glenwhilly include MacWhannel's Knowe, the Rig of the Eyes, The Black Isle, Goat Knowe, The Blood Lane and Philtoul.

Do not miss taking the twisting moorland road north from New Luce towards Glenwhilly and Barrhill. The Portpatrick-Girvan railway, opened in 1877, follows you most of the way, and the view as you approach Barrhill Station is very impressive. Unfortunately Glenwhilly station is closed, but it would still be an enjoyable ploy to take the train from Stranraer or Girvan to Barrhill and then walk south, hopefully into the sun, to New Luce. The railway line is spectacular, particularly the Pinwherry-Pinmore-Girvan stretch and the run downhill to Challoch Junction. British Rail really ought to be persuaded to offer one, three or seven-day tickets allowing unlimited travel between Stranraer, Barrhill, Girvan, Maybole and Ayr, perhaps linked to the Western bus services between Stranraer, Newton Stewart and Girvan.

Visitors and holidaymakers staying at the Newton Stewart and

Stranraer end of Galloway might enjoy taking a day off to explore Carrick and its castles. Starting from the A714 at Barrhill, note the late sixteenth-century L-plan tower house at Pinwherry (197867). Continue north to take the B734 along the Stinchar valley to Barr, generally regarded as a most picturesque and delightful village, and then north-west to *Penkill Castle* (232986). It has a remarkable collection of pre-Raphaelite paintings brought together by the 14th laird, Spencer Boyd, who entertained, at Penkill, Holman Hunt, Dante Gabriel Rossetti, William Morris, Edward Burne-Jones and many other prominent artists and writers. The new owner, Elton A. Eckstrand of Detroit, welcomes visitors who apply in advance by telephone for admission between May and September. The tapestries by William Morris woven for Alice Boyd, the mural paintings by William Bell Scott and the Rossetti Room are especially important.

Take the side road before Old Dailly north-east along the Water of Girvan, passing Bargany (NS 243002), a late seventeenth-century mansion house set in eighteenth-century parkland. At Dailly take the B741 by Trochrague to Girvan, passing the shell of Robert Adam's magnificent Dalquharran Castle (NS 270021) built between 1778 and 1792. Adam enthusiasts, of course, will not require to be reminded of the most romantic of all his great houses, *Culzean Castle,* on the coast north of Maidens, built between 1777 and 1790, and the castellated tea-house at Auchincruive east of Ayr designed in 1778.

Joining the A77, turn north passing the site of Roman marching camps on Girvan Mains (191991 and 188990) to the famous Turnberry Hotel, opened in 1906, and the golf course which hosts the Open Championship, and Turnberry lighthouse and castle (NS 196072). In the Girvan area there are mottes at Dowhill (NS 202029) and Dinvin (200931), and the famous Ailsa Craig, nine miles off the coast, both further out into open sea and much bigger, at 1114 feet high and two miles in circumference, than it looks from Girvan harbour. Fishing boats take small groups out, very much weather permitting, in the summer months to see the castle and lighthouse and the curling-stone quarries.

From Girvan take the spectacular A77 coast road south by Kennedy's Pass and Lendalfoot. Carleton Castle (133895) is a fifteenth-century, five-storey tower house with a motte to the east of the ruined tower. Continue south by Bennane Head. Epicureans who want to know more about the Galloway cannibal, Sawney Bean, should be directed to the cave south of Bennane Head at 091861. There is, of course, no 'real' Sawney Bean cave, so this one will do just as well as another. Sawney Bean barbecues should be held on the shore.

Girvan harbour c.1905. Note the photographer's lady assistant in the centre foreground.

Take a breather in Ballantrae to visit the old parish church (083824) with the Kennedy Aisle Renaissance tomb built for Gilbert Kennedy of Bargany between 1601 and 1605. The Scottish Wildlife Trust reserve (080820) at the mouth of the Stinchar is open to visitors. From the fifteenth-century Ardstinchar Castle (086824) take the B7044 following the river to the A765 at the seventeenth-century and earlier Knockdolian Castle (122853) and continue east by the late sixteenth-century L-plan Kirkhill Castle (145859) to Colmonell. Return to Galloway either by Pinwherry and the A714 or by Ballantrae and Glenapp on the A77.

CHAPTER 20

Inch, Stranraer, Leswalt and Kirkcolm

The urban sprawl of Stranraer and the scale of the ferry terminal installations come as a surprise to most first-time visitors. And indeed Stranraer as a service and communications centre dominates western Wigtownshire to an extent few would have thought possible even forty or fifty years ago. With local bus services for Glenluce, Girvan, Kirkcolm, Portpatrick and Drummore, and the train link north to Barrhill, Stranraer is a good centre for exploring the area without relying on a motor car. The main roads, the A75, the A77 and the A716 are not really suitable for pedestrians, but the side roads, especially on the west side of Kirkcolm, Stoneykirk and Kirkmaiden, have many delights for walkers.

Starting on the A75 west of Dunragit you cross into Inch parish at Drumflower Bridge (139578) over the Ballancollantie Burn. The parish boundary runs north by Glenwhan Moor well to the east of the Chlenry Burn, Glentirra and the Auld Wife's Grave. From the A75 take the side road at Planting End (122586) south-west by Mark and then north-east by Mahaar along the west side of Soulseat Loch and Loch Magillie. The peninsula at the south-west end of Soulseat Loch (101587), formerly cut off by a deep ditch, has the old manse (1838) and churchyard on the site of Soulseat Abbey, the monastery of the Green Loch or Stank *(Viridis Stagni).* The little water outlet at the south end (101582) was known as the Green Ford. The uncertain Cistercian abbey founded in 1148 by St Malachy of Armagh did not develop and instead the Premonstratensian white canons came here to the *Sedes Animarum,* the dwelling place of souls, in 1175 or earlier and directly from Premontré. Soulseat itself was a parish until it was merged with Inch as part of a series of changes about 1628 when Portpatrick and Stranraer were detached from Inch as separate parishes.

Other sites north and south of the A75 are disappointing. The motte on Cults (123599) had been ploughed out long before the wartime airfield removed the last traces; the remains of the 'motte' at the top of the Galla Hill (092594) west of the old road running north from Low Boreland are insufficient to allow for any positive assessment of its nature or origins; and nothing is left of the motte or homestead south of Culgrange (082564). Aerial photographs suggest a possible native (Iron Age or Bronze Age?) settlement at Culgrange (084567).

At the north end of Loch Magillie you may join the Southern Upland Way which continues south-west towards Culhorn Mains and Whiteleys on the A77 south of Stranraer. Nothing remains of the rambling redbrick Culhorn House (079590), the principal residence of the Earls of Stair from the loss of Castle Kennedy through the fire in 1716 until the building of Lochinch Castle in 1867. William Adam worked on alterations to the house and perhaps on landscaping of the grounds. The oval mound at 078593 might be the remains of a motte or part of the estate landscape created for Field-Marshal the 2nd Earl of Stair. As an alternative walk to the Southern Upland Way take the Old Military Road route into Stranraer by Two Mile Howe (088601) and Aird Cottage to Bridge of Aird on the A75.

Castle Kennedy (111609) and *Castle Kennedy Gardens* are so magnificent that they require several visits. The castle, built by the Kennedies in 1607 on what was originally an island and quite probably the site of an earlier 'manor place of Inch', is now the centrepiece of the gardens between the Black Loch and the White Loch. The main block with two east towers is a good example of symmetrical planning on a fairly grand scale. The castle and estate were purchased in 1677 by Sir John Dalrymple, who became the 1st Earl of Stair.

The 'dressed' or pleasure grounds laid out after 1733 by the 2nd Earl of Stair (1679-1747), and restored by the 8th Earl after 1841 following the original plans, are remarkable for their sheer size and scale as much as for their grace and precision. The avenues radiating from the old castle and from the two-acre 'Basin' or circular pond with water lilies, the 'canal' linking the two lochs, and the huge terraces, ramps and fortress-like 'mounts' (Dettingen Avenue, Mount Marlborough) were dug out and built up by men of the Inniskilling Fusiliers and the Royal Scots Greys stationed in Wigtownshire. The lines of great conifers, the monkey puzzle avenue, the vast range and variety of rhododendrons (one of the largest collections in Britain), the azaleas, the magnolias and the embothriums are outstanding. And to the north Lochinch Castle (1867) lends a seemly air of reserved Scottish baronial dignity to the flights of fancy and delights of the gardens.

Heron Island (113611) in the Black Loch is an Iron Age and later crannog, excavated in 1870-1871, which may have had the equivalent of a chevaux de frise of pointed wooden stakes in the water around it; and there was another crannog in Cults Loch (120604) to the east. Inch Crindil island (104608) in the White Loch may have been the site of a palace of the mediaeval bishops of Galloway. On the shore opposite, the old church (1770) and churchyard of Inch may be, like Soulseat Abbey, a very early Christian site. It has some good eighteenth and early nineteenth-century stones, including the upright by William McGeough or McGeoch for his son Robert (1809) with various tools. The modern parish church (1861-1862, rebuilt 1896) is on the far side of the A75 to the south (100602).

From the long straight on the A75 west of Castle Kennedy take the (A751) road by Clachanpluck and Inch Parks down to the A77. This gives you a superb view of the great twelfth-century clifftop motte (084633) and the site of the town of Innermessan. The top of the mound was excavated to a depth of three feet by the parish minister, Mr James Fergusson, in 1834. The mediaeval town—the earliest written record is in 1426, but the burgh is probably older—was on the plateau east and north of the motte. Late sixteenth and early seventeenth-century protocol books have a number of references to the tenements and streets and closes (Borgill McClune's 'kill' or close near the motte in 1611), the 'foregait' on the west and the 'hiegate' on the east, and to particular houses, including the abbot of Glenluce's 'slaithous' and the place and fortalice occupied by Uchtred McKie in 1603; and the names of the town's shoemakers, masons and blacksmiths, and the armourer or 'polliter', John Kennedy, in 1606 and the tailor, Martine McCullie, in 1597. A 'causey' called the 'Bray' at the south end of the town led to the walkmyln and grain mill below on the Kirclachie Burn. The town declined and then disappeared from history as Stranraer grew and prospered in the late seventeenth and eighteenth centuries. The tower on the site of the farmhouse of (Roads of) Innermessan was last occupied in 1687. A few houses and the mills survived until much later, and the O.S. 1849 map shows a bone and carding mill near the shore and a tuck mill up the burn near the present A77. Ainslie's map (1782) shows a road along the shore west of the motte where the line of the Cairnryan Military Railway was laid between 1941 and 1943.

From the A77 walk or drive along the narrow road passing the dear little tower house at Craigcaffie or 'Killechaffe' (088641), built in 157- by John Neilson on a marshy wetland site. The tower is very compact yet the builder/architect managed to squeeze in a vaulted kitchen, a first-floor hall all of sixteen by fourteen feet, and second and attic floors, crowstepped gables and a wall walk with corner turrets and even machicolation above the doorway. The road climbs steeply up the hill with excellent vistas over Loch Ryan. Very little is left of Teroy broch (099641), and to get to it involves a long detour to avoid the Kirclachie Burn. To the north the deserted farm with a lime kiln at Shinriggie (099659) may be a mediaeval or earlier defensible site, and there is another deserted settlement with a corn kiln at Braid (099658) south of the Beoch Burn. Nothing is visible of the line of the Deil's Dyke which Train suggested lay north of Beoch coming up the hill from Leffnol Point.

Continue north on the A77 by Leffnoll Point for Cairnryan or, using the old name for the fishing community on the shore of Loch Ryan, Machiryskeed. The Agnews of Lochryan obtained a charter in 1701 for the burgh of barony of Cladahouse or Lochryan, taking the former name from the Clady House Burn south of the present village; but 'The Cairn', later Cairnryan, remained throughout the eighteenth and nineteenth centuries essentially a small village of oyster fishermen and slate quarriers from the workings on Cairn Ryan Hill (067687), near the Glen Burn (069693 and 069698), and on the shore near Polymodie Bridge (058703). The great Military Port (1941-1959) and, more recently, the European Ferries Terminal for traffic to Larne and the shipbreaking operations at the other north end of the village have meant enormous changes.

To try to capture something of the 'conservation area' quality of Cairnryan drive past the whitewashed single and two-storeyed cottages to the car park and picnic area north of Cairn Point and the lighthouse (1847) and Lochryan and Glenapp church (1841). Lochryan House (064687), just visible beyond the boundary wall, is an outstanding Queen Anne and rather Flemish-style building with a high central block and lesser wings completed for Colonel Agnew in 1701. The gardens and grounds include a Victorian dovecot and a 'Vault' or 'Summer House' (066688).

The A77 continues north along the shore of Loch Ryan climbing up and on to the Ayrshire border at Galloway Bridge (057712). Note the line of the old road taking the high ground up a steep hill to Laird's Hill, Polymodie and the Taxing Stone (062710), a six feet high standing stone north of Little Laight. The hinterland to the east has more hut circles and cairns and another six feet plus standing stone known as 'Long Tom' or 'Tom Slowan' (081718). The Black Cave (058708) with outer and inner 'rooms' running back into the cliff face may have been occupied as early as the Neolithic or Bronze Age periods.

The Roman marching camps at Girvan and the route west from Glenlochar to Gatehouse-of-Fleet make it highly probable that there was a 'Reregonium' on Loch Ryan in the sense of a marching camp or a fort or a naval base. However, in spite of the tradition identifying Innermessan as Reregonium, there is no necessary correlation between the mediaeval importance of the former and the location of the latter. Stranraer is almost as likely, and another unfortunate possibility is that the Roman camp/fort may have been part of the considerable acreage of land lost to the sea on the east shore of the loch even since 1800 near Innermessan.

Returning to the south end of Loch Ryan—and it is difficult to remember that the Irish ferries sail *north* up the loch before turning round

Milleur Point—continue into Stranraer along the seafront to the Market Street car park opposite the Education Office and Queen Street and west of the old 'Burnfoot'. The mediaeval waterfront villages of Chappell (from the late fifteenth-century chapel dedicated to St John) and Stran Rawer on the opposite side of the burn which is now under South and North Strand Street, became in 1595 the burgh of barony of Stranrawer under the auspices of the Adairs of Kinhilt and then in 1617 the royal burgh of Stranraer. During the eighteenth and early nineteenth centuries the 'villages' to the west at The Clayhole and south-west at Hill Head in Leswalt parish and at Tradeston in Inch parish became part of a virtually continuous urban conglomeration. The Town Council Minute Books from 1766 to 1778 and 1780 to 1788 give a good picture of the old town with little stone bridges and narrow eleven and fourteen-feet-wide streets with ash and dung hills and peat and turf stacks opposite the houses, and much tighter closes (Jean McMaster's close was three feet seven and a half inches wide), and a new tanworks with a 'lymehole and tan trochs' in 1767.

The first quay, later the West Pier, was built only as late as 1820, but long before then Stranraer was a busy shipping and shipbuilding centre. Eight vessels were built, probably at the Clayhole Bank end, between 1791 and 1806, including the brig *Providence* of 81 tons in 1806 owned by A. J. and A. Agnew, and seven vessels between 1816 and 1819, including the brig *Douglas* of 120 tons in 1818 owned by Colquhoun and Douglas. And shipping registered at Stranraer in 1820 included the brigs *Alexander* of 227 tons owned by A. McDougall and Company and the *Scotia* of 206 tons owned by C. and W. Morland, probably both operating on the Baltic timber trade to Danzig and Gothenberg or across the Atlantic to Prince Edward Island, Nova Scotia and Quebec.

By the 1830s and 1840s steam-packets from Stranraer, using the West Pier as a 'Steam Boat Wharf', were offering a wide range of services, including the *Lochryan* to Ballantrae, Girvan and Glasgow and also to Belfast, the *Maid of Galloway,* launched in July 1836, doing the Stranraer to Glasgow run in eight or nine hours, and the *Nimrod* running between Glasgow, Greenock, Gourock, Largs, Millport, Ardrossan, Troon, Ayr and Stranraer.

The official Irish ferry service started in 1862, using the East or Railway Pier (now absorbed in the vast seven-acre modern terminal complex) built between 1861 and 1863. After early problems with the 500-ton *Briton* (1862-1863) and the paddle steamers *Alice* and *Fanny* in 1865 on the Stranraer-Belfast run, the Stranraer-Larne route opened in 1872 with the *Princess Louise,* the first of a series of 'princesses', and the *Princess Beatrice* in

J

The R.M.S. *Princess Victoria* in Loch Ryan. This, the first *Princess Victoria*, was on the Stranraer-Larne crossing between 1890 and 1904. The photograph is from the *Views of Stranraer and Vicinity* published by William McLachlan.

1875. Others included the first *Princess Victoria*, a two-funnel paddle steamer of 1096 tons in 1890, the *Princess Maud* in 1904, and the *Princess Margaret* (latterly a ferryboat between Hong Kong and Macao) in 1931. And even in the railway era the *Albion* in the 1870s and the *Pirate* in the 1900s kept on a Glasgow-Campbeltown-Stranraer service. The great days of the railways have gone now with the closure of the Portpatrick line in 1950, the Dumfries line in 1965, and Stranraer's second (Town) station in 1966, but the Irish ferries have grown enormously in the last twenty years. A mini-cruise to Ireland, perhaps using Northern Ireland Railways to Belfast, is just as feasible as the more popular reverse journey. For reading en route *the* book for timetable enthusiasts is the detective story, *Sir John Magill's Last Journey* (1930, 1966) by the admirable F. W. Crofts, who undertook an enormous amount of research on the steamer and railway services on which the plot depends.

On your Stranraer perambulation note the splendidly irregular pattern of the streets, perhaps the result of five 'villages' combining into a single urban unit, and the number of good, solid, reassuring later eighteenth and nineteenth-century stone buildings with sometimes elegant plaster or stone mouldings around windows and doorways, and the inevitable twentieth-century 'environmental improvements' and shop and office frontages in the 'shoebox style'. The series of now some four hundred old photographs by J. P. Milnes of Stranraer, George Washington Wilson and many others reproduced weekly in the *Free Press* has provided a most interesting and useful record of old Stranraer, and for further reference the Regional Library in London Road has inherited the excellent Muir collection of Galloway books from Wigtownshire County Library. Unfortunately the museum, at one time one of the best-run museum services in Scotland, and which had a very fine local collection, was required to vacate the Library premises (museums being a District function). Hopefully it will soon be possible again to see the marvellous old heavy wooden Scotch plough (c.1793) from Chilcarroch, the flaughter spade from Craigcaffie and the other agricultural implements, and the tenth/eleventh-century wayside crosses from Larg Liddesdale (045617) and Glaik (about NW 991595) which possibly marked the line of an old route from Loch Ryan towards Killantringan Bay north-west of Portpatrick.

Start your perambulation from Harbour Street east of Market Street by noting between Princes Street and North Strand Street an unexpectedly fine three-storey house (Wellington House) with an ashlar front facing west. It is a great surprise as you have to walk along the street behind the garage to discover it. From Market Street turn up Queen Street, formerly the Mid Vennel where several local lairds had their town houses, to George Street. The crowstepped gabled Golden Cross at the corner has the date 1803 on it, but the title deeds suggest that it goes back to 1780. The Old Town Hall opposite at the corner of Church Street was built in 1773 with additions in 1802. It probably had shops on the ground floor then as now. The George Hotel is a fine eighteenth-century coaching inn with a three-storey symmetrical frontage and its stable entrance in Church Street. Continue east along George Street by North Strand Street. The Abbey National Building Society in the former and the Bradford and Bingley in the latter have impressive houses above them.

The Castle of St John, built about 1520 as an L-plan tower house by Ninian Adair of Kinhilt, has a chequered history as not only was it heightened in the seventeenth century but it was used after 1815 as a prison by the Town Council and then became a merchant's store into the 1910s and 1920s. The interior with prison cells on the upper floors is unusual and worth preserving. Note the roofline with a corbelled parapet walk and the birdcage belfry. The bell was made in Glasgow about 1800 and is inscribed with the arms of that city.

From George Street turn right up Castle Street. (Turn left for Hanover Street, Dalrymple Street, Ivy Place with the handsome 'L'Apéritif', formerly Ivy House, and London Road.) Turn right at the top of Castle Street on Bridge Street passing the Clydesdale Bank and the Royal Bank of Scotland and, on the right, South Strand Street. At the top of Bridge Street turn left along Lewis Street to note the pleasant cottage offices of Ferguson and Foster, the New Town Hall (1872-1873) in blistering red sandstone, and the excellent terrace block from 21 to 25. Retracing your steps continue down Church Street by the three-storey District Council offices built for the City of Glasgow Bank in 1832, the Old Parish Church (1784-1785, but rebuilt in 1841), which is probably on a much older church site, certainly seventeenth century at least, and the churchyard, kept locked, which has a number of eighteenth-century stones for the merchants and burgesses of the town, including Thomas White and his wife, Grifsell Baird (1730).

Turn left along George Street and up the High Street to the junction with Sun Street, and at the crossroads turn right along Leswalt High Road passing on the left the eighteenth-century Park House, formerly the dower house of the Agnews of Lochnaw, and on the right the High Kirk (1843) with a grand open view over Loch Ryan. Continue along Leswalt High Road to Park Lane and hence downhill to Agnew Crescent and the waterfront. A brisk walk east towards the modern ferry terminal takes you to the North West Castle Hotel, incorporating the house built between 1815 and 1825 for Captain (later Sir) John Ross (1777-1856), the Arctic explorer. His expedition in 1818, and his epic voyage and residence in the Arctic region between 1829 and 1833, described in his *Narrative of a Second Voyage in search of a North-West Passage . . .* (1835), made him a popular national hero.

For Leswalt and Kirkcolm take the A718 road from Market Street along Agnew Crescent and up the hill out of Stranraer. The golf course at Creachmore, laid out in 1951, was one of the last to be designed by the great James Braid before his death in 1950. At the circle continue straight on towards Leswalt to the parish church (1826/1828) and take the unclassified road through the village to the churchyard (015638) with the remains of the old (sixteenth/seventeenth-century) church and some eighteenth-century stones. On a good day it is enormously worthwhile to walk on up the steep hill road to the Tor of Craigoch (008646) with the sixty feet high monument (1850/1851) for Sir Andrew Agnew of Lochnaw on the top of a hill fort with magnificent views to all points of the compass. Aldouran Glen to the south was laid out by Sir Andrew with exotic trees and rare plants and paths running between the steep banks. Probably the best walk into the glen is to take the B7043 up through the woods until you see a rough road on the right leading to Glenhead of Aldouran farm. The path down into the glen cuts off from the stony (possibly car parking) area at the side of the road, which you can also follow down to the crossroads near the farm and then go up the hill to the Tor of Craigoch road to return to Leswalt. The Iron Age or Dark Age promontory fort with triple earth ramparts and stone walling known as Kemp's Graves (008635) is at the top of the bank on the north side of the glen.

Continue on the B7043 for Lochnaw Castle (Hotel) at NW 991628, the Agnews' fifteenth or sixteenth-century rectangular tower with cape-house and wall walk at the south-east end of the east and south range added in 1663. The massive nineteenth-century buildings were demolished after the end of the Second World War. The terraced site above the loch is spectacular. The earlier castle on the island (NW 993632) in the loch was taken and dismantled by Archibald the Grim in 1390. The promontory, Sir Stair's Island, on the east side of the loch, may have functioned as a bailey to the island castle. Craighead or Kinsale Tower on the wooded hill (NW 994624) to the south may have been a look-out point. The B7043 by Garchrie Lodge to the junction with the B738 is a wonderful blaze of colour from the massed rhododendrons in the early summer.

Take the B738 north-west to the road signposted for Meikle Galdenoch, Galdenoch Castle and Salt Pans Bay. The castle (NW 973632), which is beside the farm, is an L-plan tower house built by Gilbert Agnew between 1547 and 1570. Note the unusual 'filleted' crowsteps. The site of Little Galdenoch corn mill (NW 973634) is on the burn to the north. Take the footpath across Galdenoch Moor to Salt Pans Bay. Uchtred Agnew's salt pans (NW 965615) cut out of the rock below the cliffs and used to obtain salt from sea water by evaporation were in operation from about 1637 up to the early years of the nineteenth century. There is also an Iron Age promontory fort (NW 963615) at Fort Point just above the pans. The west coast in Leswalt parish from Strool Bay, Sliggery Knowe, Slouchnaglasson and the Kiln of the Fuffock, Slouchnawen Bay, Wee Portbeg and Cranberry Point south to Black Head was known as the 'Black Shore'.

Continue north on the B738 by High Auchneel, Mains of Cairnbrock, Little Airies and High Ervie to the junction with the B798. Castle Ban (NW 966678) on the coast west of Mains of Airlies looks more like a motte than a promontory fort. Salt Pan Bay (NW 964674) is another industrial site with salt workings and a small enclosure. To the north the Dounan of Dally (NW 967688) is another promontory fort. The 1849 O.S. map records a 'Potter's Kiln' (NW 967690) at a deserted site at Laggan north-east of Dally Bay.

Taking the B798 south-east by Ervie Bridge there is a very complex group of *sites* at High Milton including the nineteenth-century corn and carding Mill of Craigoch on the Craigoch Burn (probably a mediaeval mill location as well), an Iron Age circular stone fort or dun, and the 'House-on-the-Rock', which may have been the location of the supposed Craigoch Castle (all at 012667).

Continue north of Ervie on the B738 by Drumdow farm and its roadside workers' cottages, passing the Marian Tower (NW 995688). McIlwraith (1875) calls it the 'Marien Tower' on 'Marian Hill' and suggests that it was erected by 'a fond husband in memory of his wife'. The two cross-slabs from the site of Chapel Donnan (NW 998692) are in the National Museum in Edinburgh. Balsarroch (NW 993691), the country house of the Ross family, was one of Galloway's most interesting 'lost houses'. The photograph in William Learmonth's *Kirkcudbrightshire and Wigtownshire* (1920) shows that it was a classical old Scottish two-storey house with crowstepped gables, a thatched roof and very small windows. Unfortunately only the memory is left. The road west to Dally and Dinbonnet takes you by Knocknassie Hotel west of Garlies Round Hill and Little Slewmuck.

For the north coast take the side road north from the B738 by Cairnbowie and the site of Inchbane (NW 994696), then right by Knockneen, West Kirkbryde and the former Curates Nook smithy, and left by Five Shilling Land and Damhouse to Corsewall Point. The site of St Bride's church and well (004707) is on the east side of the farm road at East Kirkbryde. Corsewall Castle (NW 991714) in a field on Barnhills is an early fifteenth-century rectangular tower house with a simple wheel stairway in the wall thickness at the north corner. Aerial photographs show the line of a fosse and subsidiary enclosures. Corsewall Lighthouse (NW 980726), built in 1815-1816 to plans by Robert Stevenson, was an important aid to navigation on a treacherous stretch of coastline. There were many wrecks, however, long after this date, perhaps the best remembered being Wigtownshire's own *Whisky Galore* ship, the barquentine the *Firth of Cromarty,* which went on to the rocks at Corsewall Point in August 1898. The locals, knowing a good disaster when they saw one, did their best to ensure that most of the whisky en route to Sydney was diverted towards an orgy of over-indulgence that remained a toper's dream for many years to come. The wreck was recorded in a photograph by J. P. Milnes of Stranraer.

Going round the north coast, there is a promontory fort at Dunskirloch (NW 982727), a St. Columba's Well (NW 989726) west of Port Mullin, a promontory fort at Caspin (004732), Milleur Point, The Beef Barrel (024728), Broad Port (027721), Lady Bay east of Low Portencalzie, where

Barney McGhie's cottage, Portmullin, Kirkcolm east of St. Columba's Well, c.1890. Note the boat and the details of the thatched roof and the primitive chimney. Portmullin was a salmon fishing station.

the O.S. 1849 map lists a bone mill, and a promontory fort or dun at Jamieson's Point (033710).

From Corsewall Point return on the road by High Ardwell to the A718 east of Mahaar. Corsewall Mill (020701), the most exquisitely picturesque of all the Galloway water mills, was gutted by fire in December 1969 and subsequently demolished. Only the bridge below the mill site with millstones built into the parapet remains. The mill was run by the Hannays, who also had the Sheuchan mill, from about 1820. They were very enterprising, for example taking a schooner with a cargo of oatmeal up the west coast of Scotland, selling directly off the boat and then coming back with a cargo of dried fish; and the Hannay and Higgins shellers and grinders were used by millers in many different countries.

Continue south on the A718 to the far end of Kirkcolm village or, to give it its old name, Stewarton. As Stewarton it became a burgh of barony under Lord Garlies in 1623, confirmed in favour of the Earl of Galloway in 1633. Many of the single or two-storey painted terraced cottages were built in the early nineteenth century when Kirkcolm was, as it remained well into the present century, a village of fishermen. The deep water south of 'The Wig' at Glenside became a flying boat or seaplane base during the Second World War and it continued until 1957.

The parish church (1824) is on the hill (027687) above the village; the old church (030688), built in 1720 and demolished in 1821, the old churchyard and another St Columba's Well are in the grounds of Corsewall House east of the village. Eighteenth-century stones include an upright for the children of Niven Ker and Jean Wallace, Tenants in Douloch (1747), and a small stone with a four-horse plough team for James McKarzie, 'farmour in Cnockcoyd' (1764). The tenth/eleventh-century Kilmorie Cross, from the site of St Mary's church and well (033658), was used as a lintel stone in the doorway of the eighteenth-century church and after 1821 was placed in the grounds of Corsewall House. The workmanship is poor, with on one side a cross and panels with Anglian scrolls and plaits and serpents, and on the other side at the top a cross with extremely crude human arms and feet protruding and, underneath, a little figure with rounded shoulders and grotesque arms and smith's tools on one side and ravens on the other. Was this a pagan defacement of a decadent Anglian cross, or a Norse adaptation mixing pagan and Christian styles? The former is a radical concept in that it carries with it the suggestion that pagan religions, as well as Christianity, could be culturally aggressive.

From Kirkcolm continue south on the A718 by Soleburn Mill Croft to the circle south-east of Leswalt and take the minor road, now reclassified in signposting as the (A764), by High Challoch and Glenstockadale to the west-coast road at Larbrax. Kemp's Walk (NW 975598) is a large promontory fort with triple banks and ditches. There are two forts or earthworks west of Portslogan (NW 983590 and NW 983585). After Portslogan Bridge over the Knock and Maize Burn and the private road to Knock House you cross into Portpatrick parish.

CHAPTER 21

Portpatrick, Stoneykirk and Kirkmaiden

Portpatrick is a small parish, basically the lands of Kinhilt, Portree and Killantringan detached from the rest of Inch in 1628. The old term for it as the 'black quarter' of Inch probably refers to the grey moorland encountered on the old road from Stranraer to Portpatrick by Ochtrelure Hill, the Piltanton Burn at Crailloch, Airriehill, Knockglass, the Pinminnoch Burn and Craigenlee. This, largely the line of the Old Military Road, is a much more exciting drive than the A77 by Lochans, at the junction with the A757, and Colfin. The site of the castle of the Adairs of Kinhilt (Kilhilt), who also built Dunskey Castle, was located somewhere to the west of Lochans. To the north Cairn Pat or Piot (044563) with the wireless station was an Iron Age hill fort.

The Portpatrick railway (1862-1950) ran south from Stranraer parallel to the A77 to Whiteleys and then west of Lochans to Colfin before turning off where the B7042 joins the A77 and down to the spectacular cutting near Dunskey Castle and in to the terminus near Dinvin Mill. An excellent history of the line is contained in H. D. Thorne, *Rails to Portpatrick* (1976). Railway and cinema buffs would enjoy going through the old *Free Press* files to discover that, for example in March 1935, 'Special Cheap Train Fares' were available for patrons of the Regal Picture House in Stranraer on Saturdays leaving Portpatrick at 5 p.m. for Stranraer (Harbour) 5.18 p.m. and returning from Stranraer (Town) at 10.30 p.m. to see the great Conrad Veidt in *Jew Suss*.

Southern Upland devotees may follow the 'Way' from Ochtrelure by Greenfield, Little Mark, Knockquhassen and Knock and Maize to the A764. The best section to the viewpoint on Mulloch Hill is only a stroll from the side road (004590) near Knock and Maize. The 'Way' from the A764 at 000574 to Black Head at the south end of Killantringan Bay along the cliffs to Portpatrick is one of the best coastal walks in Galloway. The sandy bay may have been a landing place for Irish saints and pilgrims en route by Glaik and Loch Ryan for Luce Bay and St Ninian's shrine at Whithorn. Killantringan Lighthouse (NW 981564) was built in 1900. Continue south by Cubbie's Hole, Portavaddie, Sloganabaa, Gate Crease and Gatebraid Cave, Port Kale and Dunskey Glen, Port Mora and Sloganaglassin to the Portpatrick Hotel. The famous Dropping or Ouchtriemakain/

Uchtriemackean Cave (NW 992551) on Port Mora or Sandeel Bay was still a popular healing spring at the end of the eighteenth century frequented 'at the change of the moon' by the infirm, and by 'ricketty children' in particular.

The car park in Portpatrick beyond the outer harbour behind the south pier and beside the site of the Admiralty workshops is the starting point for the footpath to Dunskey Castle (003533). The Adairs' castle of c.1510 on a spectacular and exposed promontory site with a deep ravine on the landward side was ruinous by 1684, and it is surprising that so much of the fabric of the building is intact. Even before the north wing was added it was a spacious residence on a variation of the L plan with an unusually splendid staircase to the first floor. Like many other castles it had a resident ghost, a 'hairy man' or brownie, and the perennial servant problem in the form of another nursemaid who dropped her young charge on to the rocks below. An earlier castle on the same site was besieged and destroyed by McCullochs and McDowalls in 1496.

The view of Portpatrick from the Dunskey Castle path suggests both its attractions as a port and its major weakness, vulnerability to south-westerly sea storms which brought with them the devastating destruction of elemental forces. Portree or Portpatrick became for a short time the burgh of barony of Montgomerie under the charter of 8 February, 1620 to Sir Hugh Montgomery of Newton House (c.1611-1618), Newtonards, County Down. However, the Montgomerys, who purchased the Adairs' estates about 1620, were not a lucky family. Newton House was gutted by fire about 1664, and Sir James Montgomery, who died in 1652, has one of those perfect epitaphs:

> Sir James by pirates shot, and therfore dead
> By them i' th sea was solemnly buried.

The port and estate were acquired by Mr Blair, the parish minister, about 1648 and subsequently.

The cross-channel traffic from Portpatrick to Donaghadee increased in frequency and regularity towards the middle of the seventeenth century with an official weekly postal service packet from 1662 and a government subsidy from 1677. The golden years, however, were the 1770s to the 1830s with vast numbers of Irish cattle coming through Portpatrick, for example 18,301 between January 1784 and January 1785, until the direct steamers from Ireland to Glasgow and Liverpool by the 1830s captured the trade; with eight to ten thousand letters daily passing through to Ireland in the 1830s; and as late as 1837, 3,974 and 4,618 passengers to and from Ireland. There was also some local coasting trade and an attempt to establish a shipbuilding tradition. Of the four sloops registered at Portpatrick in 1820, the *Vanguard* and the *Venus* were built in Ramsey and Stranraer and the *Earl of Stair* of 50 tons and the *Batchelor* of 41 tons were built in Portpatrick in 1790 and 1811. And Portpatrick was also the western Gretna Green for Irish travellers and fortune-hunters, with the Church of Scotland, until 1826, operating a highly profitable facility (used by 198 gentlemen, 15 Army and Navy officers and 13 noblemen between 1775 and 1826) for quick marriages at a fee of £5, later £10, for the minister and £1 for the session clerk—'landed on Saturday, cried on Sunday, and married on Monday'.

John Smeaton's 'old pier' of c.1774 was scarcely adequate, and after the survey (1814-1818) by John Rennie vast expenditure was incurred on new harbour works between 1820 and 1846. The technology used was interesting and David Gibson describes two diving bells in the harbour in 1831 with teams of three men in each bell operating from 3 a.m. to 9 p.m. in two four-hour shifts each day. Massive damage in 1839 and the in the long term better facilities at Stranraer for steam packets led to the withdrawal of the official Admiralty mail and freight service in 1849 and the end of Government interest in the port in 1873. A later attempt to revive the Donaghadee route with the paddle steamer *Dolphin* in 1868-1869 was a failure. To-day only the scattered boulders and stonework in fragments of the north pier and sections of the south pier survive to indicate the Cyclopean scale of the harbour works.

Starting your Portpatrick perambulation at the south pier and the late nineteenth-century yellow brick lighthouse, note the twenty-feet-high old lime kiln near the 'Lighthouse Pottery'. The kiln is a prominent feature in Daniell's print of the harbour sketched in 1815. Barrack Street on South Crescent and Colonel Street take their names from the site of the military barracks which were used in the eighteenth century, and possibly in the later seventeenth century as well, to accommodate troops in transit to or from duties in Ireland. In the 1800s the first floor of the old barracks was used as the parish school above, on the ground floor, a distinctly disreputable lodging house; and, from the ridiculous to the sublime, in 1836 the same premises were used on Sundays as a temporary chapel or preaching station to accommodate the overflow from the parish church which had only 300 sittings. The site of St Patrick's Well was above Barrack Street.

Continue round South Crescent with its mix of smaller eighteenth-century or early nineteenth-century houses and their Edwardian neighbours. The present road is much higher than the original level, and the high pavement on the harbour side is dangerous if you step backwards over the edge while admiring the view. The Scottish Record Society volume, edited by N. L. Tranter, *The Urquhart Censuses of Portpatrick 1832-1853* (1980), is a fascinating study of the street by street and house by house private records in 1832, 1844, 1846 and 1852 taken by the Church of Scotland and then Free Church minister Andrew Urquhart. It includes, for example, details of the 'prison' or 'lock-up house' in Barrack Street and the occupations and 'scholarship' attainments of the inhabitants of the parish. Urquhart would not have made a good tourist officer. Indeed he describes the parish in the New Statistical Account (1838) as having 'upon the whole ... a healthy climate ... But rheumatism, dyspepsia, consumption, fevers ... are not unfrequent'.

However, Portpatrick developed in the later nineteenth century as a leisure-orientated village, and the Portpatrick Hotel (1901-1905) by J. K. Hunter high above the inner harbour and the Lifeboat Station (1877) was the splendid Edwardian culmination of this new way of life. Do not miss the curious statue of 'Robbie Burns' found in 1929 in a disused stonemason's yard in Stranraer and returned after repair in 1981 to its place for half a century beside the Bowling Green.

Turn into Main Street by the Harbour House Hotel, Anglesea and Rockville and take Saint Patrick Street on the left to the churchyard and the old parish church (1622-1629). The cruciform plan with the round (watch/belfry/beacon) tower with string courses and a steep slated roof at the west end of the church is most unusual. Did the round tower follow the plan of an older mediaeval or Irish Celtic church on the same site, or was it rather an idea introduced from County Down by the Montgomerys? The church has been repaired and the site cleared and excavated in 1985. The churchyard has some good stones describing disasters at sea, including the wreck of the Glasgow steamer *Orion* (1850), when over fifty lives were lost, and the loss of the clipper ship, the *Lion of Boston* (1835). The best inscription reads—

> I thank my God for poverty,
> For Riches and for Gain,
> For God can make a Rich man Poor,
> A Poor man Rich Again.

Ingleneuk on Saint Patrick Street was formerly the manse. Continue to the bow-fronted 'Fruit Shop' at the corner of Saint Patrick Street and Main Street beyond the four-storey Downshire Arms Hotel. Note the single-storey and basement Ivy Cottage with conical roof next to the Commercial Inn, and up the hill the parish church (1840-1842) by William Burn.

Stoneykirk (Clayshant, Stoneykirk and Toskerton amalgamated in

The round church tower at Portpatrick.

1650) is a large parish from Port of Spittal Bay and Freugh in the north to Kirkmadrine, Ardwell House and Drumbreddan in the south. With Kirkmaiden parish making the southern Rhins, this is from the air a patchwork of rich green hilly pastures between the blues of Luce Bay and the Irish Channel, dotted with the browns and creams of cows and the grey strips of dipping, twisting, climbing narrow roads, and exotic semi-tropical gardens, a 'Palm Tree County' which allows visitors to the far south end a feeling of remoteness and isolation from Stranraer and the horrors of the A75. It was also over the centuries a rich cradle for settlers from the Mesolithic world to the Iron Age of forts, brochs and defended promontories, for the early church with its inscribed stones and chapels and holy wells, for pilgrims on a route from Port of Spittal Bay east by St

Catherine's Well (061543), Eldrig Hill or Eldrickhill, Kilbreen and Kildrochat to the Piltanton Burn and Luce Bay, for the builders of the early earthwork castles, and for collectors of folklore although the data and tales collected in the later nineteenth century were no doubt less and less reliable as Rhins folk became more and more literate and sceptical.

To explore Stoneykirk and Kirkmaiden start not from the east coast road, but rather by following the almost secret byways down the west coast rich in wild flowers and happy cows and deserted cottages and crofts. From Portpatrick take the road south-east by the old Port Patrick Common and Portree Bridge (009536) to meet the side road from the B7042 above Port of Spittal Bay and Knockinaam Lodge Hotel. The 1850 O.S. map records a Lady Well (019526) above Morroch Bay and the Port of Spittal carding mill (023521). There is a possible fort site to the south at Dunaldbays (021517). Continue on the road over Port of Spittal Bridge and take the road to the right at the next junction (035522) up Knockteenan; and right, that is south, at the next junction (043519) by the former Meoul school (043512), now housing Invergyle Jewellery. The school opened in 1863 as Meoul Unsectarian School and closed in 1968. There is a promontory fort with triple ramparts at Kirklauchlane (035505).

Continue south by Cairnhill, Cairngarroch and Meikle Float. There is a standing stone with a deep circular depression on one side on Whirlpool (067492) and large stones in the field dykes which may, or may not, be remnants of a stone arrangement. To the west there are a number of cairns and hut circles recorded on Cairnmon Fell (047487). Take the road to the left, that is south-east, before (067479) Little Float, and then east by Mid Ringuinea to the road junction at 075476. There is a possible fort site at Dove Cave Head (060472), a promontory fort with triple ramparts north-west of Kenmuir (065469), and a cairn south of West Ringuinea (070471). The Good Wife's Cave in Float Bay is an interesting placename, suggesting that it was the retreat of a local wise woman or white witch, the equivalent of a male 'Bob Annat'.

The coastline here is dotted with caves, so perhaps one should be claimed as the Rhins retreat of that committed troglodyte, Sawney Bean, the shining star in the firmament of mythical Scottish rogues, whom at least one writer, John Wilson of Gatehouse, wanted to place in the southern Rhins. His *Strains o' Galloway* (1914) has a superb description of Sawney's cave with

> The limbs o' men, women, an' weans on the wa's,
> Like beef that is dried were hung up in grim raws,
> An' some laid in pickle fu' sune tae be ta'en
> By that horde in the Hades o' aul' Sawney Bean.

Take the road south from Mid Ringuinea and then east up Frecket Hill for *Kirkmadrine Church* (080483) and the collection of early Christian stones. The little dark-grey building on a hillock approached through a gloomy avenue of trees was the mediaeval (thirteenth/fourteenth? century) Toskerton parish church, allowed to fall into ruins after 1650. Restored by Lady McTaggart Stewart, it now houses—behind glass—a group of ninth to eleventh-century cross fragments and the three outstanding fifth-century funerary monuments found in use as gateposts for the burial yard and as a stepping-stone for a dyke. Kirkmadrine was an important Anglian and mediaeval period religious centre, but whether the original early church site was at this particular spot or nearby is a more difficult problem. The pillars did make very functional gateposts and might quite easily have been brought here for that purpose. A coastal location (compare Low Curghie near Drummore) between Sandhead and Ardwell seems more likely than the bleak exposed hill at Kirkmadrine. The pillar commemorating, in Roman capitals, the chief priests (or bishops?) Ides, Viventius and Mavorius also has a cross within a circle with the Chi-rho monogram, that is the first two letters in the Greek form for the name of Christ, and the letters A and O (The Alpha and the Omega). A second pillar commemorates ——S and Florentius, and the third smaller stone has the 'Initium et Finis' (the beginning and the end) inscription to be read, with the 'A et O', in relation to *Revelations*, XXI, 6.

From Kirkmadrine return down Frecket Hill and take the road to the left by Awhirk to Clachanmore (083467), where there was formerly a school at the crossroads. The road from Low Ardwell and Pans goes to the shore where Salt Pans (070462) are recorded on the Ainslie map (1782) and on the O.S. 1850 map. The road by High Ardwell goes down to Ardwell Bay for access to Doon Castle (067446), a broch at the end of a promontory with a trench on the landward side. The thirteen-feet-thick double walls and the entrance at the seaward end are clearly visible. Round the coast by Bandoleer Slunk there is another promontory fort at Grennan Point (076437) west of Drumbreddan. From Clachanmore continue south-east by Kirnaughtry Corner to the A716 at Ardwell.

The richer east coast has most of the sites of castles and mills, a sure indication of good land. Going south on the A716 from Culmick Bridge (077565) east of Lochans you pass Garthland Mains, the site of the important castle of the McDowalls on the Garthland Burn (077554) demolished about 1840. Take the side road by Craigencrosh through Stoneykirk village. The parish church (089532), built in 1827, has a Dutch bell dated 1663 and made by Gerard Koster II of Amsterdam for the City of

Glasgow's tolbooth and therefore carrying the coat of arms of Glasgow. Return to the A716 at North Milmain. The Windmill Plantation (094522) opposite Low Culgroat has the remains of a windmill tower, possibly for a scutch mill for flax. The A715 from Sand Mill Bridge goes by the sites of the nineteenth-century Culmore tile works (101515) and Clayshant church and churchyard (108522) beside the burn south of Clayshant Bridge. To the south the Sand Mill Burn is shown on the 1850 O.S. map as powering a corn mill (100506) near the shore.

Balgreggan motte (096505) on the ridge above the A716 is the first of a line of early castles along the eastern shore of the Rhins. The top was used by the Royal Observer Corps during the Second World War as a lookout point. To the west off the B7042 there is the site of Kirkmagill church and churchyard (085502) at Mains of Balgreggan. Further west there is another of these difficult Iron Age or Dark Age or mediaeval rectangular homesteads on Doon Hill, Kildonan (059523). The massive earth ramparts with rounded corners were still clear when visited in 1970.

Going south on the A716 go through Sandhead, which had developed as a strip village with a smithy and a school by 1850. The bay was used for landing lime and later coal. Note the alternative approach to *Kirkmadrine* from the A716 by Cairnweil and Dunting Glen. The old landholding or settlement of Toskerton (092482) was in the field next to the road north-west of Kirkmabreck. Continue south on the A716 passing Ardwell mill (101486), in use as a meal mill up to 1967. The 1850 O.S. map also records a lint mill on the shore (103487), and a waulk and dye mill on the Alwhibbie Burn (106475) where perhaps they used natural dyes from seaweeds, lichens and mosses.

Ardwell is a good area to pause to explore at leisure. There is a fine motte (107455) in the grounds of Ardwell House, again on the ridge above the road, with possibly a bailey to the north. *Ardwell House Gardens*, which are open all the year, are especially good for rhododendrons and azaleas. Note the row of single-storey cottages on the east side of the A716 south of the 'Murder Plantation' (109460) as described on the 1850 O.S. map. Did the placename relate in some way to the traditional 'Leek Fair' held at Ardwell in the spring for the sale of plants and often an occasion for vile intemperance and fighting? Another old market was the 'Sooty Poke Fair' held at the gates of Kirkmadrine churchyard for the sale of woven cloth. Next take the road west by Ardwell Mains to see the charming Ardwell *quoad sacra* parish church built by Sir Mark and Lady McTaggart Stewart (1900-1902). South of the church a mound of rubble and stones marks the site of the fifteenth/sixteenth-century Killaser Castle (096450), which was

Port Logan village c.1910. Note the second row of cottages on the hill behind.

held, as was Ardwell, by the McCullochs. Again this is an example of a ✳
tower house on originally a swamp or marsh site.

Continue south into Kirkmaiden parish by Chapel Rossan (ecclesiastical architecture) and Auchness (castellated) to the B7065 road junction at Balkelly Bridge. The beautiful little toll house with a rounded gable end was sadly and unimaginatively removed over twenty years ago to make way for the road improvements here. The most important feature of the complex of industrial buildings to the east is the famous Logan Windmill (115437) built c.1670. The nineteenth-century meal or corn mill and saw mill below were powered from the mill lade and pond.

Take the B7065 for the almost sub-tropical *Logan Botanic Garden* (096425), without question the most surprising, the most exotic and the most exciting corner of Galloway which should give even the most unimaginative historian more than a touch of the Tahitis. The McDowalls had in Logan House an excellently proportioned late seventeenth or early eighteenth-century Queen Anne style residence, now again, minus the 1870 additions, restored to its full elegance. A fragment of the older Balzieland Castle survives from the 1500s at the end of the terrace garden. The Garden itself, however, is a comparatively recent creation dating from the work by Mr. R. C. Hambro after the late 1940s and, since 1969, by the Department of Agriculture and Fisheries for Scotland. Outstanding features are the rows of Chusan palms from China, the huge tree ferns, the Cabbage palms growing again after severe losses in the hard winter of 1980, the

Age and innocence. A beautifully composed Edwardian impression of the Logan fish pond.

hydrangeas and the rhododendrons, and just the overall effect of the series of separate gardens with many rare and special plants.

Continue on the B7065 by Ballochagunnon Plantation and Mount Sallie for Galloway's longest-running tourist attraction, *Logan Fish Pond* (092412) at the north end of Port Logan Bay. The circular tidal basin, over fifty feet in diameter, was first stocked in 1788 with cod and blockans or coal-fish which wobble up to the surface for limpets and crabs. It is a curious phenomenon, as David Gibson observed in 1831, as 'the large codfish allow you to stroke their heads, and take meat out of your hand'. The deep-sea fish, however, also become blind with exposure over a long period of time to strong light in shallow water. Round the coast to the west beyond the Mull of Logan is the Dropping Cave or Peter's Paps or St Peter's Well (076421), which was resorted to as a healing source for 'chincough' or whooping cough. To the north there is a promontory fort at Duniehinnie (076425). A small pier is marked on the 1850 O.S. map at Port Gill (077430).

Port Logan at the south end of Port Nessock or Port Logan Bay is a typical small planned village—one main street along the front and a second row of cottages up the hill—laid out by Colonel Andrew McDowall in 1818. Little is left now of his new pier for the Irish ferry traffic he hoped to bring to Port Logan. (Robert McDowall had tried out the same scheme with a small pier in 1682.) The bay is too exposed in rough weather and it is amazing that the picturesque lighthouse with external stairs and a decorative stone-lantern has survived the storms over the years better than the rest of the pier.

From Port Logan take the B7065 east up the hill passing the side road for Killumpha and Terally Bay. It is not easy to pass Killumpha without remembering that the best people receive the best insults, and indeed the local exchange for crying at Killumpha folk was truly splendid:

> There's muckle splay feet in Killumpha,
> There's noses set on wi a gley;
> But what can ye look for o' Kyloes
> That's fed upon pratas an' whey?

These and many other outrageous and irreverent tales of ghosties, fairies, witches, and mermaid-hunts at East Tarbert, probably collected from Dominie Todd of Drummore, are included in Robert de Bruce Trotter's *Galloway Gossip Sixty Years Ago* (1877). Trotter is excellent also on the peculiarities of the Galloway dialects, for example the use of 'intensifiers'—by Miss Hannay to Mrs Smith—

'They say she's gaun to be married in a month.'

'That's a melodious lee, whaever said it . . . I never heard her even't tae a lad yet, nor naebody else.'

His classic test for Machers folk can scarcely be bettered—

'Luk in the n'yuk,

An' g'yim me the cruk,

Or A'll hit ye on the faice wi a raid blaizin pait, so A wull.'

In Kirkmaiden, as in Stoneykirk, take the west coast ways first and continue on the B7065 by Kirkbride Hill and Garrochtrie for superb views to the south. Many of the old placenames and holdings on the 1850 O.S. map, Berehill, Burnthill, Mugloch, McMan's Croft, Inchmulloch, Macherally, have disappeared or been absorbed in larger farming units. At the road junction (114377) take the circuit west to Low Clanyard and back by High Currochtrie to the B7065 at Kirkmaiden. The site of the Gordons' tower house, Clanyard Castle (108374), was east of Low Clanyard. There may have been a motte at High Clanyard or Coreholmhill (107372), but the existing remains are not convincing. Clanyard Bay was reputed to be a smugglers' landing place and the Breddock Cave (091372), now accessible only by sea, was reported to have been fitted out for storage of contraband.

Trotter, in a perhaps not-too-serious passage, distinguishes between the original long-legged, fair-haired natives, the Fingauls or 'heehh-enders' south of a line from Clanyard Bay to Kilstay Bay, and the Gossocks or 'laihh-enders' who were descendants of the Kreenies. Both the Fingauls and the Gossocks looked on a journey to Stranraer or Glenluce as the equivalent of a journey to a foreign land! But this, of course, is mythology not history.

The A716 from Balkelly Bridge by Myroch Point to Drummore is a much easier road for car drivers and nervous passengers. The small motte (122411) beside the burn on Terally Bay is now suffering from severe erosion. A long cist cemetery (122412) near the standing stone on the raised beach to the north was excavated in 1956. To the south the nineteenth-century Terally brick and tile works (120407) with clay pits and workers' cottages made a most interesting group. The brick works was revived after the War until 1953, but unfortunately the kilns and the chimney were dismantled in 1968. The site of Kirkbride church (120404) was on the hill to the south. Continue south by Grennan, where there was a nineteenth-century slate quarry (126394), to Kilstay Bay, where a chapel and burial site is recorded at 126381, and Low Curghie, which was the probable location of an early Christian station and of the burial ground where the lost fifth-century stone for Ventidius the deacon *(subdeaconis)* had stood.

You are quite liable on a fresh day, let alone in a south-easterly gale with 21 or 22-feet spring tides, to get a free car wash from the sea in Kilstay Bay, and indeed coastal erosion is a problem from Sandhead to Drummore with the road having had to be diverted inland in several places over the last two centuries. The road, for example, from Low Curghie to Drummore along the shore by Clashwhannan had to be abandoned for the present A716 line, and in Drummore itself the road at the north end of Shore Street up to the A716 has recently suffered severe damage.

The coach for Stranraer (with at least fourteen people on the top) and the unfortunate horses at the Queen's Arms Hotel, Drummore c.1900.

Park in Drummore on the hill near the Queen's Arms Hotel, the terminus for the horse-drawn coaches which ran from Drummore to Stranraer. The service, inaugurated in 1892, offered coaches leaving Drummore at 7.30 a.m. and 4.50 p.m. and reaching Stranraer at 10.30 a.m. and 7.25 p.m. respectively. The motor bus service which began in May 1907 did rather better, leaving Drummore at 9.30 a.m., 2.00 p.m. and 6.00 p.m. and taking an hour and a half to get to Stranraer. Plans and a route were also prepared in 1878 for a Stranraer-Drummore railway and the project was considered again in 1918, but perhaps fortunately for potential shareholders did not get beyond the planning stage. Coal and lime continued to come in and farm produce went out by sea from the harbour below Shore Street. The (south) quay was probably built in the 1840s, when there were four small sloops working out of Drummore and belonging to the port, and it was extended in 1889 when the north breakwater was also erected. One sloop, the *Trades* of 39 tons, was built at Drummore in 1816. The eighteenth-century grain mill was demolished in 1969, but the three-storey Wyllie's (formerly Marshall's) mill and store above the harbour at the corner of Shore Street is an impressively massive building. The last remnant of the Adairs' tower house, Drummore Castle, at Low Drummore farm was removed in 1964.

Kilstay Bay, Maryport Bay, Mull Glen and Drummore Bay, where Dr Gemmill, the local medical practitioner, collected flints during his rounds in the 1880s are possible Mesolithic sites. For Maryport Bay (143343) and Cailliness (Killiness) Point take the minor road off the B7041. Cairn Aine (141347) between Cairngarroch and Maryport is a denuded cairn site. To explore the area between Kirkmaiden and the Mull of Galloway on foot or by car start by going up the B7041 by High Drummore motte (130359). The gold torc in the National Museum in Edinburgh was found on High Drummore. Turn right onto the B7065 and take the side road (123365) before Kirkmaiden west by Inshanks Fell towards Barncorkrie, passing the site of Kirkleish chapel and well (108355) east of the Mulrea Burn and the Cairn More denuded cairn site (102361) on Cairn Fell. The road by Knockencule, Inshanks and West Muntloch to Damnaglaur passes a number of important sites. The fort on Crummag or Crammick Head (088340) is a circular dun or broch on a promontory site cut across by a trench; and to the south-east Dunman fort (097334) above great seacliffs is even more spectacular. The 1850 O.S. map includes a disused mill at Low Slock or Slockmill and 'The Auld Kilns' (mounds) on Auchneight Moor south-east of Dunman fort. The Muntluck Well (111338) in Kilbuie Moss was a famous healing well, and the water in the Bat Well (112334) east of Auchneight was used for horses suffering from worm disease and for humans with colic.

William Todd (1774-1863), the parish dominie from 1799 to 1845, mathematician, antiquarian, maker of clocks, sundials, globes and beehives, author of a manuscript parish history, founder member of the Kirkmaiden Temperance Society (not a success) and a truly great man, was also a collecter of local tales and traditions. Some he passed on to Joseph Train (1779-1852) and others were published in the 'Galloway Traditions' series in the *Galloway Register*. They include the Brownie of Breddock at Portencorkrie, a demonic creature in the form of a pig at Brocklan Brae near Dunman (the last possibly badgers), Hallowe'en apparitions at Terally and Auchneight, and reports of the witches Luckie Agnew and Luckie Lymeburn and Meg Elson. His verse on the last-named is particularly good:

> Kirkmaiden dames may crously craw
> And cock their nose fu' canty,
> For Maggy Elsons now awa
> Who lately bragged sae vaunty—
> That she could kill each cow or ca'
> And mak their milk fu' scanty,
> Since death's gi'en Maggy's neck a thraw
> They'll a' hae butter plenty,
> In lumps each day.

The distinguished folklorist, the Reverend Walter Gregor (1825-1897), who undertook two Galloway tours in 1895 and 1896, staying with Sir Herbert Maxwell and with clergymen at Kells, Minnigaff, Mochrum, Soulseat, Logan and Kirkmaiden, seems to have collected some of his liveliest material here in Kirkmaiden parish. Some, for example the cure for deafness and the means of protecting cattle from ill-luck, are so coarse that they might have come from some mythical 'Coordistan' rather than from douce Kirkmaiden. They can scarcely be repeated before a genteel twentieth-century audience. However, their fascination may be suggested by three examples of local cures: for whooping cough—'Place a slice of raw pork ham on the chest of the patient'; for the sting of an adder—'Tear a fowl sindrie, i.e. asunder, and put it hot and bleeding over the wound'; and for warts—'Rub the wart with a black snail, and then hang the snail on a thorn-bush. As the snail wastes, the wart wastes till it is gone'. Many examples of traditions associated with farm animals are included. This one on domestic fowl is typical—'When a hen crowed she was killed at once. Such a thing was accounted very unlucky. *A crawin' hen's no sonsey* and *A crawin' hen an' a whisslin' lass is no sonsey* and *Whisslin' maidens an' crawing hens are no lucky aboot ony man's hoose* are three saws'.

The folklore aspect aside, the most striking feature of Kirkmaiden parish is the sheer number of chapels and holy wells, reaffirming the importance of the peninsula in the Dark Ages and the early mediaeval world, and the line of Iron Age/Dark Age promontory forts to defend communities all too vulnerable to Irish or Roman or Hebridean or Norse raiders. This pattern is more than maintained in the last lap towards the Mull.

From Damnaglaur take the B7041 south by Creechan Park to the road junction (130336) at the former school at Castlemoor, and then the Mull road east of Auchie Glen. The site of the mediaeval parish church of St Catherine is on the south side of the Kirk Burn in Portankill Glen (138324). Only very slight turf walling is left to mark the graveyard and the later St Catherine's Croft. There is a small promontory fort, The Dunnan (141322), south-east of Portankill. Continue along the shore for the famous St Medan's Chapel and Cave (143316) under the cliffs south-east of Mull Farm. It is difficult to find, and the old track down the cliff has long since disappeared, but it is quite possibly as old and as important a site as St Ninian's Cave at Physgill. It was excavated by the Marquis of Bute in 1870, but tragically a broken sandstone slab with the figure of the Virgin, stone lintels, and some brass mountings were left there unprotected and the local yokels, in a frenzy of no doubt alcoholic piety, threw the lot into the sea. The Chapel Well is actually three natural rock basins which fill with sea water at every high tide. Both the Chapel Well and the splendidly named Kibbertie Kite Well (131316) on West Cairngaan south-east of Knockantomachie were popular healing wells.

Back on the road note the row of old workers' cottages and the nineteenth-century threshing mill building below the mill dam at Mull farm (139319). Continue south to the still spectacular double rampart earthworks (143307) across the isthmus between West and Easy Tarbert. The best section is just to the east of the road. Try to see the lines in a sharp late summer evening sunset to pick out the details. The ramparts probably are the landward defences of a huge promontory fort or *refuge area* embracing the whole of the Mull of Galloway, which would make it one of the largest and most spectacular Iron Age strongholds in Britain. There is a hut circle or enclosure (142306) at the south-west end of the ramparts. The sixty-feet-high Mull of Galloway Lighthouse (157303), standing 269 feet above the often stormy seas with powerful tidal currents, was built in 1828.

Working back from the Mull, the 1850 O.S. map records a quay at East Tarbert (144309). There is a defended homestead or fort site (138310) above the shore south-west of Mull Glen, and promontory forts at Dunorroch (130310) and Carrickamrie (129310). Following the cliffs west above Old Mill Bay, the Cave of the Biawn and Port Kemin takes you to the Nick of the Kindram south of the site of the denuded Eagle Cairn (110324) on Cardryne Hill. Does the placename refer to a long-forgotten (sea?) eagles' eyrie on the cliffs or to eagles' talons found when the cairn was removed?

From Drummore village walk up the hill to the right at the top of the main street passing the old school (128369) built in 1887, and turn left on the B7065 to the old parish church or Kirk Covenant (124369), built between 1638 and 1639. Immediately to the south note the Iron Age/Dark Age hill fort (123468) with triple ramparts on Core Hill. The view from the churchyard, where William Todd taught in his parish school for the best part of his life, is magnificent. There is a good collection of funerary monuments, including Sara Corkran (1698) and a memorial in the form of a lighthouse (1852). The church has a classically simple Presbyterian interior with the pulpit in the centre of the small building which had only 275 sittings. The bell, dated 1534, was a wedding gift from the Gordons of Lochinvar to Alexander Gordon of Clanyard Castle. The wooden panel on the north wall belonged to Patrick Adair of Drummore Castle and carries the inscription

PADR O God Mak Me To Heir In Faith And Prackteis In Love Thy Holy Wird And Comademetis. Thou Art Only My Supoirt. God Mak Me Thankful. 1618.

The perfect winter scene on Carlingwark Loch, Castle-Douglas at an inter-county bonspiel (Wigtownshire and the Stewartry of Kirkcudbright) dated December 1961, with at least twenty-five rinks spaced out over the loch. Indoor curling at, first, Ayr and now Stranraer has meant that it is exceptional to find local ponds and lochs being used for the 'roarin' game', but during occasional severe winters with prolonged cold spells the larger lochs may freeze over sufficiently to allow this major event to take place. Galloway has indeed a tradition of curling going well back into the eighteenth century, and a number of clubs with a great history, for example Parton (1834), Kelton (1831), Penninghame (1828) and Glenluce (1839). So long may the old phrases ring out—'Gie me the oot turn', 'Come a yaird on', 'Crack an egg on it' and 'Soop, man, soop'.

APPENDIX

Scottish Monuments, Country Houses and Gardens open to the public

An essential preliminary before setting off on an excursion is to visit one of the Tourist Information Centres in the larger towns to confirm the opening and closing times of the various castles and abbeys and gardens on your list. Arrangements vary considerably. Some are open all the year; others close from October to March; and some close on particular mornings or for whole days; for example in 1985 New Abbey Corn Mill was closed on Wednesday and Thursday mornings.

A check list of official monuments in Galloway and adjacent areas should include:

Ruthwell Cross
Caerlaverock Castle
Lincluden College
Lochmaben Castle
Morton Castle
New Abbey Corn Mill
Sweetheart Abbey
Drumcoltran Tower
Orchardton Tower
Threave Castle
Loch Doon Castle
Dundrennan Abbey
Maclellan's Castle
Cardoness Castle
Cairnholy Chambered Cairns
Carsluith Castle
Torhouse Stone Circle
Laggangairn Standing Stones
Whithorn Priory
St Ninian's Chapel
St Ninian's Cave
Rispain Camp
Barsalloch Fort

Drumtroddan Standing Stones and Drumtroddan Cup and Ring
Marked Rocks
Wren's Egg Standing Stones
Druchtag Motte
Chapel Finian
Glenluce Abbey
Castle of Park
Kirkmadrine Church

Country houses to visit include Blairquhan Castle, near Straiton, which
has an important collection of examples of the work of Scottish painters
including Raeburn, Patrick Nasmyth, Sir David Wilkie and David Allan,
and which opened to the public for the first time in summer 1985; Cally
House, Kirroughtree House and Lochnaw Castle, all of course now hotels;
and Drumlanrig Castle, where a complete 1st/2nd Century A.D. Roman
fort with ditches and road systems covering some three acres was located
south-east of the castle in the 1984 aerial photographic survey by the Royal
Commission on Ancient and Historical Monuments. The Roman army
units stationed at Drumlanrig would have provided garrisons for the
outposts such as Durisdeer on the road north and the newly located fortlet
near Sanquhar on the road north-west towards Ayrshire. The 1984 results
also included another fortlet at Lantonside on the Nith west of Caerlaverock
Castle.

Gardens to visit include Maxwelton House, Castle Kennedy, Ardwell
House, Threave Gardens and Logan Botanic Garden. Other and smaller
gardens may open on particular occasions.

Museums and art galleries with different virtues and strengths are
located in Ruthwell, Wanlockhead, Dumfries, New Abbey, Kirkcudbright,
Creetown, Newton Stewart, Wigtown, Whithorn and Stranraer.

Useful and inexpensive guidebooks are available on and generally at:
Caerlaverock Castle, New Abbey Corn Mill, Sweetheart Abbey, Threave
Castle, Dundrennan Abbey, Whithorn Priory and Logan Botanic Garden.

Index